Wangeli Chaaraoui

DIARY OF AN

AUTODIDACT

◉ Diary of an autodidact
© *Wangeli Chaaraoui, 2018*

ISBN: 9781976737480

To my son

Alexandros Andre Chaaraoui

On his thirtieth birthday

Introduction

I want to write a great book about life, a universal one.

This idea was born on the island of Crete in August 2015.

It is a purpose that is not easy at all, but it is possible.

Proof of this: here is the first book for you.

They are Napoleon's words: *«The impossible is the ghost of the timid men and the refuge of the cowards...*

The word impossible is not in my dictionary. »

There is no creative work that is easy and good at the same time, but nothing is impossible; you have to keep trying, and one day it will be possible. It takes a lot of will; you need to trust yourself, your ability to overcome the monotony, taking advantage of the moments of inspiration.

To achieve this goal, one must be prepared and have passed through various schools of life. I think it is possible to create a passionate work based on thoughts and memories of the past, gathering memories of the past and the present and working them in deep; it is necessary to learn from the past and look with optimism on the present and the future.

Writing a book about life is a very hard and a great work. Once is considered to be finished according to the judgment of the same author, deeply believing that the fruit is already ripe and seeing it clearly as a true depth work, it goes then to its publication.

Every day, the desire of surviving, of rising and being reborn from its own ashes - like the phoenix - is renewed based on the daily struggle and the ideas that arise every day when you wake up in the morning after taking a relaxing bath.

Without struggles and with no desire to fight and overcome our own weaknesses, we humans cannot evolve. We are obliged to face our daily problems that arise on a daily basis by the circumstances of our life and, also, because of our weaknesses. Many times we do not feel strong enough to face those problems that represent an obstacle that blocks our life and our evolution, our inner and outer growth, our progress towards the goal, where we want to reach or where we could reach. We also want to increase our mental and material productivity, expand our intellectual knowledge and our spiritual vision of the world around us. We want to advance in the long way of our life, giving, every day, a further step towards our final goal.

The general development of the world around us and the modernization ask us, every day or every time, to do more efforts and to have a greater capacity for adaptation; for example, learning how to use a new computer or a new computer system, learning to use new mobile phone applications, new media, new applications, learn to live and tolerate new social and demographic trends as a consequence of the wars in the world, the crisis and the social misalignments of the emigrating flows. Also, it asks us to learn to consume and like new modern or exotic foods that come from globalization; to learn to perform also disciplinary practices practicing new exercises and sports, also to have new habits linked to the fashion and the artistic currents. We need to spiritually meditate on the past, the present and the future, learning to live with new dangers that come from uncontrollable violence - from evilness-, new epidemics that come as a result of industrial pollution, poverty and environmental pollution.

We live the direct consequences of unjust wars that put the world's population at risk, produce insecurity and generally deteriorate the life quality.

We have to learn to live in a multicultural society where there are, on one hand, wonderful people, from whom one can learn every day about their human qualities and, on the other hand, we are confronted with different socially degenerate and spiritually ill people who can cross our path and that we can observe in several public places - as the poor people, beggars, drunkards and vagabonds. They are also well-dressed people with a modern appearance, but they are, unfortunately, dominated by evil spirits such as arrogance, selfishness, omnipotence..., evilness, in general!

In many countries there are rulers - or, rather, dictators - who themselves or their governments are continually dictating new unjust and inhuman laws that are driving the world into abyss, disaster, and the total degradation of social life.

The living costs do not stop increasing: we have more expenses for inflation, the cost of security of the states against the imminent war risk, for the treatment of garbage and toxic elements; we have to pay, increasingly, more taxes and to meet expenses for the needs that modern life requires. The cost of living is constantly and considerably getting more expensive.

The intelligent and conscious human being faces great delusions on his daily life and work; does not know where to get so much money to maintain a good living standard, so many people choose to have several parallel jobs and they work practically all the time without pauses or breaks. Others choose to immigrate into a new unknown country, where they think they will have more opportunities to work and earn a decent living.

I remember two anecdotes of past times

An anecdote from a Brazilian friend, of Lebanese origin, from Sao Paolo who said: "Every day I went to get the bread and I took it out of the mouth of a lion!"

Another anecdote from a friend of Jewish origin I met in Casablanca who said: "Every day a naive person comes to visit my shop, to which I can sell a piece of furniture, a carpet or an object of value for more value than it really is and thus bring out the bread for the day."

I do not believe that these two situations are possible today, maybe they were possible forty years ago, but the world has totally changed: there are no more lions from where to get the food out of their mouths, nor naive people who enter a bazaar to buy something for more than its real value. Every day there are less naive and people are savvier, those businesses have disappeared; perhaps there is an art gallery, where people rarely enter, and many of the owners soon close for lack of profit and the unbearable renting cost.

People just buy what they need, small shops are usually closing due to the lack of customers, and almost everyone buys on the big platforms. Although, sometimes, people spend little money on some whim, every day less!

Writing a book about life requires, without any doubt, much will and patience, especially if one wants to write something useful, refined and crystalline; something noble as gold and transparent as a pure crystal, carved like a multi-faceted diamond; something fluid as the mineral water, which comes from a high mountain source that fills our spirit quenching our thirst for knowledge. It is like drinking a good mature wine that refreshes our mood and then we feel at ease, serene, balanced, satisfied and happy.

The world of ideas, of wisdom and of modern and practical philosophy is the theme that will be mainly developed in this book; it must be meaningful and give a real value for all who are going to read this book.

Apart from satisfying the author itself, these philosophical thoughts, which come from human experience, can undoubtedly serve for the construction or reconstruction of our being. The purpose of the chapters of this book is to strengthen one's self-confidence and, at the same time, to keep respect for others, based on the principle that one does not get anywhere by itself; we can all reach the goal by working together and collaborating with each other, especially with the professionals around us and the noble, sincere and kind-hearted people who can help us.

It is very important to feel that one is useful in a society, to have a profession that serves for the development and realization of future projects. It is also necessary for us to have a unique and unmistakable character so that we can live the present and prepare for the future that we see coming.

For writing this book about life I have to be prepared, to have a clear mind and to see things as they are. It is like looking at the horizon at sea, on a clear day, which inspires me and opens my eyes and my mind enough to write an interesting book rich in content, which has a deep and true meaning for all who will read it.

My book is titled "Diary of an Autodidact"

Why? For the simple reason that I am a self-taught person who has gone through several schools of life, starting with the education my parents gave me, who tried to transmit their experience and gave me confidence in myself to be able to follow the path, and for the different schools where teachers taught me the bases of knowledge. Then, my passion for travelling and my desire to discover the world impelled me to search for the essential things and the secrets of life: there has been growing my own philosophy and perspective about things.

I am neither an academic nor a professor of philosophy, but I want to draw many philosophical conclusions from my own ideas, schools and lived experiences.

This book will discuss and develop aspects of the practical and modern philosophy of our daily life in a modern world of globalization, where we all receive information at the same time through multiple means of communication.

The equation of life is increasingly difficult to solve: it is no longer as mathematical as in the past times of the famous writer, philosopher and French lawyer, Voltaire.

Stability, security, social peace, development and living standards are directly influenced by world conflicts and the positions of the major powers and strategic interests.

The economy directly depends on wars, terrorist attacks, immigration and the mass movement of oppressed peoples; these conflicts produce poverty, hunger and social imbalances throughout the world.

Also, our life, economically speaking, depends on the oil price, the manufacturers of weapons of massive destruction; that causes us fear and insecurity. Every day there is less work, more spending, more chaos and the equations are no longer the same, what we learned yesterday does not serve us much today or tomorrow, we will have to learn constantly and also find, if possible, new sources of income.

In addition, natural catastrophes, epidemics affecting our health, such as malaria, plague, cholera, Ebola, invading insects, zika, etc. are also added.

One asks the following question often: "Why cannot human beings or great powers, governments, great laboratories and peace institutions, prevent such human disasters and why they cannot help us?

Why do more and more innocent people have to suffer from wars, hunger, disease, forced emigration, rape, massacres, etc.?

Why all this social injustice?

The answer is that the human being is the only animal on Earth that does not learn from its own mistakes because it is selfish, and therefore is not able to give something of itself to those who need it. The rich people give the crumbs to the poor, this is not a solution and it does not help to solve the problems; from there it comes chaos, injustice and social imbalance, although there are many who are generous rich, who give every year half of what they earn to others, but even so, 47% of the world's wealth belongs to only 1% of the world's population!

That is why it is important to philosophically discuss all these important issues of our social and spiritual life.

What is philosophy? Philosophy is undoubtedly the friend of wisdom and it is also the science that puts the human being in question.

We will speak in this book of a practical and modern philosophy of the twenty-first century, different from the typical thoughts of a philosopher of the Socratic era almost 2,500 years ago, when philosophers lived in a more pure, simpler and less chaotic world than now. The world was less complex and less explosive, less violent and perhaps less dramatic than our present world, although there were other great difficulties, such as incurable diseases, injustice and, no doubt, much suffering. However, philosophy continues to have the same conclusions, the words of Socrates 2,500 years ago are still valid today because the human being has simply not changed and remains the same in his spirit, although the overall picture, scope and context have incredibly changed and evolved.

Our age is undoubtedly much more modern, but there are thousands of people who daily unjustly die because of absurd wars, violence that comes from men commanded by maddened and dominated by evil leaders... The problems of these days come from poor education, lack of morality, the lack of human ethics and the selfishness of the human being and evil spirits.

This degeneration gave harmful and dangerous fruits that poison our society every day.

How is it possible to live in this terrible and insecure world? The answer is that we are, by nature, confident and optimistic, we easily forget and we think that tomorrow things will go better than before and undoubtedly better than yesterday.

Nowadays, tranquility has become a rare and scarce thing, people live in a continuous stress and there is also insecurity and fear.

In the media we hear news of human wars and tragedies, accidents of all kinds... everything comes from the mistakes of human management and also from the bad intention of the human being.

We live practically in a world of chaos and total alert, especially in the big cities; villages no longer exist, they are urbanized as small towns.

Let us not forget that everything comes from years back and from the last century, we are starting the 21st century and we are evolving with extreme speed.

In recent years, from the beginning of the 21st century until now, there has been more violence and innocent deaths than in the last fifty years of the 20th century, that is, since the end of World War II.

It is a bad sign, the world is very bad and it is very insecure, we ask ourselves: "Why is it like that?" There are many reasons, we all know them, we read the news, although there are hidden things that cannot be said in the media because they cannot justify them, those truths will come into light much later, perhaps in fifty years when the responsible people are buried, so there will be no trial, people will have forgotten the human tragedies that have harmed their beloved ones.

Those who knew the truth, fully or a half of it, are no longer living or are very old and cannot lead the guilty ones to trial for health reasons; others, who have been wrongfully mistreated, are older or are also buried, can no longer fight or claim for their rights, etc.

Most adults were born in the last century, and we continue to live on the basis of our history, learning and experiences of the previous century. We have come, most of the twentieth century, where we have spent a great part of our youth, there were great advances in this 21st century and much more chaos, and a series of great problems were born at that time, such as insecurity, which before it almost did not exist, time is also going much faster in this twenty-first century than in the twentieth century!

This book will be a dialogue between myself and I will try to teach you many truths I have found distilling or synthesizing ideas from the past, that I have acquired through my experiences and my travels to Lebanon, where I was born and performed my first studies; to Greece, where I made my first long trip to the Salamis island; to Europe, where I have received my great schools; to Belgium and Northern Europe, Spain, Morocco, Brazil (South America), Germany, Arabia and the Sub-Saharan Africa.

You will see that my language is different than the usual that is already used in general because I am not a classic or a common man, I'm not a conventional man, as my dear friend, the great playwright writer novelist from Madrid, German Ubillos, who I met in Madrid In the eighties and from which I got his literary novelistic art passed to me.

I am a different man, out of the ordinary, as many of the readers will feel and some will be able to identify within my thoughts, especially those who consider themselves different and have other interests than the majority of society.

Thus, I believe that we are many who are restless, inspired, who are self-taught thinkers. We want to learn from our environment, observing it and analyzing it, reading and searching, to discover the truths of this immense world; we can get it through our work of analyzing the things of life, where we find, undoubtedly, more and more ourselves.

The self-taught thinkers try, day after day, to develop their skills incorporating new disciplines in their way of life, to be able, one day, to achieve their goal, which is their full realization, without becoming arrogant, becoming more humble and grateful for what they have.

The language of this book is simple and practical and can be used by all readers at all academic levels.

I hope to be inspired enough to be able to write my book about life. I do not want it to be a boring book! Because, for that, I prefer not to start this work.

My goal in writing this book is that you can enjoy reading each sentence and each page, where you can find on its content clear answers to your concerns and questions.

I hope it gives you the pleasure to read it again and again, without making it a boredom, I hope it to be an exciting book and that you want to not stop reading until one chapter ends, before moving on to the next.

My desire is that my book can be read even in the last corner of the world.

A book that is a symphony of truth, where each of you, by reading it, can feel identified.

Here we go...

To the masterpiece!

Here we go!

I write this book out of love for the Crete Island and its people, who has loved me, who has accepted me and who has given me back my confidence as a Greek from Asia Minor returning to his homeland.

I also thank the Spanish people, the country that adopted me, from the beginning. When I arrived many years ago, that great country that is called Spain, it became the beloved homeland of my soul.

This wonderful Spain, which gave me all the opportunities and, above all, the language to be able to write this book in Castilian, this so beautiful, so rich and expressive language that it has become my mother tongue, from Spanish it can be translated into other languages!

Viva España, a romantic land of cultures and inspiration, land of El Greco from Crete and Toledo, land of Miguel Cervantes, Don Quixote de la Mancha and of the great inspired artists.

Long live Greece, land of philosophy, sciences and Greek mythology.

Long live Europe, land of freedoms, great civilizations and discoveries.

Long live France, land of wonderful cultures and great human revolutions.

Long live Lebanon, land of the alphabet, the Phoenicians, merchants and travelers. Lebanon is the lighthouse of the Middle East and the Arab world.

Long live Ukraine, land of great culture, with its capital Kiev, mother of the Russian cities, where Rus of Kiev was born and where Christianity was adopted for all Slavic peoples.

Long live England, Ireland and Scotland, land of great thinkers and human cultures.

Long live Africa, the land of origin of all human beings.

Long live Brazil, the Americas, long live Asia, China and Australia, lands of exotic cultures.

Long live the world of joyful autodidact thinkers who always seek truth through culture, cultivating ideas.

Best regards. A big hug for all who love the truth. I will try to do my best, my first great book of life.

«Diary of an Autodidact»
Wangeli Chaaraoui

Chapter 1: Distillation of Ideas

My first job was as a liquor distiller.

It was the job my father taught me, he was also an Autodidact.

My father was born in 1916 in Asia Minor, in a city called *Alexandretta*, a city founded by Alexander the Great in 333 BC. It is a city and a strategic commercial point of the Mediterranean; through it passed the trade routes between Baghdad of Mesopotamia and India, after the city became Byzantine. There, too, my mother, Eleni, was born. Alexandretta is called, today, Iskenderun and has been part of Turkey since 1939.

My father was called in Arabic Rizkallah, translated from the Greek *Theodoros*: it comes from *Teos Doros*, which means "gift of God", so, for me, for his friends and many people around him, my father really was a true Gift from God!

He was also Autodidact, had fewer studies than I, but it is normal, his time was different from mine.

A man, my father's friend, of French origin said that my father was *intelligent et débrouillard*, or intelligent and clever at the same time, these are two qualities hard to find in the same person; he was able to easily look for and find solutions to the problems that arose on his technical investigations, especially chemical or, rather, alchemical.

He was my first teacher, he had a small distillery, where he distilled all kinds of liqueurs and spirits; he invented everything and made everything out of nothing, with a very little knowledge he was able to achieve many successful inventions and technical developments.

He had few studies, he went to school until the age of fourteen, lost his two parents when he was only seven years old, his life was painful and very hard.

Afterwards, he had to learn everything from practice: by learning, observing, thinking, applying, experimenting and discovering.

God made the world out of nothing, he did it of his own free will and desire to create a perfect universe in which we live.

In this perfect world, each one of us is born with his virtues and his weaknesses.

We receive life from nothing, from the fertilization of a loving relationship between our parents - a man and a woman - that is ideal, that children are born of the fruit of the love of parents.

So, out of nothing or something sublime that comes from nature or from God, the Supreme, depending on whether we are believers or not, we were born in this world and, thanks to the love and care of our parents, we have grown and become adult people, prepared to survive in this demanding and multicultural society that asks us, every day, to know more things and to work more on ourselves.

Finally, all of us, and especially the self-taught people, daily try to realize ourselves as human beings out of nowhere. Starting from our mental basis, which is our level of knowledge and experience, we develop, every day, something new of what we have learned, by working and by making our future with our own hands and by applying our own ideas.

Then, comes the natural desire to someday form a family and have children, build a home, have money to spend, eat and drink, buy everything we need, go on vacation and live our dreams.

All that, which comes from nothing, becomes something tangible and substantial thanks to our will and our power of natural development.

By distilling a liquid we separate the volatile parts from the non-volatile parts.

By distilling the wine gives the alcohol, which is volatile.

Good alcohol - or the good distillate - has to be separated by the process of distillation.

The heat of the fire boils the wine and begins to emit vapors that are our ideas.

Only the volatile elements can be distilled; these are our ideas that are volatile, they are different ideas that can fly in the air like our thoughts.

Which is not volatile remains in the still: they are the residues, the ideas that weigh, that have no value and, therefore, are residual.

Residual ideas are separated from volatile ideas, but they cannot be destroyed, they are always present here, whether we want them or not, but we have to know how to separate the volatile from the residual.

The distillate - or the volatile part - has a head, a heart and a tail.

The good part is the heart, which is the good distillate that is the good ideas that we must keep, adopt and live with.

The head are superior spirits that we distill first and produce headache. The tails have acids and bad odor.

The heads and tails are put back into the next cooking period and they will continue coming out at the beginning and at the end, they are the auxiliary ideas that exist, represent the volatile evil which is very attractive but dangerous and nefarious. Tails are the degraded ideas, so heads and tails are bad ideas that cannot be adopted, as they are negative ideas that we have to reject and separate, they are bad because they poison, intoxicate and infect our lives; even if we know that they exist and will continue to exist. They are ideas that exist but cannot be adopted, are extreme and bad ideas, negative ideas for a conscious, responsible mind and human values; but these negative ideas are present in our world and belong to the evil; so if we want to stay in the good we must discard them and systematically reject them.

In the center there is the heart, which is the good and optimal part - or the best part -: they are the ideas of good, love and human tolerance.

Now, in the same ideas, the heart is where there is love, peace and tolerance.

We have to learn to distill the ideas.

We must not believe everything that the books or the media tell us.

We must be able to differentiate the truth from the lies; the good from the bad; the sincere things from the hypocrite ones.

In order to be able to separate the good from the bad, we must put everything into a still, which in this case is our power of analysis and that will guide us thanks to our scent, which is our sensitivity to be able to differentiate the truth from the lies, the good from evil, the genuine from the false; we will also need our experience and judgment.

For that, we need to have a spiritual eyes that come from the good spirit of God.

In this case, we can differentiate what is worth from what is not and thus separate the good ideas from the bad ones and order everything within our mental and spiritual system.

The distillation of ideas is the analytical process and the principle of every deep and coherent study.

Chapter 2: Trip to the Island of Salamis (Greece), summer of 1966

I remember that in late June or early July 1966 and at the end of the school year, I traveled from the port of Beirut (Lebanon) with my grandmother Irini (Greek name meaning Irina or peace), my sister Ketty (Catherine), who was then fifteen years old, in a boat called "Al Jazaer", an Arabic name that, translated into Spanish, means Algeria.

It was the first time in my life that I had been on a boat and had listened to the word "Al Jazaer", I was only twelve years old (I did not know that there was this country called "Al Jazaer" which in Arabic means "The Islands", that is Algeria!, a country that I have not visited so far, perhaps one day later. I have known in my life several Algerians, both men and women; they seem friendly, educated, noble and classy to me, which will surely come from their history and their culture.

The ship was white and the name, "Al Jazaer", was written in green.

The captain and crew of the ship were Egyptians -from Egypt- and they spoke Arabic with an Egyptian accent. The ship made the route Beirut-Alexandria (Egypt) - *Piraeus* (Greece).

Our first stop was at the port of Alexandria.

Alexandria is located in the north of Egypt, *Iskandariyya*, as they pronounce it in Arabic, is the second most important city of Egypt after its capital, Cairo.

Alexandria is a city of Alexander the Great, and bears his name; it was established in the year 331 BC, and it is a strategic port and an important cultural center in the Antiquity.

The trip lasted, I think, about four or five days in total travelling through the sea. We stopped after one or two days of sailing to spend a day in the port of Alexandria; there, in the early morning, we left the ship to the port of Alexandria and took a taxi to take a tour around the city.

The taxi was yellow and black (we first negotiated the price of the trip with the driver, this was done by the Greek man older than us), we were my sister Ketty, myself and a couple of young married Greeks, my grandmother Irini stayed on the boat; we first visited the Alexandria Zoo. I remember that they gave breakfast to a pair of big brown bears in the early morning, they were much taller than a man, they were perhaps two meters tall, and they gave them long loaves of bread soaked with milk and honey for breakfast. Since then, I like honey, which I take a couple of times a week, especially on Sundays with breakfast, on black bread with German Quark, on top of bitter orange jam, with English black tea and soy milk. After visiting the Zoo, we went to the Greco-Roman Museum of Alexandria, there were mummies and many antiques from the Greek and Roman times of the city. They were displayed, in some cases, the old gold jewelry matte gold resembling the matte gold of Crete and turquoise beetles. On the way back, we passed the *Al Zamalek* neighborhood, full of people familiar to us from the Egyptian movies we saw in Lebanon, talking about *Iskandariyya* (Alexandria) and *Al Zamalek*!

Later, in the afternoon, we returned to the ship and the journey from Alexandria to Piraeus was much longer, almost twice as long.

The trip on the boat was very nice, I slept on the bunk upstairs and my sister slept downstairs, my grandma also slept downstairs, I think we had a room with four bunk beds and there was a round closed window from where we could see the sea.

They offered us for lunch and dinner, I remember, some egg omelettes that were prepared with egg powder and the milk was also powdered - now, in modern ships, there are normal eggs and pasteurized liquid milk -, they also made spaghetti and salads, nothing was missing.

The night before our arrival at the port of Piraeus, before entering the Greek Sea, the captain of the ship called us to his cabin to show us how the island of Crete could be seen on the radar, which seems like a long shield that covers and protects the Greek Sea. It was very interesting to see the radar and how it worked, it was when I first heard of the island of Crete. There afterwards, in Greece, they talked a lot about the island of Crete, which was apparently an important island of Greece, the largest of all Greek islands and so I had the interest, which eventually became a dream, to one day get to know this famous island of Crete.

We arrived the next day at the port of Piraeus, near Athens; the customs controllers opened all the suitcases to control and looked at everything inside, they found matches in my grandmother's suitcase from Lebanon, they opened them and threw them on the ground, it was forbidden!

At the exit of customs, my uncle *Yorgos* was waiting for us, and he took us to his house in *Palia Kokinia* ("old Kokinia"), which is a neighborhood of Piraeus where lived the Greeks that came from Asia Minor; most of them were "pondios" (means Pontics), since the name of my mother and my uncle is

Andoniades, all surnames ending in "des" are pondios. We slept one night at his house and went the next day to the port of Piraeus, where we boarded the passenger ferry that took us to his summer house on the island of Salamis. The journey was relatively short, about half an hour or so, we could see many landscapes along the way, also a small island, where they said that there was an insane asylum inside!

Apparently the mentally ill were as prisoners on an island far from society, as in a great prison! It is a discriminatory thing that does not seem right!

The house of my uncle Yorgos was in Moulki and it still exists. Moulki is a well-known neighborhood on the island of Salamis.

The island of Salamis is a relatively large Aegean island. It is the largest of the Saronic Gulf islands and it is historically famous for the Battle of Salamis (480 BC), which confronted an alliance of Greek cities with Persian fleets, where the Persians eventually lost the war and since then, they did not try to conquer the Greek cities again.

I remember that my uncle drank from time to time with his friends a wine called *retsina*: it was served in the Greek taverns in cylindrical metal jars with a handle, they were copper colored metal of several measures (of a litre, half a litre, a quarter litre).

My uncle took me with him to buy groceries, with his great English motorcycle brand BSA, in the food store and also bought *retsina* on draft. *Retsina* is a white wine scented with pine tree resin, which preserves the wine for a long time, since the pine resin is antiseptic and also gives the white wine a very special flavor and touch.

My aunt, his wife, is called Ana: she was very nice, she loved us very much, she cooked typical Greek food with lots of vegetables and especially eggplants, green beans, assorted dishes, cooked with olive oil. Ana and Yorgos had two small daughters, six years and one year old, called Despina and Andigoni. They are now adults, married and have children.

Once a week, we ate meat, my uncle was a butcher, and he brought some good beef from his store. Sometimes they also brought lamb chops for barbecue, in Greece they are called *paidakia*: they are delicious, they are seasoned with salt, black pepper, mustard powder and Greek oregano, roasted over the wood fire, they come out exquisite.

My uncle's house in Moulki looked out onto the road through the garden with vineyard grapes to eat. The hawkers came every day and stopped there near the house; they were motorized cars with a motorcycle, the vegetable's car came, the baker's car, in the afternoon came the man who brought the Greek yogurt, who called it "*o yaurtás.*"

It was a country life and very calm on the sea, the house was facing the sea, it was only needed to cross the main street - that is, the road - to go to the beach and take a bath in the sea.

There, in this long stay of three months and a long summer, my sister and I learned many things like living in nature, being almost all day in bathing suit, learning the culture of the sea, learned to swim, to have an intimate contact with the sea water and nature, we learned to speak Greek well (a language we already knew from our house thanks to our mother Eleni, but it was not as good and genuine as the one we learned in Greece). We were very integrated in the atmosphere of the relatives and friends of my uncles, they all loved us, so we went deep into the Greek culture and mentality of those times, which has not changed much to this day.

There, we met a lot of people and made friends; we then made some trips around Greece. At the end of our stay, in late September, when my father came from Beirut to pick us up and stayed with us for a few days, we went to the fair in Thessaloniki (about 500 km away from Piraeus, I think, on the bus); We also went to the Acropolis of Athens, etc., and in the evenings, sometimes, to get some fish for dinner in the famous "*Turco Límano*" (the Turkish port), with its taverns facing the sea, now they call it "*Micro Limani.*" It was a very rich, precious, exciting and unforgettable trip for a twelve year old boy!

My father was joking and was as funny as he always was, he spoke Turkish to my uncle Yorgos. Also, there were dramatic moments: my father tried to reconcile my grandmother with my uncle (her son), but it was not an easy task, it was rather difficult! I remember that my father helped my grandmother repair things at home and my grandmother loved him very much.

We returned with my father from the Athens airport by plane to Beirut airport.

After this journey from Greece and Salamis, when I returned to school in Beirut, I no longer felt the same child as I had been before: a new identity had been born within me, and my Greek roots began to grow within me. Lebanon was no longer enough for me, I had seen something beyond little Lebanon: I had seen Alexandria, city of Alexander the Great of Egypt, its history and splendour; I had discovered Hellenistic Greece, its history and its glory, a multitude of Greeks, almost all were Orthodox Greek; while small Lebanon is a different country, a cultural mosaic with eighteen Christian and Muslim religious communities, united and divided by confessionalism, where there is also the feudalism of about eighteen powerful families and conflicts of coexistence are present between the different parties and Lebanese communities; These conflicts come from cultural problems and, mainly, by the ambition of the politicians and the distribution of the power.

Lebanon also has political problems with its two neighbors: Syria and Israel.

Greece and Lebanon are totally different! Although Lebanon is a very beautiful and wonderful country, a symbol of the beauty of a country that was always in its splendour in the sixties and seventies, until the war broke out in 1974, it is still beautiful and bright today. There were no comparisons with Greece and its great glorious history, where Greek mythology, philosophy and democracy were born; all Greeks have the same rights of citizenship, in Lebanon it is another world!

The two countries are nothing like it!

The president of Lebanon has to be a Maronite believer, so not every citizen could be president of the country!

As a result of this paradoxical contrast, a conflict of identity and tremendous doubts arose within me, I sought to find myself, I asked myself:

"Am I Lebanese? Am I Greek? Who am I really?"

Perhaps, I am rather a man free from all ties, citizenship or commitment or I am a traveller or a citizen of the world or, perhaps, a Greek from Asia Minor, like my uncle!

I dreamed of travelling again and embracing my body with the sea, I needed the trip and to return soon to my Greece.

I no longer had any interest in the school, it seemed a little boring to me: the new books, the school was for me like a prison, a few teachers were interesting; I dreamed of flying out of the classroom window with my desk to catch the boat and the plane again.

I could not bear any longer the Maronite priests (the Catholics of Lebanon) nor could bear their faces, nor their false beards, nor their black dresses, nor their words full of hypocrisy.

My father did not believe in the Orthodox Church or the Catholic Maronite Church and he said to me: "God exists somewhere, but not within these Churches!"

I remember that an orthodox priest came into our house every year, as usual, with his scary dress. He came with an assistant who carried with him a bucket of water, the father was throwing droplets of holy water through a cross with his hand on which were attached green branches of cypress or some similar plant; he threw the water droplets all over the house, they did it systematically every year in the houses of all Orthodox Greeks, I think before Easter. This priest was big and fat; he came every year, my father said: "Last year came a very fat priest, who could not fit on the couch, it looked a bit like you but I think it was not you." The priest replied, "No, no, it was me!" and my father laughed out loud, as he was the same priest. My father gave the assistant, who was really poor, more money than the priest, who did not need so much because he lived thanks to the Church.

What interested me most and passionately were my experiments and my inventions in my father's factory and talks a lot with him about many issues and many things. There, at my father's factory in Beirut, I had my little first laboratory: the whole factory was to me like a great laboratory.

In school, I liked chemistry and mathematics, I did not open almost any book; I lived in another world, in my world. I went out with my friends, I could not concentrate on the school, I searched for the truth, my own truth, I went up from class to class because I did not need to study so much, as I could see things coming!

I liked to travel in Lebanon, which was a very beautiful country: I went on a trip every weekend to the mountains and to the sea, the Becca valley, Zahlé, Chtoura, Baalbeck, Riak, Tripoli and southern Lebanon, to Sidon and Tire, where I had good friends throughout Lebanon.

I dreamed of one day being an engineer and working at Bosch and having a gas station in Germany; I dreamed of marrying a German blond woman and having a German Sheepdog and raising a family in *Deutschland*.

In the end, I managed to live in Germany and meet almost most of Germany, marry a German blond woman, learn to speak good German, but I did not become a mechanical engineer at Bosch, or have a gas station, or have a German Shepherd dog.

The Salamis journey marked my life. I have just celebrated the memory of fifty years of my trip to Salamis, on the island of Crete, where I was for the second consecutive time in the month of August; now my dream on the island of Crete is fulfilled in 2016, fifty years later. After traveling and discovering much of the world, I return to my Crete of Greece to plant myself again and see my Greek roots grow back into the land and sea of Crete.

On the trip to the island of Salamis (Greece), I discovered my dreams and much of myself; it was my first big trip as a kid.

Chapter 3: Learn how to cultivate the memory

Memory is basic, necessary and fundamental in every process of study or development of deep research, calculation, resolution and synthesis.

If memory fails, everything fails!

Without memory, intelligence cannot exist.

Intelligence needs memory as a database and knowledge storage; without this basis, intelligence can neither function nor give results.

Memory must also be intelligent!

Let's take the example of a pharmacist: he or she has hundreds of drawers where there is inside of them thousands of medicines stored for sale to patients with or without a prescription.

A pharmacist should memorize where each drug is placed, also know what group each drug belongs to, from there how to find it and where to find it, he must also have an order that he or she has created, either alphabetically or another order that can be used to search and find each medication without difficulty.

From there we conclude that without memory we can neither search nor find.

The same thing happens with a multilingual translator: he or she will know thousands of words in every language that speaks and perfectly dominates.

When a translator translates simultaneously (orally) or in writing, he will need to know how to look up the words inside his mind that belong to such a language and such a group of words, without the help of a dictionary or the internet translator.

The same thing happens in many cases or similar and different situations: a seller of a car spare parts shop will need to know where each spare part is and what it is for; although the hardware is very similar, each tool or each device has its utility and serves to something and he will have to know where it is, etc., etc.

So our memory has to work, we must know how to search for everything that we have already stored, look for it in our memory storage system, look for it in every corner or department within our human brain, and that without getting a headache or without having to suffer by memorizing so much useful data.

If we store the memory with intelligence, as it should be, we can store much more data and we can have several trades or professions, meet a lot of people from several countries and cities, get to know each person by his name, character and history, know the ways and being able to walk and drive in several towns, cities, countries, speak several languages, know how to cook several exotic dishes. We can have artistic facility to do various artistic tasks - to paint, to dance, to sing... -, to be able to ride a bicycle, to drive a motorcycle or a car, to fly a plane or to govern a boat, to be able to engage in conversations with different classes of people: educated, ignorant, from various religions, children, young people, adults, elderly, men, women, knowing how to deal with different types of people, etc., etc.

A man who speaks many languages does not need to repeat every day what he has already learned, once he has learned it is enough. Sometimes it is hard to memorize, you'll have to repeat it until you learn it by heart; then you should practice it; otherwise the memory will be lost over time, if it is not used often.

Memory is like a car: if it is stopped, it ages and the gums dry out; if used daily, the car stays as new for a long time.

If memory only has the purpose of memorizing by simply keeping or retaining, learning and repeating some phrases, songs, laws, stories, poems, music..., it will not be a smart memory and it will lack intelligence or logic; it will then be memorized as a song. Things must normally have some logic, some sense, and some veracity, based on principles of logic or mathematical, physical, chemical, biological or spiritual deduction.

True, there is memory without a logical sense and it is harder to memorize it for intelligent people; those who are smart enough do not usually agree to fill their memory of useless, meaningless and unreasonable things, in other words, they do not want to store nonsenses!

In the world of art, it is different: a singer has enough with memory without intelligence because he will always sing the same song and repeat it over; what he has to memorize are the notes, the melody, the tone and how to sing it; he also needs the intelligence and talent of a singer.

A scientist needs the memory of the data of a product to be able to work it, the laws and mathematical, physical and chemical formulas to be able to analyze it and to develop his experiments on this matter.

A polyglot needs to know how to memorize the words by associating them, sometimes with similar words from another language he knows.

For example, when I learned Norwegian in the years 2013-2015, the students had difficulty with the nouns *he* and *she*, which do not sound either feminine or masculine; in another language it is perhaps easier to distinguish masculine from feminine, but in Norwegian *he* and *she* are *hán* and *hün*, and it is not at all easy to know which is masculine and which is feminine, but, even memorizing them, remains difficult. The students were frequently wrong, also those who knew German *Er* and *Sie*. I was able to memorize it easily and the very nice teacher, who was called Siri, a resident of Norway for many years in a nearby town, called Alfaz del Pi - name of Arab origin - and in Valencian *Al Fares del Pi,* which means "Knight of the mount of pines", she liked the way I could memorize *hán* and *hün* directly. In German, a cock is called *Hahn* and is male, a hen is said *Huhn* and is female; so, just thinking about the cock and the hen, I could know what to use. If you talk about a man in the third person, you will say *Han*, and a woman it will be *Hün*, is a simple example of how you can memorize using the intelligence to memorize words of a language.

To learn a language, we need to memorize words, but then intelligence will help us to choose the right words for each situation and how to construct the sentences.

In other words, memory is the basis of knowledge or the instrument; it is the fundamental tool to perform the work.

Now, how to cultivate the memory? There are several methods to do it.

Going to the movies and watching movies from time to time, watching television on all kinds of topics that are interesting attracting for us, artistic, scientific, economic, political issues... but we must recognize that politics, many times, it lacks logic and is governed by hypocrisy, interests and is, often, ruled by the law of the jungle or the sea law, where the big ones impose over the smaller and the stronger over the weaker.

In an informative newspaper, they talk about time, repressed popular movements, events, murders, accidents, ugly and unpleasant things, politics and, above all, wars and terror of all kinds.

Memory will continue to function as long as we continue to use it.

Memory has enemies, like, for example, being surrounded by idiots, that does not help the memory; if we live with mental or spiritual patients, we can get contaminated by their mental or spiritual illness; that is why it is ultra-necessary to surround ourselves with intelligent, spiritually healthy, sensitive and creative people, and not mentally ill people - that there are in quantity in our multicultural society -, those people are weak from their birth or have had serious trauma or serious accidents that affected their nervous system and intelligence in general, and they often become bad or simply mentally ill.

Drugs impair memory; for example, smoking, although it is not considered a drug socially speaking, it is indeed: smoking destroys brain cells and smokers lose their memory or their ability to memorize; abusing the consumption of alcohol or natural alcoholic beverages, even wine or beer, in considerable amounts, can greatly damage the memory according to the brain mass of the person. The great philosopher Socrates drank wine more than anyone and did not get drunk, is a sign that he had a large, superior brain mass.

The concentration of alcohol in the blood does not help the work of memory.

For the memory, a lucid mind is necessary, an inner peace and also being able to concentrate.

Holidays away from your surroundings are good for healing and regenerating the memory, it is like washing it and detoxifying it from all the stress and routine of everyday life.

The use of Ginkgo biloba or soy lecithin are also good for memory: from a certain mature age, taking them regularly undoubtedly helps the capillary circulation within the veins of the brain and, therefore, helps in keeping the memory alive and young.

It would be good to eat fish (containing phosphorus), nuts, goat cheese... cheese is a good food for the brain if taken in the morning and at noon, but if taken at night it causes fattening and producing cholesterol.

We must eat little meat, at most once a week, and not eat pork, maybe a good ham, that once in a while, but avoid the fats; eating a lot of meat causes an aggressive behavior, it is better to get some lamb or, better still, chicken or rabbit.

In order for the memory to continue working well, it is necessary to use it, it is like any machine or vehicle: if it is not use, it oxidizes; the gums or the joints are dried and no longer work. The same thing happens inside our brain: if you stop using it, your memory will lose quality.

To have an elastic brain, it is necessary to have elastic or, rather, flexible memory power; it is important to be able to memorize the words we hear after a few minutes, so it is important to know how to repeat phonetic sounds well.

People who do not listen well have difficulty learning a new language, a song, holding back words and repeating them.

I remember that when I was young, I could memorize what a customer told me on the phone and now also, if he even gives me a phone order; therefore, it is necessary to know how to listen and concentrate on the conversation.

Intelligence separates useful memory from useless memory, it is like selecting trash, it is just like selecting glass bottles, cans, PVC or tetra Brik, metal cans, paper or cardboard, biological waste..., every garbage will go in the appropriate container.

Thus, it is grasped what is useful is saved and the useless is discarded.

What is useful is what serves us and what we need as knowledge and tool for the development of our universe, our intelligence, our inner peace, our relationship with the others and particularly with the people we love, for our life in couple; we also need it to develop our spirituality and our relationship with God, so our wisdom can grow.

What is useless is what can confuse us, which is immediately seen as worthless, it is useless to have a false content, hypocritical or liar, even diabolical.

You cannot believe in the lie, you must believe and be based on the truth!

Memorizing useless things will weary our mind and get it away from the truth and from God.

Memory is trained from a young age.

When a human being listens more, the more he will be able to learn, especially if he listens to different things, different languages, if he had different schools, if he learned different trades, different cultures, if he were interested in different religions.

A child born in a multicultural environment develops a better memory capacity than a child who is born and grows in a simpler and less culturally diverse environment. He may develop other skills, in this case, artistic and others, depending on where he lives and who he frequents.

If one relates to artists, unwittingly will become an artist.

An intelligent person normally focuses less time to craftwork and more time to difficult and more coherent things, which need a high capacity and mental concentration.

Artisans are very patient people with their artwork.

There are also genius artists who have both: intellectual ability and patience and artistic talent.

For example, Leonardo da Vinci was both a scientist and an artist.

Einstein was only an intellectual scientist.

Socrates was a sculptor, artist and philosopher.

The ideal thing is to practice both things: science or logic and art, which depends on beauty, that develops the inner part of a person - as his mind - and that enable oneself to have spiritual peace.

Memory is basic and fundamental; it accompanies us throughout the evolutionary process of our professional, intellectual, artistic, sentimental and spiritual life.

Chapter 4: My first laboratory, my father's Factory in Beirut

In this chapter, I will talk about my early research I conducted in my youth and my first laboratory at my father's factory in Beirut.

As a child, I liked to go with my father to his factory, it was a liquor factory and a small distillery, it had many barrels of oak wood where they rested and matured the distilled spirits like distilled wine spirit, malt, *whisky*, *brandy*, etc...

My father was a great genius, an inventor; he had invented by himself and conceived everything.

When he was twelve years old, he helped in the small factory of his Uncle Manoli in *Alexandretta*, where they distilled the *arak*, which is a distilled wine spirit with anise seed, it is the traditional anise seed liquor typical of the Middle East, In Turkey they call it *raki*. On the island of Crete, they also call it *raki* trough the Turkish-Ottoman occupation and influence of the island of Crete, but the *raki* of Crete does not contain anise, it is comparable to a Galician marc spirit or an Italian grappa, a little finer and has a very refined aroma and taste.

Since my father was still a child, he could easily enter the copper boiler of the alembic to clean it after having distilled or, perhaps, even before. To clean the copper, it is necessary to use an acid solution; the vinegar is equal and is almost better than a chemical acid and is more natural. Imagine the experience and hard obligations of my father when he was a child of twelve or thirteen years old!

The word "*arak*" is an Arabic word meaning sweat. They referred to the alembic sweating when distilled, subjected to the heat of the fire and, when the wine comes to the boil, inside the boiler the vapors are released that arrive at the serpentine bathed in cold water; then the process of condensation of the vapors begins by the sudden change of temperature, it is as if the alembic was sweating: hence the word "*arak*".

<u>All of the words</u> "*alembic*", "*alcohol*" and "*arak*" are of Arab origin.

My first laboratory, at ten years of age, was a cardboard box where I kept (inside of it) all the utensils and chemicals from my little boy's laboratory. I remember well that the box was small and rectangular, perhaps twenty centimeters wide and forty or fifty centimeters long. Inside of it, I had my whole laboratory in, it was composed of several tiny bottles of fifty ml each, containing acids - such as sulfuric acid, hydrochloric acid... - and bases - such as caustic soda, baking soda... - they had all been collected or discreetly stolen from somewhere in my father's factory. It had on each bottle a label that indicated its contents and they were covered with aluminum screw caps. My father let me have access to everything so that I could develop and he would keep an eye on me so that nothing bad happened to me.

The first thing I wanted to test was the phenomenon of electrolysis, so I took an electric wire, I placed a plug on it and put it inside a wall socket.

The current in Lebanon, in the mid-1960s, was biphasic and 110-volt alternative. I placed each of the two bare wires of their plastic protection inside two bottles, containing a solution of acid diluted with tap water, vapours flowed into each bottle, where the gases that evaporated by the electrolysis produced the electric current . This phenomenon gave me so much joy, and I was beginning at that moment to realize myself as a child scientific autodidact researcher.

My father, seeing everything, was shocked and scared for me, because I could get electrified or burn my hands with the current or the acids, and he dismantled the box from my first child's laboratory.

Later, I learned many more things as I grew up!

My first laboratory, at fourteen or fifteen years of age, was composed of a small glass alembic that became after a while into my great real laboratory. There was also another copper alembic for testing, which my father did later on. There were also alcoholometers, boilers, probes, gas fires, and so on. I also dreamed of becoming a chemical engineer because I read the French books my father had on the fermentation of malt must and they were written by French chemical engineers, but it did not become so. I do not regret not having been an academic as I had to leave university courses and leave them half-way through, for the circumstances of my life; that is why they called me "the autodidact researcher."

My father's factory had an area of approximately 250 m², it was a basement of a three floors building, it was located in the *Achrafieh* neighbourhood and it had two entrances and shop windows to the main street. The small factory still exists, it is now owned by my brother André, who uses it as a warehouse and office.

Upstairs, on the third floor, lived a family of a Lebanese taxi driver married to a blond, beautiful, intelligent German woman, they called Ortancia; it is a name of a pretty flower to adorn the entrances of the Andalusian houses of Granada, but I do not think this is her real name because I did not meet women with this name in my long stays in Germany. Ortancia had three little boys, as handsome and intelligent as she is.

She was a very nice woman, she loved us very much and we loved her too.

She helped us, from time to time, to translate German letters that came sometimes from Germany, from the suppliers of the golden lead capsules for the liquor bottles like *brandy* and *whisky* that my father made and bottled. We, the three children, helped him; especially the two boys -my brother Andre, who was two and a half years younger than me, and especially me- while my mother and sister helped from home.

Since then, perhaps observing that beautiful woman and interesting person, I dreamed of living one day in Germany and marrying a blond German woman. The dream has been possible, but it was done in a different way than I had imagined or dreamed.

My first German course was at the «*Madrasat Al Hikma*» school in Arabic, in French it is «*Collège de La Sagesse*», which means «school of wisdom». We were the first generation to receive German class - it was a novelty in the history of this school - course just inaugurated in 1966; we were in the sixth class of the French teaching system, that is equal to the first of E.S.O. in Spain.

<u>We had lessons in four languages in total</u>: French for all subjects, Arabic only as language and literature, English three hours a week as a language, and German two hours a week as a language.

The teacher was big, a little robust and quite nervous of temperament, he was Armenian; I think the Armenians are the ones who speak the most German in Lebanon. I had my mind occupied on other things, as it almost always was since I was little. When I had, I think, seven years, the teacher called me in class with the name Vango. Vango was the diminutive of my name, my child's name. As my name Wangeli or Vanguelli was somewhat unusual at that time - a Greek name not common in Lebanon - they preferred to call me by this diminutive name, since it was easier, but I did not answer, I was in another world, I was on the Moon dreaming!

At school, I was an irregular kid, depending on the fact if the subject was interesting or, on the contrary, boring to me. When the subject was boring, I liked to talk during classes with other students to distract me; some teachers kicked me out of class with other talkative guys like me. The German teacher, besides kicking me out, also slapped me!

At that time - we talk fifty years ago - it was normal and allowed in schools to hit the children with the ruler on the hand; now, in our present time, that is no longer admissible!

At that time they said: "Whoever has hit you, loved you," that is, whoever hits you wants to educate you for love and interest; now students are educated with words and valid arguments.

It was also a phase of adolescence and puberty. At the age of twelve, when the children wanted to have more freedom and to develop at all levels, I asked my parents to sign a letter for me, as did the parents of other students who did not want their children to attend this German class with the nervous and rough teacher. German was an optional subject and was not mandatory like the others; English was mandatory.

In this school *Ecole de la Sagesse*, we were formed to be the elite, all my classmates now have high positions in society: they are doctors, engineers, have high rank in the army... Unlike them, I had two occupations or concerns: school and factory, so I did not have enough time to open the books at home, I only concentrated on the subjects that really interested me!

I remember that my sister Catherine taught me all the chemistry of the high school year on a night before the final exam in June of 1973 and I passed the bachelor of the Mathematics field on my first trial. I liked chemistry and mathematics; I solved problems in my own way, and came to the right solution because I could not do it any other way because I had never opened the book, just by listening to the teacher when I could concentrate!

My father was a tireless researcher as I have been all my life too. I was trying to correct his faults.

My father had done many tests of distillates of different grains and even dried vegetables. Sometimes I would open the test bottles, each bearing a label stating the content and date of the test. I smelt the distillates and was sorting and selecting the results according to the labels, I concluded that my father had obtained a good result and, as they say in English, "he had nailed it"... However, as my father distilled with his traditional method of distillation and burned the must of barley and other cereals, almost all the tests had a taste or smell of burning!

He did, at the time, try several attempts to correct his distillation technique, but he could not solve this serious problem he had.

To solve this problem, I proposed a distillation to the bain Marie or water bath with a boiler of double bottom of copper bathed in water by outside; but the problem was that the water in the water bath evaporated and got lost. I was fortunate enough to find, thinking and analyzing, that the alcoholic solution of the must boiled at a temperature less than one hundred degrees Celsius or centigrade; so the water did not necessarily have to reach the boiling point or a hundred degrees Celsius in the first phase of the distillation, but the water in the bath Maria should boil at the end of the distillation, when the alcohol contained in the wort was evaporating little by little after a few hours of distillation and the must would lose its concentration in alcohol and needed to reach a hundred degrees to be able to boil.

I then proposed a water bath in the closed double-bottomed outside with an exhaust valve, which I regulated as I needed it. I had to change the spring for a looser one, so that the valve could open from a slight pressure of accumulation of water vapors. That was possible and the invention was successful!

This invention would not be possible without the help of my father, who had faith in my ideas and made this new great alembic; he did it in the workshop of an Armenian coppersmith - at that time and up to now, the Armenians were the great craftsmen of Lebanon and they still are. He did it as I conceived it: with a closed bottom double chamber for the water bath where water was poured in from above and could be emptied from a faucet below, I remember that I had, apart from the exhaust valve, a Boiler thermometer and pressure gauge for boilers. It was a great invention, an innovative machine, in this alembic the must was no longer burned as before and the distillate was perfect!

This is to tell you that my father's factory was a large laboratory within my reach where I could carry out all the investigations I wanted with the help of my father.

From the small laboratory of my box at the age of ten, I came to make a great invention at my twenties. Later, I went to Belgium to study at the Catholic University of Leuven; there began my life, which was full of endless adventures that continue, to this day, being inspiration to write this book and performing a thousand and one experiments.

My father's factory, apart from being a great laboratory, was also a place for social gatherings: there were friends of my father who came in the afternoons, almost every day of the week, to put labels on the bottles; it was an entertaining manual work at that time.

The labels were pretty from *Whisky* Brands *Queen Helen, Evangelos Brandy, Town Hall London Dry Gin,* etc.

First, the liqueur glass bottles were filled and sealed with printed and lacquered aluminum capsules. Before, in past times past, it was made with cork and covered with lead caps of gold color and printed, my father did everything himself and we helped him.

The labeling was done with almond tree resin glue, which was diluted with water, a layer of liquid glue was distributed on a large square glass tray and the labels were placed, which were moistened with this glue solution; then the labels were removed from the glass tray and placed correctly on the full and closed bottles of liquor. There were glass bottles of various sizes: 0.75 L large bottle, half bottle, quarter bottle and 50 cc or 50 ml bottles.

There, too, in my father's factory, during the bonding of labels, there was a social atmosphere of daily chatter; there was a talk about everything - in Arabic or Turkish - of politics, criticism, socio-political affairs... they were not philosophical dialogues, but often they spoke with mixed irony and perfumed it with a lot of humour and they all laughed in a friendly and healthy environment.

There were occasional sporadic meals after work; they were very happy and entertaining moments, there even was a person, Abu Leila, who sang in the small parties.

There were very interesting people coming to sit, talk and help; most of them emigrants who were friends of my father, from *Alexandretta*, his childhood, like Abu Eli, although his name was Georges, but they used to call him as usual at that time: father of Eli or Elias (who is his son). There was also another funny friend named Abu Leila (the one who sang), his real name was Hanna - like Juan, in Spanish or John in English; also Abu Freijo (the cousin of my father), his name was Etienne and his son Freijo (my cousin), who died more than fifteen years ago very young. All these people have died, but their memory is eternal, that is why I quote them in this chapter, because all my father's friends loved him and us, the children, and we equally loved them.

My father's factory, apart from being my great laboratory and a small liquor factory, was also my first great technical and practical school, a place of social encounter where positive thoughts and much love were exalted, a place where the soul could rest.

Chapter 5: The Three Great Secrets of Life

What are the three great secrets, the most important, of our life?

I have had the answer inside of me for many years. That is what I was looking for all my life: to find God, myself and find true love.

In these three great secrets are all the mysteries of life and all the truth that we are looking for.

The Lord Jesus Christ said: "I am the Truth; who follows me has eternal life."

I am totally sure and convinced that there is nothing that is bigger, more important and deeper than being able to seek and find these three great truths or three great secrets of life.

In the meanwhile, one continues to search within these three wonderful worlds: God, oneself and love. If one could become immersed in the relationship with God, with himself and with true love, one could start feeling like a hero who has the great privilege of being able to swim in those three immense divine oceans that form our human truth and our divine reality.

If one could get to understand these three great secrets and see them clearly with his spiritual eyes, and if one continues to work on himself, seeking to reach the depths of these three deep truths... If one were to be able to see clearly in the horizons of these three immense seas, after having gone through long difficult paths, after having gone through great disappointments and sentimental, psychological pains and having gone through failures on his professional life, after also have lived joys, happiness, even children's dreams, physical pains and psychological traumas in his long journey of the search for truth and through his own circumstances and the conditions of his life... could one day undoubtedly come to decipher these three great secrets, from which derive all the answers to our major questions about the great mysteries that revolve about the life of the human being.

If we come to discover those three great foundations that dominate our life - which are God, ourselves and love - and if we come to know and live these three truths with love, joy, harmony and serenity, there will be nothing more to look for or anything else to find.

God is in the first place, as the Gospel of Jesus Christ says: "*You shall love the Lord your God with all your heart, with all your soul and with all your mind. This is the greatest and first commandment*" (Matthew 22: 36-38).

God has given us life, He is our heavenly father - although we all have or have an earthly father - God is the creator of the universe, God is an eternal Father.

First we have to look for God, pray to God every day so that He will listen to us and hear our prayers, He knows what we really need, He is the only one who can help us more than anyone else in this world.

God must always be present in our life and in our heart.

We discover God through what our great teacher, Jesus Christ, the Son of the living God, taught us about Him, who came to earth to tell us about God the Father. Then followed the work of Jesus his Apostles preaching the Gospel and the teaching of Jesus Christ all over the world to the ends of the earth.

Discovering God is being able to see the daily miracle that is alive within us and in our environment, in our family, in nature. Thank God, we have creative gifts and faculties; the miracles of God are seen everywhere: within ourselves and around us.

God is always present; we feel Him when we need Him and He, from above or from close, lends us His help and does not let us fall.

Without God, the human being is lost, it will walk in the darkness, in ignorance, in uncertainty and chaos. Without God, we are depending on the prince of darkness, who is Satan. Satan was an important angel of God who rebelled against God the creator, but God let him loose for a time so that man is free and can choose between the true God and the other god of evil: the god of selfishness, the god of power, of materialism, of injustice, of hypocrisy, of lying, of omnipotence, and of falsehood.

If the human being comes to find God the supreme and if he can live in harmony with God and his son Jesus Christ, he will also have the help of the Holy Spirit, who is God's spirit on Earth; he can have the protection of the angels of God and thus he will be able to find the first most important foundation of life.

The second important foundation is to know oneself

What does "Know yourself" mean? "Know yourself" comes from Greek antiquity, it means that the main need of a person to gain access to philosophical wisdom is to know himself.

How can we know ourselves?: discovering ourselves through our daily work and human experience.

For example, we are in an emergency situation, we need to be able to save a human life or simply help a friend, family member or ourselves. Suddenly, we discovered within us a faculty or talent that we did not know before, nor did we know that it existed within us.

Looking for or investigating something, we surprisingly discovered something very important, totally different from what we wanted to find.

Talents are discovered within ourselves when we try to practice some art - such as singing, painting, dancing, acrobat - or being able to negotiate some important deal, or we try to solve some difficult problems that require us great mental abilities – as for example, solve some technical problems or other physical practices: sports, etc. - or when we try to be creative and we want to write a diary or make a synthesis of our life and try to draw philosophical conclusions from our own experiences.

We discover ourselves not only looking at ourselves in the mirror, which only teaches us our aesthetic side and our apparent age, but by exercising our work. If we are able to carry out difficult tasks daily solving the equation of our life - working on ourselves, doing great difficult missions, experiencing great adventures of exploration trips -, and if we discover a lot of things and get ahead and achieve good results, we could forge some unusual knowledge: we will undoubtedly satisfy within ourselves, we will be able to see that we have become important or reach something more in our intellectual or professional life - a good job position, a good profession, a good future.

We also discover ourselves through our family and our children, who we have educated according to our own philosophy and our way of seeing things, and of which we can be proud because they, although they are different from us and have their own personality and character, continue to be our reflection and the projection of our own person in the future. Just as an Arab proverb says: "*Who has begotten is not dead,*" so our children can keep our memory alive through time.

One can discover himself in social life: when people accept him, love him and listen to him, especially those who are intellectual and healthy in spirit; those who are open and willing to learn. It should not matter to us to be despised by the naive lost or by those that envy us or those who cannot bear our way of thinking and how we see things, because we see beyond the sight of a simple human being who only watches and contemplates every day his banking account and what he has achieved materially: those are the naive, spiritually blind that do not see beyond their nose. We need, on the contrary, to be appreciated by great thinkers, visionaries and philosophers; then we will have been able to pass the great test of life to discover ourselves and become heroes or great artists, and above all, when we see that God accepts us, when we can feel that God loves us, He listens and supports us and we continue alive and healthy walking the roads of life.

The third thing to look for is true love

Love is about loving God, loving your neighbour, and loving yourself.

Here comes the second commandment of Jesus Christ: "*Thou shalt love thy neighbour as thyself.*"

Love has to be mainly towards others: in the couple, in the family, in the circle of friends, in social life and in our relationship with others. This love consists in wanting to help those we know or do not know, but who we know need our help, and do it with love and selflessness.

Discovering love is being able to love, to know how to love and to feel loved. That is why it is important to give and know how to make yourself loved: if we do not know how to give from ourselves, we will never have the joy of receiving something from a loved one or another stranger we did not expect, who can make us feel happy.

Discovering love is also being able to find the couple that we have always sought because we do not want to be alone and we want to form a family and feel happiness in life.

Discovering love is also being able to make friends -true friends- and to know how to take care of friendship.

Socrates has many phrases about friendship. The one I like most is "*Go slow when you choose your friends; but when you have them, stand firm and steady.*"

God is love, that is why we must love Him and thus we can feel the love of God within us.

Love contains the first two important things: God and self.

The three secrets of life are practically united in love and life with God, in life with oneself and with others.

The three great secrets of life are just as important...

God, yourself and love.

Chapter 6: My pilgrimage journey to Jerusalem, Easter 1967

Here I am going to tell you about a pilgrimage trip that the whole family did to Jerusalem in 1967.

This trip took place during the Holy Week, at the Orthodox Easter of 1967, just the following year after my sister and I, along with my father, returned from our long summer trip to Greece in 1966; my grandmother Irini stayed in Piraeus, where she lived in her house until she died, I think in the year 1980.

This family pilgrimage journey to Jerusalem was done by all members of our family: my father and mother and the three children - my sister Catherine, my brother André, who is two and a half years younger than me, and I. We all left Beirut, passing through Syria and Jordan, until we reached Jerusalem. We were also accompanied by a Lebanese neighbour, who we had known for a life time, who was called Saide, synonymous with Our Lady Mary; Saide is the same age of my mother Heleni, the two are now ninety and they are still alive. Saide had a sister who was a nun, a leader of a Catholic convent in the well-known city of

Irbid in Jordan, which caught us right on our way to the holy city of Jerusalem.

The purpose of this trip was to visit the holy city of Jerusalem and donate a rooster to the monastery of the nuns. It was to fulfill a promise that my mother made many years ago, when she was pregnant with her second child (who was me); my mother then made a promise: if she had a son, she would donate a rooster to the monastery of the nuns in Jerusalem. It was also a journey of thanking the beloved God and His angels, as the entire family went through a serious traffic accident, which occurred just two months before this trip, completely harmless.

When I was born on April 2, 1954, my sister Ketty was three years old. Thirteen years later, in April 1967, came the possibility of realizing this promise and this journey of pilgrimage to Jerusalem.

In winter, in early 1967, I think in February, our entire family had a serious traffic accident. My father drove his car on a Sunday afternoon, it was an Opel Record model 1959-1960 two-coloured with coral red and white imported from Germany, it was a very nice car at that time. The car was almost a total loss, the whole family was inside the car, the blow was on my side, I had a wound on the chin and they gave me two or three stitches, which they took away in a few days; the scar is still present to this day, but scarcely visible.

People were talking about a miracle, a fatal accident! The whole family left unharmed, my father also had a wound in his foot, but it was not serious.

I was the cause of this accident, as I insisted all that winter Sunday, I wanted to go and see the snow of the mountains of Lebanon. After the long journey from Greece, I could not stand still, the world no longer fit for me! I needed to travel, it was my drug, my great need, as it is still so far, I need to continuously trip, every now and then I get this idea and need to travel, it is a drug and a passion for which I could never resist!

My father was tired of hearing me repeating and insisting about it and - also because he loved me very much - he then took the decision to take us all to see the snow of the mountain of Lebanon, where in winter, from about 800 meters of altitude could be seen and touched the snow, and see it from afar on the high mountains of Lebanon. I remember that we went out in the afternoon, after eating, we got there at dusk, we saw some very white, wonderful snowscapes, we saw from afar the Mount Hermon (*Yabal al Shaikh*).

When we got back, it was night, the road was new, there was no light and, wanting to cross the main road on the coast, a car hit us at full speed on the left back side (right where I was sitting) and where the Driver (my father), in front of the same left side of our car.

As a result of this accident, my father looked for a substitute car while repairing the ragged old car, which he used for the distribution of his liquors.

After a couple of months, he found, with the help of his cousin Etienne, a second-hand car that was brand new, owned by an Arab prince from the Persian Gulf -Kuwait- who wanted to sell it. The prince used this luxury car in his instances and vacations in Lebanon, the car was a Mercedes 220 S 1964 petrol black color with all the extras, upholstered in natural cream colored leather, with hydraulic steering, etc. There was all the extra equipment that existed at the time!

We went on a trip to Jerusalem, early in the Orthodox Holy Week, after Palm Sunday, which was April 23th, although Orthodox Easter Sunday was April 30, 1967. In that year, the difference of the two Easter dates -Catholic and Orthodox- was five weeks, the difference between the Georgian calendar of the Catholic Church and the Julian calendar of the Orthodox Church.

This trip has been crucial to me, it was my first and only trip to Jerusalem. Then I could no longer visit this holy place, which is the city of Jerusalem, because, after some forty days of our journey to Jerusalem, the

Six Day War broke out between the Arab countries of the Middle East and Israel.

It was the famous Six Day War of June 1967, faced by Arabs and Israelis. This war was a total failure for those Arab countries: the Arab coalition of the United Arab Republic (Egypt, Jordan and Syria) against Israel. The coalition was led by political leader Jamal Abdel Nasser, who, through his actions, only succeeded in making relations between Arabs and Jews worse off. There were many human losses and territories lost by the Arabs and the Palestinians, there were irreparable dramas and frustrations for the countries of the Middle East, Jerusalem was no longer Jerusalem before this war. Although it remains a holy city for Jews, Christians and Muslims, it has been under Jewish control since that war, when it should be a free city as it was before, but it is no longer a free city.

After this famous Six-Day War, the political situation degenerated into several regional conflicts which gradually gave way to a sad and nefarious regional panorama that led directly and indirectly to the civil war in Lebanon, which began in 1974 -1975 and its consequences are still present to this day, after more than forty years!

Lebanon remains an unstable country. Although the war officially ended in 1991, conflicts and wars in the Middle East area are still news of every day, seemingly interminable. Lebanon hosts 1.5 million Syrian refugees.

<u>Now I get back to our journey of pilgrimage to Jerusalem</u>:

Our pilgrimage trip to Jerusalem was very nice, very pleasant and very interesting, we were sleeping several nights in the monastery of the nuns of Irbid; next door there was a catholic church that we visited once.

My father taught me a little to drive his car when I was only thirteen and I was already able to take it. Then, at the age of fourteen, I would take turns, from time to time, with my father's cars. Driving was my passion and it is still so!

We went to Jerusalem by day, I think it was Holy Thursday or Good Friday, very early in the morning, we got there in the middle of the morning. First, my father bought a rooster at the market; it was a little, since the big roosters were sold very expensively because of the great demand at Easter, so my father said: "A rooster is a rooster, no matter how big or small. The difference between one and the other will be better for the poor! "

He bought a small rooster and we gave it to the nuns of the convent, it seemed to them a little donation! Later on, my father gave the difference to the poor beggars who were there, they seemed really poor and really needed help; well, the promise was fulfilled.

We visited in Jerusalem the Church of the Resurrection and the tomb of Lazarus, in Bethany. There, there were guides who taught that from a window of the Church of the Resurrection, there were always sunshine constantly and there was light.

We were in the Christian neighborhood, where the big churches were.

There are five neighborhoods in Jerusalem: the Armenian quarter - the small quarter of the old city - the Christian Quarter - where the Church of the Holy Sepulcher stands -, the Jewish quarter - where the Lamentations Wall stands -, the Muslim neighborhood – the largest neighborhood - and the Temple Mount -Esplanade of the Mosques, which is a sacred site for Muslims and Jews.

There, in the Christian quarter, we saw from afar a cousin of my father's named Elenitsa (diminutive, in Greek, "little Heleni"), a very believing woman who was always present in those holy places in these dates; she saw us from afar and greeted us, it was not possible to approach her, there were hundreds of thousands of pilgrims in that Holy Week of 1967!

Elenitsa died a few years later, by a fate fact, with a bomb that exploded in Beirut in the year 1979, I believe, in the Achrafieh neighbourhood, during the civil war in Lebanon, where instantly died in this cruel and sad act more than seventy people; they were all inside their vehicles stopped by the traffic. My father's cousin, Elenitsa is undoubtedly a saint; she appeared to me after having died, a couple of years later, in a dream in Madrid at the end of 1981, a few weeks after arriving in Madrid, where I permanently lived; I will tell you about this dream and the consequences it had in my life in the next chapter "My dream of Madrid, late 1981."

Afterwards, we returned in the afternoon to the Irbid convent, where we slept a couple of nights and the nuns treated us very well. I think the trip lasted about four or five days in all. On the way back, we stopped in Syria, in the town of Houran, I think, near Daraa, it was a pause on the way to visit the family of a Syrian worker who had worked for many years in my father's factory; his family was very modest, they welcomed us very well, they invited us to a cafe, my father made them a thank-you gift that gave them great joy. Afterwards, we return blessed from this holy journey to our house in Beirut.

So it was our pilgrimage journey to Jerusalem in Easter 1967.

Chapter 7: The Mediterranean languages and civilizations

This chapter is very large and very extensive.

Personally, I had the luck or the opportunity to live in a great part of this wonderful world, but not in the whole world. I know most of the Middle East, much of Europe, much of Africa and Brazil.

I will be able to write about what I have seen, what I have perceived, what I have experienced, what I have felt and what I have lived in countries where I have been living for short and long seasons.

I have been able to learn the languages of almost all the countries where I have been living, I loved learning languages. I was not interested in dialects, since they have no horizon, since they are only spoken in certain regions. When one leaves the region or the country, hardly anyone speaks them outside, unless it is an emigrant that comes from this place or of this specific region where it is spoken such dialect. Thus, dialects were not interesting to me, although I had to learn some naturally, as the Lebanese dialect, which is a dialect spoken in Lebanon, which comes from Aramaic and Arabic, is spoken in some countries of the Middle East (like Lebanon, Syria, Jordan and Palestine, although the accent changes and some words depending on the country). My passion was and continues to be communication and to engage in conversations and dialogues with people from anywhere in the world.

My father once told me: "Go to the world, learn everything."

He liked to know and learn from everything, the circumstances of his life were not the same as mine, his conditions did not allow him to travel so much or learn so many things that he wanted to learn. But from the few things he had learned, he did wonders, he spoke three to four languages, he was very intelligent.

He wished I could learn about everything.

I remember that he sent me a lot of money to live very well in Belgium and to live well for more than six months in 1976, when I was studying at the University of Louvain. He was the most generous father of all the fathers in the world, he gave me the newest of his cars to drive and use it, while he stayed with the oldest. I think I was the most beloved among the three children of my father or he loved me in a special way, perhaps because I was the first male and bore the name of his father, Vangelis. I also loved him very much and that is why I write this book: for love and homage to my father who taught me so much and loved me very much.

With the money he sent me, in early 1976, I bought a used car and traveled to England and Scotland to visit the *whiskey* factories in the Highlands, the high mountains of Scotland. It was my first solo trip around the world. It was an unforgettable two week trip that I did at the end of March 1976, where I learned many things, including practicing English and discovering a new, very interesting and wonderful world.

My father is present in my mind and heart since I was born and will remain until the end of my life and, also, in the hereafter!

I also write this book out of love for my son Alexandros. I named my son Alexandros because I loved the character of Alexander the Great when I saw his great statue in a monument on a horse in the famous city of Thessaloniki. I dreamed, since then, of having a son and calling him Alexander.

My son is big and beautiful like Alexander the Great, but he is still young and I hope he grows up with the wisdom that I try to influence him. We are joined by the same love that my father taught me and that I taught my son.

I practically speak all the languages of the Mediterranean. The ones I do not speak are Hebrew and Albanian, because I did not have the opportunity to visit those countries or live in them.

Some languages I learned as a child - such as Greek, Arabic, French, English and Turkish - and other languages I learned as adult - such as Portuguese, Spanish, German, Italian and Norwegian. I tried several times to learn Russian, but I could not continue for lack of time and for not having lived in Ukraine, the country where my wife Marina comes from. Thanks to Marina, her love and her patience with me, I have been able to write this book about my life.

There, in Ukraine, I only had a long vacation and I followed Russian courses in Kiev for foreigners. There, in Ukraine, one speaks Russian and Ukrainian at a time, since they are very similar languages. This creates confusion for foreigners who are new to the country and makes it difficult for them to quickly learn Russian, although it would be possible to learn Russian if one lived a long season in Kiev, where good Russian is spoken and without accent.

Our house in Beirut was like a language school: my mother Heleni speaks five languages. At home, we learned Greek from my mother, Arabic - a language spoken in Lebanon - for talking to my father and at school, and Turkish to hear it. Turkish was the language of communication between my parents because they were both born in Asia Minor, my mother is Greek of Greek parents, my father was Greek for the two grandmothers, and so her parents were the children of Greek mothers.

The Chaaraoui family comes from Aleppo, now Aleppo is in ruins by the Syrian Civil War. It was a rich family of cotton merchants; they were of Greek Catholic confession. My father's grandfather was married in the late 19th century to a Greek woman, and his son Vangelis (who is my grandfather) was baptized in the Greek Orthodox Church. The Aleppo warehouses of the Chaaraoui family were set on fire at the end of the 19th century, they were insured for 100,000 pounds of gold, but there was an error in the document. The insurance company compensated them with only 10,000 gold pounds, since zero in Arabic numbers is written with a dot on the right and, apparently, they had forgotten to put a zero, that is, one more point to the right! Thus, the fortune of the Chaaraoui family was suddenly divided into ten. They happened, suddenly, to be rich to be middle-class! Perhaps, that's why they were forced to move to Constantinople - today, Istanbul. There, my grandfather Vangelis grew, he spoke Greek and badly Arabic and with an accent, he naturally also spoke Turkish like all those who lived in Asia Minor under Ottoman domination; as for profession he was a carpenter, he made the trunks for newly married brides.

My grandfather Vangelis married my grandmother Caterina, who had a Greek mother and whose father was a Christian of Greek Orthodox confession of the Abiad family (Arabic for "white"). This family was originally from Tripoli, a northern city of Lebanon, they had emigrated to Alexandretta, they were a very rich family. Caterina's father, the maternal grandfather of my father, was a very strong and a very rich man, he unloaded the ships in the port of Alexandretta, but his fortune vanished at once, like my father's other grandfather. He had been endorsed by an Armenian, the son of a friend of his, who wanted to get a job, wanted to work as an official in the Turkish Ottoman administration. This Armenian did something very serious: he apparently stole money from taxes; it is not known whether it was true or not, but the tragedy was when the Turkish administration confiscated all the goods of my father's maternal grandfather. The Abiad family was left with nothing of the grandfather's fortune, but they continued to live comfortably, fortunately, thanks to the few properties grandfather put in the name of his wife, my father's grandmother, Caterina's mother. Thanks to those properties, they were able to survive!

Thus my father's grandfathers lost their immense fortunes by bad luck, which I consider a good thing because if my father had been born rich, he would not be the father I knew, and if I had been born rich, I would not be the man that I am. It is better to be born with less money and earn yourself your future, but it is always good to have something, it always helps in something!

Alexandretta was and remains a port city of Turkey in the region of Adana, where at that time lived several Christian communities: Greeks, Armenians, Arab Orthodox Christians and Catholics, as well as Arab Muslims, Jews and Muslim Turks.

Let us start in the Middle East, because here, in this part of the world, Lebanon, is where I was born on April 2, 1954, just ten years after Lebanon gained independence in late 1943. I studied and grew up in Lebanon until the age of twenty, there begins my history of travel around the world to finish where I am now, going through Salamis in 1966, Jerusalem in 1973, Leuven (Belgium) from 1974 to 1966, England and Scotland in 1976, France in 1976, Spain in 1976, Morocco in 1976, Brazil in 1976 and 1981, Spain in 1981, Germany in 1986 to 1988, Arabia in 1990, Germany in 1992 to 1998, Italy and several countries in sub-Saharan Africa from 2008 until now. I have been living in Spain since the end of 1981 and I continue to travel several times a year throughout Sub-Saharan Africa without forgetting my beloved island of Crete in Greece, which gives me all the inspiration to write this book.

In the school where I studied, which is called "*Collège de la Sagesse*" (School of Wisdom), studied the famous Lebanese writer Jibran Khalil Jibran, who wrote a very famous book called "The Prophet" and other famous books. In this school, we were formed to be elite; my class friends of my generation are all engineers, doctors, senior army officers, and so on. Everyone ended up being elite, while I was the only autodidact because I dropped out of college, I left when I was halfway wanting to discover myself and the truths of this world.

I am not from a single country or a single profession, as Socrates said, I am a citizen of the world.

I remember that in Beirut, in the family liqueur factory that my father founded in the 1945s, we had, in 1980, two doors that opened onto the street. A door and a shop window were from the goldsmith shop that we founded my brother and I with the help of my sister Ketty –the jewellery no longer exists, lasted only a few years-, the other door was from the liquor factory behind the jewellery. The factory still exists, now it belongs to my brother André, transformed it into a small liquor factory and alcohol store for pharmacies and hospitals.

As you will see, they are two trades practically far from being compatible with each other. What does a liqueurist distiller have to do with an alchemist goldsmith?! They both have something in common: chemistry; if you do not know a little chemistry, physics and mathematics, you cannot be a good distiller or a good alchemist goldsmith.

Now we return to our main theme: the languages and civilizations of the Mediterranean.

Why do I group these two giant things together? Because without a spoken language, people would not be able to communicate. A community communicates using a language, a city needs to have order and laws, a people has its identity, its origins, its history and its mentality related to its culture, a people has its religion... From all that arises its philosophy and way of seeing and conceiving things; all this represents the culture of a people.

If a people is large, it becomes a nation and a great civilization, such as, for example, the Phoenician civilization, the Greek civilization, and the Roman civilization. These three Mediterranean civilizations influenced the birth of the great civilizations of modern times, such as the civilizations of France, England, Germany, Austria, Russia, Ireland, Spain, Portugal, etc.

When we say "civilization," we also say "nation" or "people."

The Phoenician people were craftsmen, travellers and merchants; they needed language as a means of communicating with one another and with the other peoples of the world.

The Phoenician civilization was very advanced in its time - it continues being in the current Lebanon -, 10 000 years ago BC the Phoenicians had mercenaries for their wars, the native people were peaceful and did not like to war.

The alphabet, according to History, was born on the Phoenician coast, in the city of Byblos (in present-day Lebanon), which was once Phoenician or much of Phenicia.

The Greeks were the first to adopt the Phoenician alphabet and made with it their own Greek alphabet, which comes from the Phoenician alphabet; later the Greek alphabet was translated throughout Europe.

From the Phoenician alphabet of the city of Byblos, several alphabets derived from the Middle East: among them the Aramaic alphabet and the Arabic alphabet. Arabic and Hebrew are languages derived from ancient Aramaic.

Arabic then spread throughout Arabia and the Middle East with Islam in the 7th century and reached Europe and the famous Al-Ándalus of Spain.

The languages of northern Europe, such as English, German and Scandinavian languages, are of Germanic origin, but they are written in Latin alphabet.

From the Greek derived Latin, Greek and Latin derived the southern Mediterranean languages like Italian, French, Spanish and Portuguese.

In Spanish and Portuguese, we can see the great influence of the Arabic language. That comes from the Arabic domination in the Middle Ages.

The Cyrillic alphabet was also derived from the Greek, which was created by the brothers Cyril and Methodius of Bulgaria in the 9th century, for wanting to translate the Gospel into the Slavic language. Then they came to Kiev, where Queen Olga and her son Vladimir adopted the Orthodox Christian religion and the Ukrainians of Kiev were baptized on the Dnieper River, *El Dnipro*.

Russian cities received from Kiev both the language of *Rus of Kiev*, from which derives the present Russian language, as the orthodox Christian religion that they adopted. All this, thanks to the civilization that was in Kiev that is today the capital of Ukraine and that is known as the mother of Russian cities.

Thus, the Russians should have a special respect and admiration for Ukraine, with its capital Kiev, and treat it as a mother and not consider it as they do, as if it were a small brother.

Russian cities are considered as the daughters of the city of Kiev of Ukraine, who became great thanks to what has given Kiev, as basis and cultural foundations.

But the history, unfortunately, was not like this: there were no thanks, on the contrary, there were punishments!

Stalin's regime caused a great famine to the Ukrainian people. The "*Holodomor*" was his opposite form of gratitude, where four to five million hungry Ukrainians starved to death. The regime took away all wheat grain stocks from the barns of the poor Ukrainian farmers, who were then sold on world stock markets.

There was such a famine that the parents left the children loose in the woods to live with the help of God, because they were not able to feed them. The hungry people ate everything: grass, cats, dogs, rats... There was even anthropophagy, apparently hunger did not forgive! It was an unimaginable and indescribable human tragedy!

All the intellectuals of Kiev and of the great cities of Ukraine that had ideas against the regime of Stalin were systematically eliminated. That is why the Ukrainians supported Adolf Hitler's Nazi army in their invasion of Ukraine in World War II: to come out of the Soviet domination of the Stalin regime, and did not hesitate to express it for many centuries, until now. With the present Russia, heiress of the Soviet Union, has not changed anything, they also expressed it again with the Orange Revolution in the year 2004. Then came the Revolution of Maidán or Euromaidán in the year 2013, in which it was deposed The pro-Russian president, Victor Yanukovych.

The same thing happened with other oppressed peoples, like the Armenians by hand of the Ottomans. Turkey today is the heir of the Ottoman Empire.

The Ottomans have received the language and religion of the Arabs, their letters were Arabic, their language came from Arabic, Persian and Ottoman. Although the Ottomans received all that is culture of the Arabs, they also punished the Arabs, Greeks and Armenians. There were, according to History, genocides to people like the Armenians, and massacres and mistreatments to Greek and Arab people.

Turkey today does not officially recognize the Armenian genocide from 1915 until 1923; there were brutal massacres to Armenians, Christian groups like the Assyrians and Greek Pontic groups. The Pondios, although they recognize that there were many deaths of Armenians, do not recognize that it was a massive genocide.

Thus, we conclude that, although great peoples such as the Russian and the Ottoman received language and religion - fundamental foundations of other peoples for their civilization - their responses have unfortunately not been adequate for recognition or gratitude. We conclude that pride makes leaders blind and transforms them into egocentric and omnipotent characters.

Now we return to our main theme again:

All languages are means of communication, we cannot say: "That language is beautiful and another is ugly," as long as it serves to communicate, it is good and useful. Now, naturally there are languages that are more liked by the ear than others, that is obvious. But knowing a language is always good and positive, it is a fundamental tool: without it communication could not be performed.

The more languages we know, the better we can communicate with people or citizens of nearby countries and far away countries.

Scandinavian languages resemble German and English and resemble each other. The difference is small, those who know German and English can easily learn Scandinavian languages like Norwegian, Swedish and Danish, which are derived almost from the old German.

Now that we have a general overview, we will begin to define peoples and civilizations:

People have to do with their history and where they come from.

If we start in the Middle East, we see that from there, apart from the birth of the alphabet and commerce, the three great monotheistic religions that have a common history are also born.

The Jewish people were the chosen people of God until the Messiah, Jesus Christ came. The Jewish people were led through the desert and God worked miracles so that the Pharaoh would free the Jewish people from slavery, and was led by Moses through the wilderness for forty years. Once they arrived in Israel, there were kingdoms of David and Solomon, there was a great Jewish nation and prophecies of the coming of the Messiah. Afterwards, there were divisions and Palestine was for centuries under Roman rule and then the Messiah, Jesus Christ came. Then, centuries later, it came the conquest of the *Byzantines*;

then came Islam and, with it, the Muslim Arab Empire; then came the Ottoman Empire.

The Ottomans brought degradation to the Arab-Muslim Empire, they often burned books as a form of repression, because they did not want anyone or any intellectual to lift the people against them. They were savages and barbarians, they killed many Greeks in Asia Minor and threw them from their lands, and treated the Cretans very badly. On times of Ottoman domination, there was hunger and lepers, as in all the territory under Ottoman dominion, and they exterminated to the Armenian people. From there come the genocides during the Ottoman rule.

The Turks of today have not yet recognized these genocides of the Armenian people, or the Pontic and other Greek peoples of Asia Minor. They also attempted to destroy Greek culture, Arab and Armenian cultures, which remained in the books kept in the monasteries of Greece and Mount of Lebanon.

In Germany, there was a great civilization from the Middle Ages and it had its glory with industrialization in the eighteenth century, as happened in France and England.

There were world wars: World War I (1914) and World War II (from 1939 to 1945, lasted six years and one day).

The German people have partly followed their *Führer* Adolf Hitler blindly, who were of Austrian origin - some media say that Hitler was the son of a Hebrew mother – they followed him out of obligation, out of fear or conviction. It was a diabolical spirit, there were German heroes who tried to kill Hitler and protected the persecuted Jews, but they could not stop Hitler and Hitler triumphed in Germany, but in the end Germany lost the war and the German nation paid a very high price to those who won the war. There was the Marshall Plan to lift the German economy at the end of the war, Germany had to pay a lot of money to Israel to repair the damage done to the Jewish people as compensation for the crimes of Nazism and will continue to pay so far.

Other nations, such as Leopoldo II's Belgium, ordered barbarities against the poor African workers, inhabitants and citizens of the Democratic Republic of the Congo: he ordered to cut off the hands of those workers of the rubber plantations who refused to work to sow the terror among the poor Africans. The Belgian Government continues to pay homage to *Leopold II*, calling it "the builder king" (*"le roi bâtisseur"*) because he built cities with the illegal money stolen from the Republic of the Congo which he considered his property with its inhabitants in the condition of slaves.

Neither the Russians recognize the crimes of Stalin in Ukraine and continue to pay him homage, nor do the Turks recognize the crimes of the Ottomans of their predecessors and consider themselves as a great civilization with a history of which they remain proud. There are also other nations with similar stories.

Here I do not want to criticize anyone, but we wonder: Why is there so much malediction in the world?

Jesus Christ said: "Every soul is worth more than all the treasures of the world." Imagine dictators who launch their bombs every day on the pretext of wanting to eliminate the terrorists: in the most of these acts, die innocent civilians. How many treasures are here, only God can do justice, laws and the human right are not capable of judging such crimes, wherever.

Now, in The Hague (Netherlands), only criminals of Africa and Eastern Europe are judged! Lately, there were countries that withdrew from the ICC such as South Africa, Russia and other African countries.

Why do not they also judge people from Europe or the West?

I have no answer to this question.

Maybe I'll continue in another occasion; my soul is tired of so much bitterness.

It would be noble and honored for every nation to recognize its mistakes as the Germans did, even the French in the war in Algeria. Each nation should recognize its mistakes of the past and try to repair the mistakes of its ancestors, even if it is symbolic, and thus they will be able, in this way, to reconcile with its past.

Chapter 8: My trips and stays in Belgium, 1974-1976

When I was a small child and I was six or seven years old, I had a friend from school, who was also my neighbour, whose name was Jacques Ward. Jacques was the same age as me, but he was two weeks younger. He liked to eat chocolate, while I was addicted to nuts: I liked pistachios, peanuts, almonds, etc., and I still like them. We went to school together, the school bus came to pick us up early in the morning, under his house in the Achrafieh neighbourhood in Beirut, I had to walk a few minutes from my house to reach the meeting point.

I remember that I cried the first day I arrived at the new school. I used to go to a nuns school for girls in the same district of Achrafieh, where my sister Ketty was studying, as the pre-school section - three to six years old – it was mixed.

I remember that my mother took me by the hand, the first day of school, to the new great school of almost a thousand students; it was, I believe, October of 1960, when I was only six years old. The school is called, in Arabic, "*Madrasat Al-Hikmat*" or, in French, "*Collège de la Sagesse*" which means "College of wisdom." In this school, studied great personalities of the elite of the Lebanese society; there also studied the famous great Lebanese writer, playwright, essayista and painter Jibran Khalil Jibran. It was a school that had fame and so much history, as it was founded in the year 1875.

Wisdom is the knowledge of the truths of the human being, it studies thoroughly all the elements of nature, literature and the sciences; however, I consider that wisdom is equivalent to closely knowing the truth. Truths are not only learned in the school, in the school the bases of knowledge are learned and the pupil is taught how to think, how to act, the personality is forged, the rest is learned in everyday life and in the world.

I almost lost contact with my friend Jacques. We were friends, we escaped together from school some evenings, and we were the two rebels. I just called him right now to his house in Belgium, in Louvain, to get back in touch; he does not call me as I call him, but he remembers me, he never forgets. He is Aries, like me; he was born on April 16th, true friendship is not lost, it is a rare thing that can happen!

At that time, in 1960, we had too many school hours, in the morning and in the afternoon, the briefcase with the books was very heavy. We studied in primary classes in two languages - in Arabic and

French - then in secondary schools we went to three languages - with English - but in our case, our generation had to study four languages - along with the German- . At first, I was good at classes, I think I was studying enough and with that I got good grades, but from a certain age (I think at eleven or twelve), before and after my trip to the island of Salamis, in Greece, I did not open almost any book, I only read what really interested me, the books were more for decoration. I dreamed of traveling the world, doing great experiments, I dreamed of having my own laboratory, discovering the world, I wanted to fly with my desk through my classroom window, I dreamed of being a mechanical engineer in Bosch in Germany, having a gas station in Germany, getting married to a blond German woman and having a purebred German Shepherd dog. I liked to read "Tintin" and his adventures in Gabon, Congo, etc., I was more identified with Captain Haddock, I liked the trip and I still like it, it is what I am most passionate about in life, along with investigation.

I was interested in discovering the secrets of life and philosophy, understanding politics, what is happening in the world.

I was very busy with my father's factory. During the summer holidays and on Saturdays and holidays, my brother André (younger) and I helped my father in the liquor factory; but since I was older than him by two and a half years, it was my job to do much more than my brother.

Despite almost never opening the books, I approved the first course of the scientific high school; a year later, I got my second bachelor's degree in mathematics thanks to the help of my sister Ketty, who taught me all the chemistry in one night, the day before the exam.

In 1973, when I finished my second year of high school, I had bad luck or good luck. It was my duty to do military service, something I did not want to do willingly in a country sold to all the nations of the world, to the Arab countries and to the great powers, since each powerful or influential country had its agent or its direct or indirect representative In Lebanon.

The idea of the mandatory military service was something new, never seen before in Lebanon since its independence in 1943, more than thirty years since its creation as a state.

In 1916, there was the Sykes-Picot Agreement between England and France, which divided power over the countries lost from the domination of the Ottoman Empire, which they called "the sick man." It was when the ancient mother of present-day Turkey had lost World War I and had disintegrated, so Lebanon was liberated from the tyranny of the Ottomans, but it was after twenty-seven years under French mandate, it was a phase of transition and preparation for its independence at the end of 1943, which was obtained after a national political movement, international negotiations and agreements between the different religious facets of the country.

The idea of military service was an action and a plan to teach young Christians from eighteen to twenty years to learn to fight and to use weapons, and then to fight during the civil war, as the high political and military leaders knew that war was coming soon and was almost inevitable, given the political situation of that time.

It was a camouflaged plan, we were Christians and Muslims, but I think most of us were Christians, perhaps because the high school students who ended up were mostly Christians, or did so in order for more Christians to learn to fight.

There were lists of names of students and a lottery; I had to perform the military service for my bad luck. There were systematically absolved only children and the students who were to be engineers or doctors; all the others had to do a year of military service. My friend Jacques was an only child, although he had two sisters, so he did not have to go to do it! I, on the other hand, was not an only child having a brother and a sister.

Thus, Jacques could go - and has gone - a year before me to study at the Catholic University of Louvain. At first, I thought of studying oenology at the French university of Bordeaux, which went well with the office of my father and the family business, but there in Bordeaux I did not know anyone, I preferred to go where my friend Jacques was. I had to wait another year, once I had finished my year of military service.

In this year of the military service, I made several friendships and I learned to have patience with the time and to endure the hard life.

My specialty in the military service was the military ground transportation in the barracks where I was, so I learned to be a driver of a large American Army Reo brand ground truck, as I see it is the **REO M35 2-1 / 2 ton cargo truck.** I remember that I really liked mechanics and thermodynamics, I was the first of my promotion, we were, I think, more than thirty or forty students, they gave me the prize for being the first with the best notes in the mechanics, maintenance and driving test, the prize was a seventy-two hour leave to go home and enjoy freedom!

I think the military service was positive for me; it gave me time to meditate and reflect, especially during the hours of the guard at night as a sentinel. Every four hours of guard and four hours of rest, I looked at the stars and made and imagined my plans and dreams of the immediate future, just out of military service. The waiting time was long and endless; I realized that nothing was easy in this life. Once I cried in anguish because they did not give me permission to go out, it had been a long time and several weeks without permission, the barrack was for me like a great prison - if not a real prison. Thus I had more reason to leave my native country, which had disappointed me, which had deprived me of my freedom for a whole year by a simple law which was, in my opinion, senseless and useless; but perhaps it made sense to the parties involved in the civil war in Lebanon, who thought about their future and the future of their country, but that was not my future, I have not served them at all! Maybe, just now, including and remembering that time within my memories.

As soon as I left the military service, in early August 1974, I decided to leave Lebanon. I had very good contact with my friend Jacques and had asked him to register me at the Catholic University of Louvain in the Faculty of Agronomy, which he immediately did as he was a good and true friend.

I then applied for a student visa to the Belgian Consulate in Beirut and, as Jacques came to spend his summer vacation at his parents' house in Beirut, I took the opportunity and we went together in August 1974 to Brussels with a KLM Flight Beirut-Amsterdam-Brussels. Arriving in Brussels, we took a train to Louvain.

Upon arrival, I had to sleep as a guest a couple of nights in Jacques's room while I was looking for a student room to temporarily settle. At the same time, I enrolled in college in the first year as an agronomist.

At the Catholic University of Louvain, I made some friends and, among them, a special friend with whom I lost contact, was called Antoine Siage. He is Syrian, from Damascus, from a Christian family, he was very good to me, he helped me to find permanent accommodation that suited me and where some Lebanese students also lived.

A few months later, I had to leave the agronomy course for several reasons: I had several concerns, it was very long to me having to study five years to finish the course, my father was sick and I knew, unconsciously, that he was not going to live much longer.

The courses of the university of Louvain francophone were, at that time, taught in two different places by the linguistic conflict between the Francophone and Flemish communities of Belgium, something absurd that I still do not understand. It was the transitional phase of the total separation of the two universities, courses were taught at Louvain the Old Town - where we lived - and other courses, according to faculties, were taught in Louvain the New Town, twenty kilometers farther. The following year, in 1975-1976, most of the students were already in Louvain La Neuve where everything had moved there, so I had to wake up, some days, very early - at six in the morning - to go on the train to Louvain the New Town; in winter it was very cold and there was snow. I wanted to discover the world in my own way and to find the roots of wisdom and science from its depth, from its definition, it is the autodidact way of discovering the world, the things of life, their secrets and what they mean.

I remember that once I was walking in a forest of very tall oak trees, near the university city of Louvain the Old Town, the nature of it was such that I said to myself: "I want to discover the truths from the bottom, from its roots." Now, talking to my friend Jacques, I told him that I would like to live on the island of Crete one day, he thought it was because of the temperature or the landscape, but I said, "No! It is not like that! It is neither because of the temperature nor the landscape, which are undoubtedly important and very favorable elements, but rather by the magnetism, inspiration, roots and history of the island of Crete and its people, who have something common with my history, as being largely formed by Greek people from Asia Minor, since many micro Asian Greeks have returned to live in Crete. There, on the island of Crete, there is a village near Heraklion called

Nea Alikarnassos, alluding to the ancient city of Alikarnassos in Asia Minor. I have not yet been in this town, I will go to see it out of curiosity on my next trip as usual on holidays in the month of August». Nea Alikarnassos was founded in 1925 as a shelter for the refugees who came from Turkey after the persecution of the Greeks, after being forced to leave their lands by the hand of the Turkish barbarians of that time, there were many massacres and many dead, many martyrs and victims of violence and injustice.

On a Saturday or Sunday at the Brussels market in the autumn of 1974, I bought a second-hand motorcycle, I think it was a 50 cc Honda with gears, in red and black, I think it was worth about 4,000 or 6,000 Belgian francs, I do not exactly remember it. The bike apparently had many mechanical problems: it was not in good condition. I got sick afterwards, I had a bad cold and I was in bed, my friend Jacques came to my aid, he brought me food and he got me an appointment with a good Belgian doctor who gave me, I think, antibiotics and a syrup elixir for the throat. So, between Christmas and the end of the year 1974, I returned to my parents' house, from Brussels to Beirut via Genoa (Italy). The plane had to make an emergency stop at the Genoa airport because there was a lot of wind and a storm. After a few days of arriving in Beirut, I decided to stay in Lebanon to work with my father. My father was alone in the factory, he needed my help a lot, I stayed a few months, we renewed and we developed many things together; but afterwards I had again a great disappointment, at the end of 1975, when the civil war broke out again in Beirut and rains of projectiles began to fall over all Beirut from both sides. I decided, then, to go back to the Belgium I knew, at the end of 1975; my father supported my decision, although it hurt him to be abandoned, as he unconsciously knew that he would never see me again and said: "Go to the world! Learn everything!"

Arriving in Louvain again, I checked in, this time, at the Faculty of Veterinary Medicine in the first year. I could not continue, I finally knew my destiny, I had good intuition, I saw things coming. I enrolled in the institute of living languages to learn two languages: Spanish and German; two important languages of two countries with which I would be linked all my life. Five years later, in 1981, I was already living in Spain, and five years later, in 1986, I also lived in Germany. By now, I have lived in Spain for more than thirty-five years since 1981, but there were also intervals where I lived - in total seven years - in Germany, I was naturalized German in 1997, a curious thing about the circumstances of life, but when I sleep, when I think or when I write, I am not of any nationality, I am neither Greek, nor Lebanese, nor Spanish, nor German: I am myself. As Socrates said: "I am a citizen of the world, an autodidact."

From Belgium I made some trips to Amsterdam and made a major exploration trip to England and Scotland in April 1976: it was my birthday, I made a twelve-day trip from the end of March to the beginning of April.

I remember that we had a friend who was renting a room in the same house where my friend Jacques lived, his name was Salam Abdel-Ahad, he was an architect and he was doing his doctorate of specialization in prefabricated reinforced concrete to build modular houses that are fixed with Screws. He was very nice and very intelligent, he was an Iraqi, Orthodox Christian from the city of Mosul, a good friend. Jacques told me that he got married and that he has children, now he lives with his family in Canada, I am happy for him and for his destiny, that he is far from the problems and insecurity of Mosul, of Iraq.

I knew that my world or my life were not going to end in Belgium, I knew that I was expecting much more world that I had to travel, to know, to discover and to live. I was not satisfied with this small country that was Belgium, despite all the economic and social guarantees that this country offered at that time, while my friend Jacques stayed in Louvain: he married in the same city with a Flemish girl from there, he worked for almost forty years as a technician on the Brussels railways, he had three children who are all well placed and brilliant, he is now a grandfather, he has two grandchildren, he has recently retired, his wife Janine is retired too, they have a very good life together.

In Louvain, I frequented *Le Cercle des Étrangers*, there was much talk of politics and the future of the world. In 1976, they said that, within twenty years, the Soviet Union's steel wall was to be dismantled and disintegrated, and it was really collapsed into disintegration in 1991: it was a good vision. They also said that Spain was the China of Europe because everything was cheap in Spain; comparing the cost of living in Spain at that time with the cost of living in Northern Europe. Spain attracted me a lot because of its Latin roots and its magnetism, I wanted to one day go to know this fantastic country and that was possible from Belgium.

In Belgium, I looked for the truths, I sought to discover the three secrets of life: I was looking to find God, looking for knowing myself and realizing myself as a human being, I was also looking for true love. Speaking of that last secret, at the beginning I fell in love with a German girl who studied there in *Louvain La Neuve*, it was rather a platonic love, a friendship and a feeling just on my side, in the end I discovered that she had a boyfriend in Germany, it was a great disappointment, I left the university to not have to see her anymore or to cross her way. After a few months, I met, at the beginning of May, on a Saturday night, in a dance hall and German music from Bavaria of the Dortmunder Union, a Brazilian girl from Santa Catarina. The musicians had leather shorts dressed in Bavarian tradition, I invited her to dance and we became friends and we loved each other very much. She was the friend who accompanied me to Granada and the one who was waiting for me on my first trip from Brazil to Santa Catarina.

This has been the story of my two long trips and stays in Belgium.

Chapter 9: Learn how to analyze the spirits

It is very important to know the spirits of the people with whom we live, relate and work, the companies we work with, the city or country where we live, the countries and cities we visit, the places we frequent – as the restaurants where we go to eat, bars where we go to have a coffee and where we make a pause of spirit - the identities that lend us a service, and even the temples of God we visit to receive grace, forgiveness and blessing.

If the spirit does not suit us, we will have to leave and not return to that place, or have close contact with those negative people, entities or companies, or stay in that place, in this city or in this country: that is, distance ourselves from those places. It would be, better still, to cut through the healthy, to leave and never get back in there.

As Jesus Christ told to his disciples, when they were going to preach the Gospel, in the Gospel of Luke 9: 5

"If people do not welcome you, leave their town and shake the dust off your feet as a testimony against them."

In other words, where they do not welcome you, shake off the dust of your sandals and leave the city.

I, personally, leave many countries and cities after having lived short or long seasons, months, years... according to place and according to the circumstances of that time of my life because I suffered and felt the weight and pain of the spirits, which were not good for me.

How do you analyze a spirit? It is easy and difficult; it will depend on our spiritual experience!

Those of us, who have a long spiritual experience, we have, no doubt, rather easy because we have elements of comparison: we can compare new sensations with perceived and lived sensations of our past. If we also have the Holy Spirit who acts within us, it will be even more easy for us to analyze and perceive the spirits, we will be able to obtain quicker answers to our concerns, the Holy Spirit guides us and the sensation - or the *feeling* - is much greater. People who have not received the Holy Spirit can also have the same faculty, because there are spirits comparable to the Holy Spirit who act in a similar way, depending on their divine nature. Those spirits classified as good, do not lead to the goal that Jesus Christ is preparing for all who wish to be saved, perhaps go in different ways, but also recognize that Jesus Christ is the Savior.

Now, if we want to classify and group the spirits, we can do it this way:

Holy Spirit or Spirit of God: There are also other good spirits that come from other beliefs - from other religions other than the Christian religion, which was instituted by Jesus Christ and His Apostles. These are the different religions that preach tolerance, love and forgiveness.

Confusion spirits: They are spirits who try to confuse us and divert us from the path of the Truth or the Gospel of Jesus Christ.

Evil spirits: They are spirits that come directly from Satan, from the prince of darkness.

Bad human spirits: They are evil-minded spirits that were invented by man and have, as their objective, to dominate the world with a plan of action based on lies, deceit, falsehood and hypocrisy.

We can classify the first ones as good spirits. We have to be careful with the last three groups of spirits and try not to fall into their traps.

Finally, there is the spirit of the non-spirit or spirit of the spiritual emptiness: It is the spirit of materialists or scientists who do not believe in God, who believe and consider that everything that cannot be seen with the eyes or be felt with the hands, or with the human senses, or that is not demonstrated by science is neither true nor credible. There is the case of atheists and agnostics, who are the undecided. This spirit can be called "the spirit of no good or no evil": it is the spirit of the man or woman who wants to ignore or not recognize God, could also be called "the spirit of ignorance," those who seek where there is nothing to find, of those who seek God in science, of those who feel neither cold nor hot.

Revelation 3: 15-19

"I know your deeds, that you are neither cold nor hot. I wish you were either one or the other! So, because you are lukewarm—neither hot nor cold—I am about to spit you out of my mouth. You say, 'I am rich; I have acquired wealth and do not need a thing.' But you do not realize that you are wretched, pitiful, poor, blind and naked. I counsel you to buy from me gold refined in the fire, so you can become rich; and white clothes to wear, so you can cover your shameful nakedness; and salve to put on your eyes, so you can see. Those whom I love I rebuke and discipline. So be earnest and repent."

What is the use of recognizing the nature of spirits?

It helps us throughout our lives, in our daily struggle, as we seek solutions to all our daily problems and on our long journey to eternal glory with God and His Son, Jesus Christ. It serves us to make decisions, to reject evil offers, to take or abandon paths that arise in our material, professional, sentimental and spiritual life.

In the couple, the same thing happens: If the spiritual union is heterogeneous, sooner or later the break will come; it is like wanting to mix oil with water, the two liquids end up separating no matter how much we shake them. It is normal for the same spirit to reign between the two united people, there cannot be two different spirits, as love can do everything to a certain point. A couple can survive spiritual differences, but love loses strength over time: a couple of newlyweds are not the same as a marriage of many years of coexistence. There are marriages that are reinforced with time like two rocks in the sea water that calcify each other and become a single rock; but if the spirit that acts is the same, the couple can be even more spiritually affirmed and will survive the passage of time.

The Holy Spirit is the Spirit of God who left the Lord Jesus Christ on earth to guide his people and prepare them for the day of the First Resurrection, when Jesus Christ will come in a lightning to take his own to the heavenly Jerusalem.

There are also other spirits that are evil, like the spirit of materialism - which we all have - we all need money in the account to face so many expenses, but this spirit should not move us away from God and Truth.

There are also other evil spirits, like those of exaggerated ambition and envy, of which we must be very careful! The temptations are many: clothing and luxury items, houses, beautiful and attractive people... We must know how to guide our ship into a sea of many waves and storms, which are the temptations of evil!

Thus, there are several spirits that can coexist within us, that is why we speak of two personalities within the same person and two different spirits. We live in a materialistic world, where many walk over souls and corpses to reach their materialistic goals, many have sold their soul and their freedom to achieve their dreams, which are to materially enrich themselves and become Influential and important, it is better to sell your productive ideas than to sell your soul and your freedom! It is better to work on yourself and let the work working.

What does it mean to sell your soul? A person, for example, is able to sell his soul to his boss or to the company where he works; his boss become the absolute masters of his soul, they are people who live for their work, who work long hours -even Saturdays and Sundays- where there is no freedom or rest for their soul or their spirit.

Sunday is a sacred day of the rest of Christianity, before it was the *sabbat* in the Hebrew time of the Old Testament, until the coming of the Messiah Jesus Christ. From the resurrection of Jesus Christ, Sunday is the day of the rest of the soul to hear the divine word, receive the sacraments and forgiveness and come out blessed.

Our soul belongs to God, our spirit is in our hands; we can live a better spiritual life, but that will depend on us.

An intelligent and self-confident person, with a good heart and strong, spiritually speaking, will perhaps find this a lot easier: he or she can choose where to stay and where it is convenient for him to be spiritually speaking; God has given him more faculties of choice and realization. While a person limited in his intelligence and rather weak mentally and spiritually is subject to luck, wherever destiny takes him! If you are lucky enough to fall into a company where a good spirit rules, then you could have a better spiritual life; if you fall into a company where the boss is dominated by the spirit of materialism which only look at the money and want workers to work as slaves, workers will suffer all their lives and, when they reach retirement, are spiritually, mentally and physically sick.

How to solve this problem? There is no easy solution for this problem; the bosses must be made more aware of the fact that they treat their workers more humanly; therefore, there are labor unions and workers' rights. For this reason, a good spiritual education is of prime importance for all human beings whenever possible.

What is the impact of the spirits in our daily life, in the work, social and spiritual aspects?

My answer is that we depend directly and indirectly on the influence of the spirits. Where we live, the neighbors we have, there are those who have good spirits - who please us - or evil spirits - that annoy us. The same thing happens in the workplace; as well as at the level of countries and citizens, when a country is governed by a governor or a dictator who runs the country with an iron hand and where people have no freedom, no security, not enough medical care, etc. in which lacks basic food and medicines, where there are epidemics like malaria and diphtheria, which appear suddenly as a consequence of poverty and hunger, lack of hygiene, which have been produced by administrative bad policies, while the Government invests immense sums of money belonging to the people in armaments of war. In addition, journalists and every free person opposed to the regime are in prisons, where there is no freedom of expression, nor what they commonly call democracy or human rights! Thus the whole country is sunk in chaos and depends directly on the spirits who work and influence within the soul of the dictator and the souls of his collaborators, who are usually no good spirits!

On a local or international trip, we depend directly on the spirit of the driver of the public transport vehicle, be it a car, a bus, a train, a boat or an airplane.

We can take the following example: The last tragedy of flight 9525 Barcelona-Düsseldorf on March 24th, 2015, of the plane of the German company Germanwings, where 150 people died, including the suicidal co-pilot, who say that he was depressive! Nobody wanted to analyze the human tragedy spiritually, the psychiatrists who treated the copilot only gave him tranquilizer tablets, nor did the governors of the countries speak of spirituality in their speeches. Everyone can think what he wants and draw his own conclusions. I am sure that the suicidal copilot had no faith in God, the Creator, or hope in his son, Jesus Christ; if that were so, he would not have committed suicide, even less he would have not killed another hundred and forty-nine innocent people!

My advice: wherever we are, before leaving our house, we should make a prayer of faith in God and His mercy, especially when we have to take a trip, whether long or is short, asking for help and protection of angels.

The spirits that live inside the people can be noticed until we hear them on the phone. If we have enough experience, we could know whether we can trust these people or not, whether they are influenced by good or bad spirits, and even easier if we can see these people and notice their spiritual nature through the movement of their body, their look and their way of speaking and breathing. Good people can be seen from the outside, and those who are false and are hidden behind a mask can be also seen from the outside, as they produce psychological irritation and spiritual discomfort.

In other words, in order to analyze the spirits, it is necessary to be an expert in them and to differentiate the good from the bad and never lose faith in God, the Creator.

That is why God sent His son, Jesus Christ, to Earth to make us spiritually rich, and for this, He left us the Holy Spirit: to guide us, to prepare us and to distance us from evil.

Chapter 10: My trip to England and Scotland, Spring 1976

My father was an autodidact, he was the first one who made whisky in Lebanon. He had a great deal of confidence in himself and his innovative ideas, he got never tired of looking for techniques to improve his liquors and bring them to the market, he himself had invented everything. His dream had been to make *whisky* from an early age: that idea came at a time when he was helping his Uncle Manoli in Alexandretta, who had a small arak distillery. At the time, in the thirties, they were talking about this dream: to be able to make a *whisky* that could equal a Scotch *whisky*, which my father managed to do thirty years later when he brought out his first Queen Helen *whisky* In the year 1960.

At first, he put on the label "*Scotch whisky*"; then he had to change it to "*Blended Whisky*" because it was not allowed and so they did not give him permission and had to reprint the labels and change the denomination.

I remember that, as my mother told me, my father had already moved from his old factory in the Badawi neighbourhood of Beirut to the new factory on Geitawi Street in the Achrafieh neighbourhood in the early 1950s and, just when I was born in 1954, he started to make the brand new Greek *brandy* with the brand «Evangelos Brandy». Evangelos is the Greek name from which my name derives, Vangelis, was for the joy of having his first son, also the name of his father and my grandfather, is called Vangelis. It was a custom - and still a tradition - in Greece and Lebanon to honour their parents and give the names of the father and mother to the son and the daughter. The 'Evangelos Brandy' was a typical Greek *brandy*, flavored with natural herbs such as ginger, nutmeg, cloves and other natural flavourings that are used for sweets and also in some countries to aromatize the tea. He macerated them in the wine distillate, to which he added dry cherries, let everything macerate for a few months, that was the *brandy* concentrate, which then added in a small proportion - about 5% - to refined grape alcohol. Then he added the caramel for the colour, it was an art of knowing how to make the caramel and the final brandy, all that was invented by my father himself and I learned a lot from him at the time.

After a few years, I believe that in 1958 or in the 1960s, he made the "Queen Helen" *whisky*, *whisky* was more difficult to make than *brandy*, because it was much lighter and less loaded with aroma or bouquet than *brandy*, it required a long research and much knowledge and experience. He had to do a lot of proofs to make a good *whisky*, which was handcrafted and can be similar to Scotch *whisky*, I remember his proofs and experiments. When I selected the proofs of my father that he did twenty years ago, I found a museum and a multitude of experiments, a myriad of tests made to find the method to achieve, mixing natural aromas, a good flavour *blending* for the palate and *bouquet* or flavour that might resemble Scotch *whisky*.

In the end, he also had to import concentrated *whisky* - that is, pure malt *whisky* from Scotland – and imported it from manufacturers exporters who have their offices in London called *'Southwark Distillers'*; he imported, from them, the concentrate of malt *whisky* branded John Pitt and the concentrated gin branded Town Hall.

Thus, he was able to make a good *whisky*, I think it was in the seventies.

My dream was to visit the *"Malt Whisky Distilleries" whisky* factories in Scotland and get to know this world so interesting for my father and me.

I did not know where the factories were, in Scotland. In the end, I had to order two books from a bookstore in Brussels that is specialized in technical books in foreign languages, which came from publishers in England or elsewhere in the world. At that time, forty years ago, there was no internet, no fax, no mobile, no Amazon as now; perhaps, everything now seems much easier with globalization and computerization, but perhaps our time is much more difficult and we must be very prepared because there is too much competition, just because of this phenomenon of globalization! In the end, with the help of the bookstore experts, who helped me and looked in the English book manuals, we found two books that talked about Scotch *whisky*; then I decided: I ordered the two books and paid for them in advance, I had to wait almost a month until they arrived. I started reading and researching the books and I found a page where they had indicated the square within the small map of Scotland. In this square, rather rectangular, there was the cradle of *whisky*: there was the town of Inverness, the city of Aberdeen and the *Spey River*, from there came the pure and crystalline water with which they fermented the malt and with which they downgraded the distilled malt *whisky* and the grain *whisky* of corn, wheat or grain *whisky*. They say that the water of the *Sprey River* gives a character and a special flavour to the Scotch *whisky* and that it is irreplaceable by any water of the world.

Scotch *whisky* rests and ages in American oak barrels of Jerez, as well as malt *whisky* aging in oak barrels, which have served to mature a generous wine, or rather an American oak barrel that has served to ripen Sherry wine From Jerez de la Frontera, from Spain!

There, in this geographic area, it was where I had to go, to this privileged and idyllic place that is in the Highlands, in the high mountains of Scotland.

Following this decision, I bought my car, a white model of the 1966 Ford Anglia second hand and with good reason, because I needed it for the long voyage of exploration. Before that, I had to homologate my Lebanese driving license to a Belgian driving license, my father had just sent me enough money to live well for more than six months and so I could buy the car and make the trip of my dreams.

Before travelling, I had to go to the United Kingdom consulate to apply for an entry visa. I still remember the old Englishman with white hair from the British embassy in Brussels who asked me a lot of questions: he wanted to know where I was going and why, the means I had, etc., I convinced him with my arguments and he granted me the visa for one month.

Now, looking at my old passport, I see that I was granted the visa on the twenty-third of March 1976, and I entered England by the port of Dover on the twenty-fourth of March, that is, the next day! I clearly see that I had nothing else in mind than to go there, where my dreams went. I left the next day, unlikely in our time now, where we have a thousand things in mind and many things to finish before embarking on a long journey. Before, forty years ago, things were different, time was not very valuable, we just immediately passed to the act, we only needed a car, a passport with a visa, enough money in the pocket and we could just run away. I remember that the night before I gave the keys to my room to my dear friend Jacques Ward of Louvain, I thought that, in the worst case, he could intervene for what might arise, he was my guardian angel, the closest and most trusted person in Belgium!

I remember that I travelled early in the morning from Leuven to the seaside town of Ostend, I left the port of Ostend on a large ferry that had its departure, I think, about noon; the ferry arrived at the port of Dover about five hours later and from there I went on my way to London. Now I see that there are about 150 kilometers by road.

When I arrived in London, I remember that I was descending as if I were descending into an immense valley; perhaps, earlier on the road from Dover to London, I was on a mountain at a higher altitude. I saw 'Victoria' signaled and I remember *'London West'*, I took this address; in the end, I arrived at a large railway station called *'Victoria Station'*. I was quite tired after a long day of traveling, I asked if they had a room to sleep one night, they said yes and they took me to the room with a manual elevator. There was a man who wielded a vertical fat rope and it was himself, as if it were the engine of the elevator, which naturally helped the counterweight, so the motorman climbed me to the top floor where my room was. When I entered into the room, I saw a bed with a very thick mattress; when I went to bed, to test it, I saw that it was coming down at least twenty centimeters and this was what they called comfort in those days. In order to be able to deeply rest, in the station, at night, there was no noise, and I could sleep, I remember, very well and dream of the angels.

After putting my things in the room, I took a taxi in the direction of the centre of London, I told the taxi driver to take me to the centre, where there was life and nightlife, and left me in a strategic place. There, I went to dinner in an Italian restaurant and I happened to meet a short Italian young man, who promised to show me London at night, as I was a new visitor. Apparently, I seemed to him sympathetic and I inspired him with confidence, I thought his idea was fantastic and I said, "*Okay.*" The two of us went walking a few meters, we entered into a large disco, there were inside the disco, maybe five hundred or a thousand people, it was a lot of people of all colours and nationalities in the dark, in a very large rectangular room of approximately one thousand square meters of surface.

The band was at the back of the room, the musicians and singers were standing on a half circle, playing and singing famous songs from that time like Barry White's song "*You are my everything*" or Tina

Charles "*I love to love, but my baby just love to dance,*" were famous songs of that time, of the mid-seventies.

Then, when the band became tired of playing, the wooden circle turned like a disk and another new band of musicians came out of the other half circle, which was behind the curtain, something I had never seen in my life, I just saw it in London!

The next day, I left the hotel and wanted to take the road north, I wanted to take the *Motorway M6*, which is the North Motorway, but, as in London, people drive on the left - as in the whole of the United Kingdom, I did not know how to get out with my conventional car, normal European type. I asked a policeman how to get out, he said: "*Go straight, left, left again, round about, to the left, etc.*"; I followed his indications and went back to the same place, I asked him again and he said the same thing to me: "*Go straight, left, left again, round about, to the left, etc.*", I returned, without realizing it, to the same place where the policeman was. In the end, I got tired of asking him, I was ashamed! I thought, then, of a solution to solve this serious problem, I remembered that I had a compass - since I was in love with those devices, such as compass, altimeter, binoculars, etc., and still passionate. I began to follow the roads that led me, more or less, towards the north as indicated by the north needle of the compass. After a few manoeuvres and with a little luck, I arrived automatically at the

Motorway M6, so I could go to Liverpool on the highway, passing through Birmingham and Manchester, which were on the way. However, I did not stop at any of these cities: my destination was the north and the city of Liverpool!

As a student, I asked how I could go to Liverpool University to sleep there a couple of nights and rest, it is always cheaper and interesting to meet students. I remember being helped by an Irish guy I met on the way and got in my car, he was hitchhiking, he was from Belfast and he had to take the boat from Liverpool port back to Belfast. He was a tall, nice and very funny guy, when he saw a pretty girl, he said "*she is beautiful, she has beautiful legs*," we had both something in common. He advised me to follow the bus that was going to the University of Liverpool and so we did: he accompanied me to the university, we arrived perfectly to the University of Liverpool following the bus. He helped me, later, to sign up, I stayed there for two nights, it was a weekend, it was a quiet and relaxing stay. I spoke with an Asian student and another interesting English student girl; now that I remember, I think she was the granddaughter of the famous British military, Marshal Bernard Montgomery, who fought in the First and Second World War, faced General Erwin Romel in World War II, in the two battles of El Alamein! He had just died, I see, on March 24, 1976; so she was quite serious. A few years later I visited my uncle Yorgos' house on the island of

Salamis, from Madrid, in 1984 and 1985, and when I told him about it, he told me that he had met, in Greece in the Second World War, Marshal Bernard Montgomery. My uncle had been a driver in World War II in Athens!

Afterwards, I moved further north to the city of Edinburgh. There, in Scotland, they pronounced the name of this city as "*Edinbura*", that is, with the Scottish accent they ignore the g and pronounce it as *a* at the end. I remember that I continued on the same M6 motorway, along the way I took a nice hitchhiking boy with me, we chatted about a lot of subjects and sympathized, he told me that I was invited to his house as a guest on my way back, to stay in his house a night or two and see how an English family lived. I was quite shy, so far I am still that way more or less, I do not like sleeping in the house of other people, I prefer to have my independence and sleep in a hotel; so I ignored his invitation, although I kept the address and thanked for the invitation. On the way, we stopped at the border between England and Scotland, but it is not a political border, but simply a district one. There, he showed me a touristy place when we entered Scotland called *Gretna Green*: it is a famous village in Scotland where the possibility of marrying young people was offered without the consent of the parents and where many people were married since the eighteenth century, it was very interesting to know!

In the end, I arrived in Edinburgh: it is an important city, the capital of Scotland, situated on the edge of the North Sea, which is a marginal sea of the Atlantic Ocean. It was very windy, as usual; I remember that I passed over a bridge where I felt that the car and the bridge were moving because of the wind that day. Above this bridge, there was a great monument of a great bronze horse that almost moved as well. When I arrived, I looked for, in the afternoon, a place to stay in a *bed and breakfast*; I found there, near the centre, one that seemed good to me: it was owned by a young family with young children, a tall woman, well educated, intelligent and beautiful. There, I met, during my stay, a couple of interesting guests and characters. Once, while watching television, the son of the owner had some homework and asked me if I could help him, I said yes and he asked me if I knew the meaning of the name Simon. I thought: "In Arabic, Simon is *Semaan*, the hearer, the old Simeon is the man who was told by the Holy Spirit that he would not see death before he had seen the Christ of the Lord. *"It had been revealed to him by the Holy Spirit that he would not die before he had seen the Lord's Messiah"* It appears in the Gospel according to Luke (Luke 2: 26-35).

I told them what the listener meant, that was the correct answer and they applauded me. Bravo!

This was the atmosphere in Edinburgh, very interesting and pleasant, civilized people, friendly and polite, and you could learn a lot of things by talking to them. Guests went to Edinburgh to heal from joint problems; there was, apparently, a famous hospital specialized in curing diseases of the joints, orthopedics and traumatology.

There, at this *bed and breakfast*, I was talking to a Jordanian military man who apparently believed in God, of Muslim belief. I still doubted the existence of God, he told me verbatim, I remember very well: "*If God exists, it is better to be a believer and, if He did not exist, you would have lost nothing by being a believer,*" I was still looking for God and the truth!

After staying two nights in this hostel, I decided to leave to the place indicated on the map, my destination was the city of Inverness. I found, on the way, two young girls, about my age, also going to Inverness. There was a lot of snow in the *Highlands* of Scotland. It was better to be accompanied than alone. When we arrived in the afternoon to Inverness, we three found a good *bed and breakfast*, they took a room and I took another one for me. The girls were very close to each other, apparently there was a relationship between the two of them, but that did not stop us from keeping the three of us together. We then went to have a typical English or Scottish *fish and chips*. There I suddenly met a young, nice and interesting couple, a rather small, blond or red-haired Frenchman with a beard accompanied by a tall, beautiful Polish girl with dark hair , we liked each other and started speaking in English and then in French. It turns out that the man had the same interests as me, but his interest was more cultural than professional. He was older than me and he knew exactly where the *Malt whisky* distilleries were, so we stayed, for the next day, to form a group of three and visit the *Malt whisky* distilleries together. We talked all night about this matter and other matters of life, time was passing, we drank Scotch *whisky* with Lager-beer -a type of a special flavored beer-, it was custom, at that time, to drink a glass of *whisky* and next to a big pint of Lager. One drink followed the other - just as it is now, too - to drink *whisky* with Lager, I'll have to go there again to check it, but I do not like *whisky* or other spirits so much, I've changed my taste over time, I just like to drink some wine with food and, occasionally, a small beer. I remember that I drank a few double *whiskys* with Lager; as my father was a *whisky* maker, I could endure drinking without getting drunk, but I felt the weight of alcohol on my head, and after a long day of driving from Edinburgh to Inverness, through the snow mountains, I felt really tired, but it seems that a young man's body can handle everything!

This was the end of the night, at ten o'clock, when they served the last drink, as it is by law in Scotland and England, then I had to return with my car to the hotel; the girls had left a long time before, right after dinner. I got in the car, I had the keys to the hotel and a slip of paper where the address of the pension was set; as I had just gotten there, I could not remember exactly where the hotel was! All the houses looked the same, I found an identical house with a similar landscape, I put the key in, but the key did not enter! Then I took another turn, always driving on the left; at the end, luckily, I found the place and the key entered. What a relief to be lucky to find it!

The next day, we met all three and went to visit a *whisky* distillery that distilled *malt whisky* for great brands of *blended whisky*. The *blenders* mixed *malt whisky* from several distilleries with *grain whisky* and thus made their blend - or *blending* - which, as a result, delivers *blended whisky*. We also visited the Ballantines *whisky* brand distillery, it was also a very interesting visit.

There, I saw how the barley was treated, from its germination and the drying with heat of the fire of the *peat* that gives the malt its special aroma. Fermentation and distillation of *malt whisky* is made in large, very tall and elongated stills, totally different from those used to distil wine spirits in France, Italy and Spain. I learned many things from this great trip.

There, in Inverness, they spoke of the *Loch Ness*, that is, the monster of Loch Ness, near Inverness.

But I could not see it in my way, even if I was looking at the *Loch Ness* and looking for him to see if he appeared to surprise me!

Once my mission was almost fulfilled, and after having stayed two nights in Inverness, I decided to return to Glasgow, which they called "*the black city*" - the black city - for the huge industry that this city had and I suppose it will continue having.

I was advised to go through Fort William to Glasgow, it was also the only way; I went through its long plains, I saw wonderful and incomparable landscapes, I keep an unforgettable memory of this beautiful nature. After a few hours of travel, I arrived to Glasgow, where I went to the University of Glasgow, where I stayed five nights, I remember that it was on a hill in the city, in the heights. When I arrived, it was a long weekend, it was good to rest.

On my arrival, I went to a Greek restaurant in the center of Glasgow, where I met a Turkish Cypriot man who spoke Greek and Turkish, he said to me: "I'm going to introduce you to a nice Iraqi student, a compatriot of yours who speaks Arabic like you, you both can understand each other and become friends."
In fact, the guy was very nice, he came from a good wealthy family from Iraq, when I met him, he invited me at night to go to the *Casino Chevalier*, it was the only place open at night where you could go out, they offered you free coffee and tea, the guy studied engineering and played roulette, he used his knowledge of mathematical odds, and he said that he could win in this way! I played by courtesy and to try to be lucky, I played at random a few times ten pounds

sterling and lost them, as is normal; then I retired from the game. Gambling was not something that appealed to me and it is still insignificant for me, I think gambling addicts are certainly mentally ill; the game is like an obsession, I think it is a difficult disease to cure, perhaps it needs psychological and spiritual treatment.

Beside me, was sitting an English girl, pretty with blue-green eyes, dressed in a light blue dress, with snow-white skin, wearing silver jewelry with turquoise stones, wearing sandals, and saying that she came from an island nearby to Glasgow and that it was the traditional way of dressing of her town, she was also an intelligent and friendly woman. She told me in English: "*You are an attractive man*" - I got weird about this first compliment that I received in my life from the lips of a woman! Her name was Victoria, she was twenty-seven years old and I was only twenty-two, she told me she had a boy, a seven-year-old boy that I did not get to know. I was a little afraid of this possible friendship, but I liked talking to Victoria, she was nice and attractive. I remember that the next day, when she did not come to the appointment at the time and place where we had stayed, I searched for her with the car all over the city; in the end, after several laps around Glasgow, I found her, as if I was a police officer or a private detective. I confess that it is not easy to find a person and find her in a city as big as Glasgow, when one is a foreigner, a newcomer, does not know the city and has to drive on the left. But I had confidence in myself and my sense of smell and I knew how to look and find, it was my specialty. Victoria was an artist, she made portraits with a pencil, I think she also painted oil paintings. She told me that she wanted to go with me to Belgium and make portraits in the main square of Brussels, the Grand Place. I remember that she drew my portrait with a pencil, I think I kept it for a while and then lost it. I was afraid of her proposal to accompany me on my return trip and come with me to Belgium to Leuven and I said no, that I could not take her with me to Brussels, it was my birthday when we had met and she was going to come to the university on the 2nd of April 1976, that day I was twenty-two years old, I was too young for this adventure. In the end she did not come to the appointment, I watched TV and waited, the next day she came and apologized, but I was preparing for the return home to Leuven.

There, in Glasgow, I also visited the manufacturer of *White Horse*, who distilled *grain whisky*. In the end, I decided to return, it was a long distance from Glasgow to Dover, over ten hours of travel, I left at dawn. The car got heated by the road, the radiator was old to pull and change; in spite of that, I was able to return. I bought a new radiator plug on the way and started the heater, so the water circuit was bigger, the water from the engine went through the heater and it was cooled by contact with the cold air from the outside and the cooler was cooled and did not raise the engine temperature so much so I could continue until arriving home.

I arrived at Dover in the afternoon, at five in the afternoon, when the ferry almost closed the doors, I was the last one to come aboard. After five hours, the ferry arrived to Ostend, it was night, from there I had to continue the journey at night until arriving at my small studio in Leuven.

On this trip, I had seen everything and learned enough English and could understand the Scottish accent well and learned many things from the life that served me on the long road that awaited me and that I am still walking.

This has been the story of my trip to England and Scotland in the spring of 1976.

Chapter 11: The Myth of Europe

In this chapter, we are going to address the issue of Europe, which is very long and very complicated.

About Europe, a lot has been said for more than eight thousand years; then there was no our current Europe, there was only the myth of Europe in Greek mythology.

Europe also existed as geographical territory from written history and in the time of Alexander the Great.

For me, today's Europe is still a myth, a project that has not yet come to perform at all!

Since the adoption of the euro as the single currency of exchange for nineteen of the twenty-eight states in the European Union - fewer than one, England, leaving the EC - today's Europe is a project that cost a great deal of money and has not yet settled. We all clearly see and realize that our own savings have been reduced to more than half, we can no longer save as before, we have to pay many taxes within this current Europe. For more than fifteen years, Europe has been built at the expense of our savings and our pockets, those of European taxpayers!

We can no longer acquire a good house or make a real estate investment in the long term, because of the real estate market and the financial crisis of 2008 and *subprime* mortgages, because we also have too many expenses; life has become very expensive. These are the negative fruits of modern Europe, although life has become more modern with the passage of time and that naturally means more expenses.

On the other hand, there are officials who have worked in quotation marks in the construction of the European Union and have made a lot of money and have not paid a cent of taxes because they have worked in the EC with headquarters in Brussels, Strasbourg or Luxembourg. These officials do not pay or have paid taxes, we are the hard workers - each one in their profession and specialty - which have struggled and worked, day and night, to build this Europe of today; we had to pay many taxes so that they can receive their astronomical salaries, free of taxes.

When the euro was born and entered into circulation at the beginning of the year 2002: one euro was worth DM 1.95 or FF 6.6 or 166.4 pesetas!

Why was not changed at a one by one rate?! Irony!

If Europe were a real political and monetary union, why not talk about a project of a European Federation or the future United States of Europe?!

No, it is not possible: Europe is simply a club of rich countries and poor countries of Europe united under the blue flag with golden yellow stars of the European community and for some determined things. On the other hand, everyone, in his house or in his country, can do as he wants and as he likes to do it.

Anyone who does not like to stay in the EC will also be able to leave and leave the club, as the United Kingdom has recently done, which has already decided to leave the EC definitively and will ratify its decision in March 2017.

Why did the British come in and why do they want to leave now?

The answer is very simple: they entered because it suited them and they were interested in entering at 1973 and now they leave because it is convenient for them to leave and they are no longer interested in remaining in the EC, after forty-three years being a permanent member of the EC. It is an illogical and absurd thing at the same time!

Now, analyzing the European project in depth, I see it sincerely without any foundations, it is totally absurd because it has no basis at all!

It has no basis because the basis must be logic and here is a project that lacks logic, which is absurd, it is paradoxical!

Why does Brussels have to be the capital of the European Union since 1992?

We understand that the common market was first made in 1957 between the six founding members of the Europe of the **European Coal and Steel Community**, or **ECSC**, energy and raw materials. It was the union for the coal and steel! Now, there is no longer talk about coal, it is a polluting energy material, no one wants it and steel alike, in Europe almost no iron is extracted, it is not profitable and also pollutes, so why Brussels remains the capital of Europe?

Now, Europe is doing very badly, it is in front of a precipice and runs the risk of disintegrating, as many sociopolitical analysts predict. There are serious problems to be solved with the *brexit*, there are many populist currents that want to make a referendum - like the United Kingdom - to consult their peoples if they want to stay in the EU or if they want to leave! There are problems that have no solution, such as emigration, the colossal debt of Greece, which reached **177.7% of GDP in 2014**, and other serious problems in Europe.

It is convenient to think: how can we repair this system, this myth of Europe that does not work?

Of course, Europe remains a myth rather than a reality! If it were a reality, there would be security and stability; but there is neither security nor stability. We are at war; it has long been declared a state of emergency in France, there is high vigilance in all European countries, high alert and fear throughout Europe!

As in every system, when there are things that are failing and there are serious functioning problems, we have to think about it and if we want to repair them. We must first look for the roots of problems, where they come from, and try to keep the good, which is good, and to discard the bad, which is not good. In other words, we must select the good from the bad and separate the mistakes of the past, from the successes and positive achievements, try to separate the positive from the negative and overcome this phase by working healthily and with conscience.

There is no doubt that the work of European construction, despite the high cost it has cost us all, has been useful in one way or another. We have very nice coins and euro banknotes, but life is worth more than three times what it was worth before and the workers do not even earn double what they earned before, so we are in a public and individual deficit of - 33% as minimum!

Honestly speaking, building Europe has cost us ten times more than it should have cost. Why? Because of the expenses of the European employees, because of corruption and bribes, because the colossal and useless bad investments, because the bad planning without having thought, without having seen things coming. Projects were made for the construction of Europe by euphoria, great investments were made in a useless way, many airports were built and colossal constructions, some good and others that are useless.

We do not know what all that has been for! If the UK is leaving now and other states will follow its example!

Since England is leaving and the official language of Europe is English, it can now be changed and become another, like French, Spanish or German!

If we had stayed as before and every state would have made its development plan in its own way and according to its criteria and financial possibilities, we would each and every one of us have five or ten times more money saved in the bank and the member countries of the EC would have much less debt than to pay in the future.

For example, if you or I now have, let us say, ten thousand or twenty thousand euros saved, we could have had, without the mistakes in planning and wrong investments, perhaps a hundred thousand euros saved or even more in our account! That money we lack is in the pockets and accounts of who took advantage of the European construction!

Let us start with Belgium, a country so rich by the tyranny of its king Leopold II. I invite you to read the story of Leopold II of Belgium, which the Belgians or the Belgian state continue to honor and praise, calling him "the king builder" ("*Le roi bâtisseur*"). You can search for it in the Internet, even his racist radio messages are recorded:

«*THE CONGO AND LEOPOLDO II. CHRONICLES OF A FORGOTTEN GENOCIDE (I)*

December, 2012. By Matías Calero. In History, (only available in Spanish, below the summary translated into English).

It is a short article where the author tries to remember an apparently forgotten event. These are the dark times of the Belgian Congo during the Belgian occupation. It speaks of a brutal genocide, planned with the agreement of the "international community." At least ten million Congolese natives died under the administration of King Leopold II of Belgium.

Once upon a time there was a little kingdom... »

Europe is the Europe of values, respect, morality and humanism; as Europeans, we cannot consent such things. Belgians should work on themselves and work on their conscience and try to repair and reconcile with their past, while Europe has to be free of those heavy moral burdens of Belgium's past with Leopold II.

Let us now turn to the true roots of Europe, here is the mythology of Europe.

You can also search for it in the Internet.

We conclude, reading ancient Greek mythology that Europe is Cretan and that she is a princess who came from the city of Tire, from Phoenicia - which is now Lebanon -, she was kidnapped by the legendary god of Greek mythology, Zeus of Crete, who was in the cave of Dikteon, on Mount Andron.

What do you think of that idea? That we propose to Lebanon to be part of Europe, since Europe is a princess of Tire, Crete, that belongs to the Europe of today. This will compensate for the departure of the United Kingdom with the entry of a new member who has more history and antiquity than the United Kingdom. Lebanon brought the Phoenician alphabet and trade as cultural exchange to the world and to the Mediterranean civilizations, from which Europe comes, which are two fundamental and very valuable elements of civilizations. I believe that the Lebanese people would be delighted with this brilliant idea and would do everything possible and impossible to enter and be part of Europe; thus they would have peace and security and a secure peace with their neighbors: Israel, Palestine and Syria.

For God to help Europe, let us put the belief in God as something fundamental. Atheism is not a religion, it is the lack of respect for God, the universal Creator.

<u>We are going to inscribe, in the charter of the foundations of Europe, a principal and first principle:</u>

First, we thank God for being Europeans and we work with all conscience and without falsehood, without lying, without arrogance, without hypocrisy, with humility and sincerity for the good of Europe and of all humanity.

The capital of Europe will be displaced by the twenty-eight Member States, it will no longer require thousands of extra officials for a united Europe, or any of that. All will return to their countries and will pay from now on their taxes and thus they will also contribute in the construction of the Europe of the future.

There will be a representation from the same countries, politicians and people of society, academics and philosophers volunteers, who will work freely and devotion, in their spare time, for the community Europe. All European affairs will be directed from member countries via the Internet, a small delegation of no more than thirty or fifty people will be present in the European headquarters for two years and will sleep in a normal hotel - from two to three stars - and will pay their taxes, will drive normal tourist class cars like a Fiat Panda or Toyota Aygo paid by the EC.

They will do tourism in their spare time on their own, not on behalf of other Europeans, they will be able to learn the language of the country with courses paid by the EC!

Thus, spending will be reduced to a minimum, all of them will be related with each other via telephone and internet (there will be no extra roaming costs, intra-European telephone calls will cost the same as local calls).

The study of the project of a future European Federation or of the United States of Europe will be put on the table to be carried out by sincere academicals, philosophers and politicians in a maximum period of twenty years.

All Europeans will have the same obligations, the same rights, the same level of salaries and the same pensions according to the work and the provision of each one.

There will no longer exist the Europe of the rich and the Europe of the poor.

There will be a single European army to defend Europe, which will be present in all countries, a single police force and services in each country and all will act with the same spirit and the same European feeling.

The first capital of Europe will be Heraklion, in Crete, followed by other capitals of all the member countries, like Madrid, Paris, Lisbon, Berlin, etc.

Psychological and social diseases such as arrogance, xenophobia, chauvinism, racism, omnipotence, disrespect, atheism, materialism and stupidity will be fought.

We will learn from philosophers such as Socrates, Jesus Christ, etc. There will be free courses in the town councils and cultural houses of each city or large European town: about philosophy, morals, ethics, languages, mathematics, science, arts, sport, humility, sincerity, it will be taught how to be generous, to know how to share and to know how to lose to win and especially to greet when we meet an unknown person, as they do in the civilized cities and towns of Europe.

Thus, Europe will be the lighthouse and glory of the civilizations of the world, and the whole world will look to Europe with respect, love, admiration and passion.

This is the myth of Europe, the Europe of my dreams.

Chapter 12: Viva España!

In this chapter, I'm going to talk about that great country that I love so much, which is Spain.

Thanks to this wonderful country and its people so special, so kind and with a great heart, I have been able to realize myself as an adult and I have been able to live the best moments of my life and I continue to live them in that great country called Spain.

Spain has a great diversity and cultural heritage; it is a unique country in the world, a very rich and varied country in all. That comes from its rich history, the conquests of the civilizations and peoples of the Mediterranean: Phoenicians, Greeks, Romans and Arabs, whence I proceed largely, that is why I am identified with Spain, by its roots similar to mine. These civilizations came here because they were attracted by the rich nature, the resplendent sun and the magnetism of Spain.

I have known Spain since September 1976, just forty years ago, when I came to Spain by car on the border of Irun coming from Belgium and passing through France. My destination was Casablanca, in Morocco.

I remember that, when entering, I saw armed soldiers; it was just one year after the death of General Franco.

At that time, I had a friend from Brazil who accompanied me to Granada, supposedly she took the photo of the cover of my book on September 28, 1976.

It was my first short trip - three days - to Spain, at the end of September 1976. We entered on September 27th and slept one night in a guesthouse in Burgos, we had little money, the hotel night with breakfast in a double room for two people was worth, I think, at that time, perhaps two hundred and fifty or three hundred pesetas. We had dinner, in the evening, in a restaurant, I think it was next to the guesthouse, they brought a Spanish Garlic chicken platter "Pollo al Ajillo", I think they also brought salad and bread, a litre of wine in a big bottle of mud or glass, I do not exactly remember it, but I do remember that it was a litre and worth fifty pesetas. Everything was exquisite, the whole meal cost something like two hundred pesetas!

The Spanish girl who served us at the table was beautiful, had long black hair, large dark eyes, a very special beauty and education. It was a wonderful and unforgettable dinner in Burgos.

Afterwards, we left with the car, a white 1966 Ford Anglia. I had bought it in Belgium for ten thousand

Belgian francs, thirty thousand pesetas; then I had to repair some things, like the brakes, the second-hand radiator, the new clutch... and then the car went smoothly.

With this car I went on a trip to Amsterdam, Holland, England and Scotland, France, Spain and Morocco.

From Burgos we went to Granada. The photo of the book cover is made somewhere on the road in the south of Madrid, in Castilla La Mancha, in the lands of Don Quixote and the famous writer Miguel de Cervantes.

Seeing the bull of Osborne so big and flashy, I liked it so much that I wanted to make a photo in front of the bull, I did not know that this photo was going to serve for my book, I remembered nothing of this photo until my sister Ketty sent it a couple of months ago. She was cleaning up our family home in Beirut; she found this photo and sent it to me through Whatsapp.

Just after looking at the photo, in a few seconds, I remembered the place and the trip and the approximate date. To be sure of the date, I looked in the stamps of my old passport, where I found the dates of entry and exit of Spain.

Spain fascinated me, a big and beautiful country, where I could develop myself as a person, with kind and friendly people, a good climate, generally dry, a good gastronomy, a good spirit, there is no racism, it is a country with a mentality similar to the Mediterranean countries where I come from, Lebanon and Greece, where there is no racism either!

I also liked to read a plaque in the Parque del Retiro in Madrid, where the words of a Spanish writer were written: *"The word "foreigner" must be erased from all dictionaries in the world."*

In Granada, we stayed one night and we ate, I remember, fish, it was golden. We should have arrived in the afternoon to Granada, I remember that we were doing, every day, about seven hundred kilometers of travel.

I remember that, in Granada, by day I cut my hair and my beard, they were both very long, as seen in the photo on the cover of my book. My father had died in Beirut on the eighteenth of August, but I was in Leuven and I heard it a month later; when I knew it, after a while I shed a few tears, I remembered that my father told me: "Go to the world! Learn everything!" It was a great commandment and a mission to perform, to satisfy my father's soul; in the end, that has become a personal desire and *hobby*: wanting to learn everything and reach the fullness of life, knowledge and wisdom.

I could no longer stay in Belgium, I had to go out on my way. I went to Casablanca, but on the way I discovered Spain, which fascinated me and still fascinates me, forty years later!

Afterwards, I stayed for about fifty days in Casablanca; From there, I went to Brazil invited to the house of my Brazilian friend in Santa Catarina.

Then I had to return to Lebanon in the war, in January 1977 at the insistence of my mother. I was the eldest son and knew of my father's factory, I was twenty-two years old, my brother was younger, he did not know anything about the factory, so I was forced back, but that only lasted four years. Then, on June 6, 1981, I went back to Brazil, to São Paolo, but in my mind was the desire to go to Spain, until the opportunity came to go to Spain on a trip that I took advantage of in October 1981. Just by entering Madrid, I felt peace and serenity in my soul and I stayed in Spain forever.

It was a long and hard road, my family sent me money to live, at first I did not speak Spanish well, I was called "the Portuguese" at first because I came from Brazil and spoke Brazilian Portuguese. Then, talking to the people and reading the newspapers, I quickly learned Spanish with practice. I frequented illustrious people from Madrid, like my great friend writer, novelist and playwright Germán Ubillos, and his friends Ernesto and Rafael, his cousin Armando, all very kind, different, but wonderful people, sincere, honest and all of them with a great heart. That is the Spain that I was lucky to find, a country that adopted me and gave me its kindness and great heart.

To gain Spain I had, apart from integrating myself in the way of life and the Spanish mentality, I also had to travel through Spain and travel the world and learn everything.

I used to say to myself and to others on many occasions: "To gain Spain, you have to gain the world!"

Thus, I had to learn, after *Castilian* or Spanish, other languages like German, Italian and Norwegian.

My world was between Europe, Arabia and sub-Saharan Africa, let us say: half the world. I worked for a long time in Germany, where I had to live a few years, living between Spain and Germany. I also made a long trip through the Arab countries of the Persian Gulf and an interesting and remarkable trip to England and Scotland, where I learned a lot from the British philosophy of life.

Now I travel a lot to countries in Sub-Saharan Africa, the West, the Center and the East.

In Spain, I lived in Madrid, Conde Duque *Street*, in front of my dear friend the writer, Germán Ubillos.

Perhaps because of the contact and friendship and for his moral support, I had the strength to continue writing this book, the idea that was born on the island of Crete and now, thanks to my friend Germán, who lends me his moral support, I am able to keep writing this book to the end.

I listened to Germán, I learned from him the good Castilian, he shared some of his lyricism as a writer and novelist. I also had friends at work, my friend Ángel Rodríguez, from Granada, who speaks good Spanish and taught me and corrected me and I was learning. My friend Ángel is affectionate, although of strong personality, he also had a great sense of humor, we had a great time together, he loved me very much and he loved me as one of his sons, he is about twenty years older than me. He opened me the doors of his Chinchón distillery, of which he was the managing director; there, after a few months, I was able to manufacture the famous Arak Al Bacha, which was manufactured under license from the family factory in Lebanon. We had to adapt the dry anise technique of Chinchón and make a special formula to distill the Arak of Lebanon; I did the tests in the laboratory of the Chinchón factory and came out perfect: an arak among the best in the world.

I was able to export the Arak Al Bacha to England, Ireland, France and Australia, thus I learned the trade of the export by myself, wanting to sell my arak in the world. I continue practicing the same trade, but I am selling other things now: I sell building materials in sub-Saharan Africa.

In Madrid, the three of us would go out at night: Germán, Ernesto and I, sometimes Rafael was also with us. We went to places where many young people of our age were gathered, in pubs or places of social gatherings. I was the star of the night; they called me "the Exocet"! I was bold, I started the conversations and introduced my friends, so we chatted with beautiful and nice girls, and we spent pleasant and unforgettable moments.

Germán would come to my studio or I would go to his apartment to have a boiled egg flavoured with curry, York ham, cheese and cabbage salad with parsley.

We had parties with Greek friends: Nicos (the Cretan), Dimitri, Vasilis (The Pontics of Ptolemais and Kozani). Vasilis no longer lives, he died in Greece of a heart attack, being so young!

Thanks to the dear friend Nikos Stamatakis of Chania, from Crete, so good, so noble and affectionate and by his memory, I came to the island of Crete looking for him, unable to find him again!

My friend Ángel, from Granada, invited me from the first year, shortly after we met, to his house at Christmas because he knew that I was alone, it was a great joy for me to be in a family at Christmas!

My friend Angel kept inviting me, year after year, on Christmas Eve, at Christmas. We remain friends until now, after more than thirty-five years, he now lives with his wife in a residence in Galicia, we continue to congratulate each other every year at Christmas and we talk from time to time.

Spain is a different country, which lives and lets live.

That is the Spain that I love, that has a great heart, I met here, in this country, wonderful and very generous people who helped me in everything; also foreign people, like me, who also helped me without interest. All I have achieved so far is thanks to the beloved God and the immense goodness of these wonderful people who live in this great country that is called Spain.

That is why I say and repeat: "Viva España!"

Chapter 13: The equation of life

I've always liked the difficult things. Between two options that came up in my life, I have always chosen the most difficult one!

Why? Because, simply, it is more interesting, more curious, more exciting and less boring.

Now I invite you to help me solve this equation, the most difficult of all equations, which is the equation of life.

It is, of course, difficult, we realize about it from the birth of a child who comes to the world, and does not stop crying for a long season.

Why children cry at birth? Because they know, unconsciously, what awaits for them in life: so much to learn, so many tests, so much to endure and suffer. Life is a long school and, at the same time, a long ordeal, although it contains so many joys!

An animal does not usually cry at birth because it does not think, it only looks for instinct to its mother; it wants warmth and milk, protection and love from its mother.

A child has its animal part and its human part. With growth, they develop their mental faculties and will lose their instincts and gain intelligence.

Now, what is the problem to solve?: human life.

I remember that, once in August 2015, on the beach of Karteros, six kilometers from Heraklion, I met a man older than me; a Norwegian man who has traveled extensively around the world. We spoke first in Norwegian, then in English, then in Spanish - he could speak fluent Spanish - we talked about the problems and news of the world a bit in general.

After a while, the man said, "But we will not fix the world, you and me, in a conversation on Karteros beach!"

It is true, in this chapter, we will not be able to solve the problems of the world, such as wars, poverty, injustices, diseases, plagues, epidemics and social, psychological and spiritual problems... or we cannot solve the whole equation of life, but what is intended is to talk about the problem and look for how to solve the problems and issues of all kinds, the ones that concern us and the others that we encounter in our daily life and everyday life and in every moment.

How to start the day: The day begins with a prayer of faith in God and His mercy, thanking Him for everything He has given us and asking Him for help and protection.

How to start the day step by step: With the desire to work, to do the work and to work on oneself, on the problems that must be solved, which emerge during the day, with faith and hope.

What should be our attitude: Always positive, open to dialogue and collaborate with others to solve collective and individual problems.

For example, if...:

You are sick: You go to the doctor.

Your car has a breakdown: You go to the garage.

You have a toothache: You go to the dentist.

You need a credit: You go to the bank.

You are looking for a job: Look for a a job with strength, confidence and optimism.

You have a serious problem: Talk about your problem with the people you trust, with your relatives, your close friends, they will try to help you and give you advice, they will teach you how to proceed to solve the problem and pray intensely to God for His help. Let God do His work within you and within your life; always follow God and the teachings of His son, Jesus Christ.

Are you depressed?: Do a deep prayer to God and try to think positively, look at yourself in the mirror, you will see that it is worthwhile to resume the path of struggle with dignity, God will help you.

You are looking for love: Open your eyes and heart and seek it, you will find, you need to have patience, never lose the illusion, you will find it!

You want to create a family: For this you need to gather so many things together: find your true love, get lucky and earn money, so you can build the new home for your future family.

You are looking for God: God is present at your side, it is a matter of faith, have faith in God, He will reveal Himself to you and He will give you signs of His power and His glory.

You seek the truth of the things of life: Ask God to enlighten you, work and seek with faith, desire and joy. God will help you to find them over time.

You seek to invent something important or to invent your own craft: It is a long way of learning and searching, trust in God and keep struggling. God will help you and you will find yourself every day closer to your invention or the person you dreamed of becoming.

You look for joys: Work and look with joy, you will find many joys.

You seek to give meaning to your life, to discover yourself: Work on yourself, take care of yourself, look at yourself in the mirror thinking that you are two people: one is the educator or the thinker, and another is the student or the worker. So you can have ideas that will indicate the path to be followed to become the man or woman of your dreams and your dreams can be realized with the help of God.

You want to be an author: Try to write and trust yourself, try it many times and never get tired of it, one day you will become a great author.

You want to be an artist: Practice your profession and your art, learn the talents of great artists and teachers; imitate them, but try to put some of yourself. Someday, you will become a great artist and have your own art school.

To solve the equation of life, it is necessary to have self-confidence and to own oneself, so that we can face, every day, the problems that come our way, from the time we get up in the morning until we go to bed at night and, at the end of each day, being able to finish the day with a satisfaction of having been able to solve some important problems of our daily life. And if they have not yet been resolved, we must pray hard, wanting to move the heavens so that God will listen to us and help us solve those difficult equations one after another in the days that follow.

Some problems are easy to solve, others need reflection, meditation and sometimes time, practice, struggle and try again many times throughout our lives.

God has given to us all human and mental faculties to face the problems of each day, each of us, human beings, carries a cross.

This cross is made to measure the endurance of each one. Even his son, Jesus Christ, God gave him an immense cross to carry, the greatest of all the crosses you can imagine! The lazy, those who do not want to carry their cross, those who do not want to work, those who are irresponsible and do not want to recognize the reality of life, which is a long school to learn and improve their spirit in order to save their soul. They do not want to face the great challenges of life, that is why they cannot go far, time will fall on them and they will stay on the edge of the road because they have not bothered to do, every day, what they should have done, an important step towards the final goal. They have been quiet, vegetated and have not worked on themselves, they have not demanded anything great to themselves, so they have not been able to move forward in their lives, they will be marginalized.

The selfish and the hypocrites, also, for a lot of money having kneaded, have not been able to triumph before God, because they kept every penny thinking of their old age and amassed great fortunes thinking that money would give them security and happiness. They did not give anything to the poor and had, in many cases, to turn their backs on God ignoring Him, simply saying that they are atheists or agnostics, who do not know God because it is no longer fashionable, those same have failed in life.

If you do not know God, it is obvious that you seek Him, because in God there is your truth, your life, your existence and your hope; one day, undoubtedly, you will find Him.

To triumph in life and before God, one must be a hero and not fear anything, only fear God and oneself, because the greatest enemy of a human being is himself when he is wrong, and try every day to make better the Life things.

Thus, and with these principles, we can solve, each day better, the equation of life.

Chapter 14: My trip and stay of 50 days in Casablanca, autumn 1976.

In 1974-1976, when I lived in Leuven, Belgium, where I went to study at the Catholic University of Leuven, I did everything but study!

Leuven is a relatively small city. Not far from the centre of the city there was a place called "*Cercle des Étrangers*", or "circle of foreigners", it was a social centre with a ground floor and a first floor. Downstairs there was a large cafeteria with large terraces; above it was a kind of shelter for students with few means or who were in transit, who slept above; there was also a large kitchen and a dining area for them.

The "*Cercle des Étrangers*" was a place frequented by few Belgians and many foreigners, the centre was open every day of the year from noon to twelve at night, and it was never closed! It was always open! Also at Christmas and New Year!

It was a social place where university students from all over the world came together: Belgians, French, English, Germans, Italians, Spaniards,

Portuguese, Turks, Greeks and particularly Arabs, Africans and South Americans.

People had beers, coffee, etc., there was also some *snacks* for those who were a little hungry. There was a pleasant intellectual and social atmosphere, I was there a lot, there was talk in many languages and everything was talked about: politics, university, society, etc. It was the only place where my soul could breathe and where I could feel social warmth, I talked and got related to almost everyone.

The Belgians of Louvain were very cold and much closed people, they hardly spoke French, or they spoke it but they preferred to speak their language, the flamenco, which is a dialect derived from the Dutch. I always listened to it when I bought something in the shops, they said "*Dach Munir*" (hello, sir) and then "*Danku Well*" (thank you very much). They said the same numbers in flamenco, to my point of view it was a sign of underdeveloped intelligence, in a university city that should be open, in a bilingual country like Belgium! There were cafes, or rather breweries where Belgians in Leuven consumed a lot of beer. In my opinion, they were quite empty of spirit, bored, quite alcoholic, they were like vegetables, they had very little culture or civilization, only money mattered to them. No doubt they were also cultivated and enlightened, such as, for example, people of high intellectual level, such as university professors, academic people, technicians, etc., who have devoted themselves to learning something in their lives; but you had to look for those people, they were not in the street or, if you went by their side, they did not greet you, if you found them in a mall. At that time, there were no shopping malls! There were only stores and a supermarket; people were, in general, very closed in Leuven!

That is why the foreigners gathered among them in this «*Cercle des Étrangers*» as they were not integrated into the Belgian society of Leuven. I believe that the "*Cercle de Étrangers*" has ceased to exist for many years.

At that time, I had enough money; my father, because he was very generous, and as he loved me so much, had sent me enough money to live well for six months. As in Lebanon there was a civil war, I spent and invited friends enough, as my father taught me when I was a child. People thought he was rich, it is true: he was rich in spirit!

Being generous and living well does not necessarily mean being rich; there are rich people who pretend to be poor because they are poor in spirit and do not like to spend money and keep it to amass fortunes.

I had other interests than studies, I wanted to travel and discover the world, discover the truths and many things from their roots. I liked business, I was looking for the first love, and I was very sentimental and affectionate!

I had met a friendly and affectionate Lebanese who appreciated me. He went out a lot with a tall, thin, well-educated and classy Moroccan. They two studied pharmacy or medicine, they were inseparable friends, they went out partying at night and slept during the day, they did not have enough time to study! Just like me!

This Moroccan boy was from Casablanca and he came from a good family, people who had good social and economic position to be able to send their son to study in Belgium, in Leuven.

When he knew that I was a distillation technician and worked on the manufacture of spirits, *whisky*, etc. -a job I learned at my father's factory- it came up the idea, dreams and fantasy, of setting up a *whisky* factory in Morocco.

Now, if I think of it, it seems to me an absurd thing: to set up such a business in a Muslim country, although it was a fairly open and tolerant country - at this time forty years ago - and people freely consumed French beer, wine and pastis, some of them also drank *whisky*, now I think it's totally different!

So he told me that I could go first to Casablanca and wait for him there, that he would soon come to find me! In fact, I went there to visit his brother in his house in Casablanca, they lived in a nice neighborhood, his brother was a pharmacist, a little older than him, I left my address where I was at the hotel. In the end, the friend for whom I made this long journey from Belgium, appeared about forty or forty-five days after my arrival, I had a few days to leave Morocco to Brazil! His appearance was no longer expected or interesting to me!

Thus, that trip to Morocco was a pure adventure and, logically, a failure. But, always behind a mistake or a failure, there is a destiny, a will of God, an experience and a truth to discover.

I remember when I left Granada on September 29, 1976 about noon, I said goodbye to my friend. I remember a landscape of Granada that got fixed in my mind, that I could not locate in future visits to Granada in this splendid city among the most beautiful cities of Spain, not to say the most beautiful and exciting of all for its strategic place, its landscapes around and its long history, etc. Perhaps, because there were many buildings during these last forty years, I think it will be somewhere behind a city wall! It was a sad farewell!

As I was going down to Motril, from Granada, from the mountain of green pine trees I saw the sea, I remembered the mountain of green pines of Lebanon facing the sea, I said to myself: "It is very beautiful! Why do I leave here, this country so beautiful? - Tears began to fall- . I'm totally alone! I just said goodbye to my friend Annette, my father no longer lives, I have no reference to anyone to ask something." I should be, from that moment, the reference for myself. It was a pretty tough experience, but I think I had enough character to overcome it by learning little by little.

Arriving at Algeciras, I got on the ferry that was leaving; perhaps, about one o'clock at two o'clock pm, I got on my car to the ferry that took us both to Ceuta. My vehicle, the Ford Anglia, was like my white horse true to me that did not abandon me! There, arriving at Ceuta, I had to wait for the line to pass the customs; after putting the entry stamp on my passport, I left on my way to Kenitra. I arrived late to Kenitra, it was already dark, I could not go any further, I had to sleep in a boarding-house that I found and have dinner at a restaurant next door.

On the way between Ceuta and Kenitra or the next day, I do not remember exactly, a policeman stopped me on the road and, seeing me as a foreign man with a beard and a car with a Belgian licence, he thought I was some kind of smuggler. He started to search and look inside my car, put his hand inside my personal things, clothes and suitcases and I said, "What are you looking for? Now it is OK!". I was nervous to see him look so much; the policeman thought he would find something for which he would receive a reward from his bosses! In the end, he left me alone and I went on my way.

A disaster, a country of fright, there was nothing to compare with Spain, it was a totally different world. Although I spoke the language of the country, I felt totally foreign, people, when knowing that I spoke five languages, thought I was a spy, in this country knowing a lot was dangerous, I think now is another modern time!

The next day, I went to Casablanca through Rabat, where I stopped and ate there in Rabat at noon. It was a rather civilized world, they were educated and nice people, and then I went through Mohammedia to Casablanca. Arriving in Casablanca in the afternoon, I searched for a hotel, I found the Al Mansour hotel, it had more name than quality! «Al Mansour» means «the winner».

The next day, I was looking to leave this catastrophic and expensive hotel until I found a hotel where foreigners slept, it was quite affordable. Downstairs there was a kind of small hall with a reception that overlooked an inner main street; next door, there was a cafe with a terrace to the street; Upstairs, on the first floor and perhaps on the second floor, there were fairly large and clean rooms.

The hotel was located on a corner of Boulevard Mohamed V, near a large round square where, behind it, there was a large mosque and next to the right was the medina, ie the *souk* or the bazaar.

When visiting again on a trip to Casablanca in 2007, thirty years later, I was looking for this hotel to remember it. I did not find it, it's like it disappeared. I also remember the central post office that still exists, it was quite far from the location where the hotel was, but the hotel had already completely disappeared, just as it would have been demolished completely and, instead, there was a new building!

I did not receive any mail at the hotel, the letters arrived at the central Post Office in the *Poste restante*, that is, the remaining mail, for the displaced people who had no address!

I was in Casablanca, abandoned in a distant world, with no family and no address! But God was present!

I went every two or three days to *La Poste Centrale*, I had to walk more than two miles to the central Post Office. There I would ask if they had any letters to my name in the *Poste restante* and they would say to me: "Yes, you have," then a joy came into my heart, or "no, you have nothing" and I got back to the hotel with sadness.

Calling my family in Lebanon was very complicated: there was a public telephone office and there was a man trying to call my home phone number in Lebanon, many times without being able to make the connection! It was the country of the impossible, there was nothing possible in this country!

The next day, when I reached the hotel, I was downstairs in the *hall* sitting in an armchair. I saw a tired man, aged over fifty, sitting in front of me, put his feet on the coffee table to rest and snore. Then he woke up and was pointing a few numbers on a piece of paper looking at a newspaper; as I was curious, I asked him what he was doing, he told me that he was targeting a game of the *tiercé*, it was a bet on horse racing in France, the famous French *tiercé*!

He said, "Do you want to play half with me?"

I said, "Okay, how much do I have to put on?"

He answered something like "five dirhams each," I do not remember exactly the amount, but it was four or five dirhams. I said, "Okay, here you have five dirhams!"

He said, "Okay," and gave me a handshake.

The next day, I asked him, "How about yesterday, do you know anything about the bet?"

He said, "I'm sorry, we've lost!"

I said, "Okay, nothing happens!"

Thus, he quickly created a trust between him and me and then a friendship that was growing day after day.

The man was called Albert Saúl, he was a Jew of origin, he was born in Egypt, perhaps in Alexandria, he fought in World War II with the allies with the Greeks against Nazi Germany. He was a diver, they gave him, as a result, a Greek passport, in fact we spoke in Greek, it was a cultural bond that united us, a language we both spoke, apart from French, and some Arabic that he spoke, but he badly spoke Arabic.

Albert then came from Brazil, where he was living, he was married to a French Catholic woman and he had three children, his family lived in Brazil. He was setting up a business in Casablanca to import products from Brazil, such as clothes and other merchandise, and he thought, once the business was set up, to bring his family to Casablanca; apparently there was a large Sephardic Jewish community in Casablanca.

His French wife was his second wife; The first one was Jewish, I think they had a son together, who lived in Germany.

This man had lived a thousand and one experiences in several countries of the world: in Egypt, where he was born; in Greece, where he fought; In

France, perhaps also in Spain; he had lived in Germany, in a couple of African countries such as Senegal and perhaps Guinea Conakry and, in the end, in Morocco after having lived in Brazil. He spoke twelve languages: Arabic not very well, Hebrew perhaps a little, French, English, Spanish, Portuguese, Italian, Greek and German; and he also spoke three dialects of African countries like the *Wolof* of Senegal and two others that I do not know.

This man, Albert Saúl, was for me a very important figure, a reference, a prototype, an example of the man that I could become. I dreamed of becoming a man similar to him, but within my personal context; at that time, I spoke only five languages, I was only twenty-two.

Afterwards, I had to learn five other languages during my travels. Albert Saúl was fifty-eight years old, he loved me as a father or a mother, we ate together every day at noon and spent the weekends together as well.

I was going to buy fish, chicken, etc. to the market that was in the interior of the city, opposite the medina, and Albert said to me: "Buy yourself a big fish and give it to the restaurant chef to prepare us food in the oven, fish, chicken, meat, etc."

Albert did not trust the Maghreb restaurants, he said that they could put you on bad food, which could make you sick; so I was going to buy fresh food at the market, the cook added the vegetables, tomatoes and olive oil and cooked our food on a tray in the oven.

After a while being in Casablanca, my friend Annette, from Brazil, started in her country the request for a visa for me, to enter Brazil, she did it with the help of her parents, especially her brother Armando. I was worried about what was waiting for me there in Brazil, I did not know if it was good or bad for me, whether I could succeed or not!

Albert Saúl reassured me and said: "Do not be afraid, you are a young man, big, healthy and intelligent, you have two hands, two feet, two eyes, there in Brazil there will be many opportunities for men like you! Do not be afraid, you will conquer it!"

Albert Saúl had a sense of humor, I had a beard. Once, he took me to a restaurant that was owned by a Greek family, who are of Greek Orthodox religion like me and told them, jokingly, that I was an orthodox priest. I did not know what to say, whether yes or no, it was a very embarrassing situation for me!

I was told that in Casablanca they lacked a priest for the Greek community; they ask me if I could perform an ecclesiastical service! I told them anything to escape and save me from this situation!

I had a great time with Albert, we laughed a lot! On the weekend we would go out for a drink on a terrace, I believe in the *Carré français*. Once, we also went to attend a French theatre in the city.

There were also guests at the same hotel who were Lebanese tourists from the Lebanese diaspora, who lived in sub-Saharan Africa, as in Senegal, Ivory Coast, Guinea Conakry, etc. They came to Casablanca for its fresh air, to go on holiday not far from where they lived, it was about three or four hours of flight by plane.

I spoke with them in Lebanese Arabic and they once asked me for a service to take them to the airport in Rabat in my car and they paid me something that compensated for the gasoline and a little more; so I gained something from time to time.

Coming from a cold country, I had winter clothes and had two coats; I sold one to a Lebanese young guy because it started getting cold in Casablanca from the end of October. I also had a *trench coat* that Albert kept, with many personal things of mine and told me that he was going to send me money to Brazil, I did not see a cent and I have forgiven him and given it away!

I also had to sell my car. A policeman appeared who paid me, at first, twelve hundred dirhams, and we agreed to this price; then later he said that he could not register the car because it was forbidden and that the car would serve his wife to learn to drive and, in the end, he offered me only seven hundred dirhams! I left it at this price because I had no better option! That hurt me a lot because he took advantage of me, it was not right, it was not a gentleman's behavior!

The young Lebanese who bought me the coat went one day with a loaf of French baguette bread, I saw him a little sad, I asked him what problems he had, and he told me that he had no more money to buy food and that nobody of the rich Lebanese lent him money. So I said, "Man, do not worry! How much do you want?" I reached into my pocket and said," How much do you need?" I took out a hundred, two hundred dirhams and said, "Yes, two hundred dirhams would do me good, I'll pay you back five hundred: two hundred plus three hundred for the coat. I said, "Okay, here you go!" And it was all I had in my pocket; I had no more money left!

I gave the last thing I had to a person who needed it more than I did!

I was not afraid, I had enough gasoline, and the next day my friend Annette from Belgium would come to visit me in Casablanca, she brought me money that I had in an old account of Lebanon that I had rescued from the same bank in Belgium and I delegated her so that she could receive it in my name. I had in this account, perhaps, the equivalent of a thousand dollars, something like that! I do not remember the exact amount! But it was something to go on for a while.

Then my friend had to lend me more money in order to pay my hotel bill and pay the one-way plane ticket to Sao Paolo, because everything I had even the money coming in from the sale of the car and the coat was not enough; Annette was very noble, she loved me very much and I loved her the same.

The time was passing and the visa to Brazil did not arrive. I visited the Brazilian embassy in Rabat, they told me that they would notify me by phone, but I could not take it any longer, I decided to go to Brazil without a visa. Albert supported this decision!

Albert told me that I could send a *Telecopy*, it was the fax that was used, it was possible to send it only from the post offices and telegram, it was a letter that one can write by hand on a sheet of DIN A4 and it was sent by telephone and the copy arrived identical to its destination. From there comes the word "*Telecopy*", then it was renamed Telefax, then simply Fax, now the Fax is almost unused, it is old fashioned! Only *email* is used!

So I told my friend with a *Telecopy* that they delivered it to her home, that I would be arrived on a certain day and time without a visa, and she called me back and assured me that she was going to wait for me at the airport in *São Paulo*, in Viracopos.

One day before I left, the Brazilian consul in Rabat called me to come and pick up my visa, which had already arrived. I said, "Okay, I'll pick it up soon," but I did not go, I did not have any more time, nor did I want to go to the consulate! I had already made my decision to leave Casablanca, I was tired of waiting so long!

The Air Maroc line from Casablanca to Rio de Janeiro was just inaugurated. When I got on the plane, they asked me if I had a visa, I said no, that I did not need it, I did not need visa as a Lebanese to enter Morocco, so for Brazil it's the same; he let me in and I got on the plane.

Thus ended my trip and stay of fifty days in Casablanca.

Chapter 15: The time machine

Time is a very important factor. Time determines everything.

It is necessary to leave on time and arrive on time.

Time hits us, time is like the waves of the sea, it never stops, we are not machines, but time itself is a machine!

That is why it is important to talk about this wild machine as time is.

No one can go faster than time, no one and no creature can survive the time.

No one or anything will be able to overcome this excessive machine that is the time.

God has created time, why? We cannot give a clear answer to this question because if there were no time, everything would be immobile, there would be no life, no pulse, no pumping of blood from the heart into the veins of living creatures; there would be no need to breathe so that the oxygen in the air acts on the blood cells and detoxifies the blood or the cells of the leaves of the trees and the plants.

Without time, there would be no life.

A valid answer comes to my mind: God has created the time since he threw Adam and Eve from Paradise.

In Paradise, according to the Bible, time did not really exist: Adam and Eve could live forever.

Ever since God had cast the man from Paradise, after the first sin, time already started to count; time already exists and counts from that moment.

Life and time go hand in hand.

A human creature needs time to be born, time to grow, time to learn, time to work, time to sleep and rest, time to grow old; until the time comes to die, when time no longer counts for a human creature, an animal or a plant, without life when the body is inert and lifeless.

Man needs time to work and time to overcome, time to heal his physical, psychological and spiritual illnesses. He also needs time to build his house and make his inventions; he needs time to repair what has been destroyed by wars or catastrophes of nature.

Man needs time to create and repair systems, time to eradicate epidemics, time to improve environmental conditions.

Time is an invincible machine, no one can beat the machine that is the time, only the Lord, Jesus Christ, has been the only one who has been able to overcome time, resurrecting the third day after dying on the cross, has gone to the Eternity to save the souls of the beyond and has returned to life overcoming time and temporality.

Time does not forgive: what you did not do yesterday you can do it today or tomorrow, but you can never do it again yesterday or an hour or a minute or a second before now, it is too late!

The past time has passed, you cannot recover, we can only learn from the past time, that new experience that time taught us!

Problems can be resolved over time, conflicts and wars need time to calm down. The sea and wind storms and the atmosphere may calm down over time.

People will be able to reconcile with each other in time, each one will eventually be able to reconcile with God and his own past. God forgives everything, provided that we are willing to forgive others, those who hurt us materially or psychologically.

Time can change in favor and become a reconciling machine.

Time overcomes all dictators, despots, unjust, liars and hypocrites, and they will all be judged, each one at his time. Time also crowns the saints, the good and the righteous, which deserve to be remembered and receive the homage from the world after a time.

Time is the prime factor of the universe.

God, all powerful, who has created the universe and time, is above time.

For God, time does not count; His system is above time or temporality. God is eternal.

We humans are governed by a solar calendar, which counts solar years, months, days, hours, minutes, seconds and even fractions of seconds.

A flower, to grow, needs some time.

A woman needs time to fall in love; a man will need, perhaps, less time!

For an idea to figure out, it needs time.

To paint a picture or compose music it requires time and inspiration.

To write a book requires inspiration, ideas, practice and time.

For fertilization, time is necessary and there is no certainty that it can occur, but it occurs frequently.

To build his ark, Noah needed a lot of time and patience.

The pyramids took a long time to be built with the hard work of thousands of men and led by great masters, as well as historic buildings and monuments.

Everything happens at its time and needs its own time. The human being lives with time and within the rhythm of time. The clock imitates time, but it is an instrument that indicates the time and the clock can fail, it cannot be compared to the machine that is time, which never fails!

Time can play in our favor or against us.

If we are right, we can overcome with time, which will be many times in our favour; it will depend on whether luck is with us!

For those who walk with lies and hypocrisy, time should normally go against them, sooner or later their lies will be discovered and unveiled.

Time helps to clarify the truth, time can be fair and often unfair, time can bring hurricanes, earthquakes, fires, violent and glacial winds, time can bring torrential rains, floods or tsunamis. Time can hardly repair injustice and restore the dead to life.

Time can be cruel, it can be harmful, just as it can be a life expectancy when the good weather comes.

Time also brings with it healthy spring air, fresh water for the plants and to drink.

Time is the number one determinant of nature.

We have to respect time, have confidence in God and know how to live with time. We cannot go against time, it is impossible.

The only thing we can do is to prevent time and work for a better future, knowing that time will surely do its job and that it will never stop, that we will all grow old with certainty, that the world's population will grow more and more with certainty and that it will need more food every time; that life will surely become more expensive and that wars will stop and conflicts will continue to exist despite time. There will never be total peace on Earth, so it is good to live the present, thinking about the future and planning a better future with ideas, which are fair and bright, healthy and good for us and for other human beings.

Jesus Christ also gave hope to the world, to those who believe in Him. This promise is independent of time: He promised to return to take His own to the heavenly Jerusalem, which is preparing with God the Father, but that day is still unknown. Only God, the heavenly Father, knows the day and hour of the first resurrection; therefore, we must trust in God and follow the teaching of Jesus and the Apostles.

Time is undoubtedly the greatest machine of nature and creation.

Chapter 16: My Trip to Santa Catarina, Brazil, 1976-1977

Here I am going to tell you the story of my first trip to Brazil, this trip was marked by great adventures, research and explorations in a new world from its beginning and until its end.

It was my first trip to South America. The American continent is totally different from Europe, which is the old continent and has a lot of history, while America is a new continent discovered by Christopher Columbus, who began the conquest of America in 1492. He was trying to reach India along the shortest route, according to his calculations; he did not know that America existed! Then there were conquests of Spain in the sixteenth century by Hernán Cortés and Francisco Pizarro, who conquered the Aztec empires in Mexico and the Inca in Peru.

When one arrives at the American continent, you immediately receive a new psychological and spiritual sensation totally different from the feelings of when one enters or lives in Europe, Africa or Asia; each continent has its own character and spirit.

I had come from North Africa, from Casablanca (Morocco), where I had been for fifty days and I was practically unsatisfied, although the stay had been very useful as I met important people like Mr. Albert Saúl, the man of Jewish origin, modern and universal who spoke twelve languages -nine of which were world languages and three were sub-Saharan African dialects. This man represented a great reference of admiration for me; I learned many things from him, from his long life experience and from his travels, by listening to him and watching him. I also learned more things during my stay in Morocco: not to trust anyone else, since I was so disappointed in general, although, despite this, there were nice people that crossed my path, both Moroccan citizens and foreigners. I remember a curious and pleasant moment: some young girls of my age - perhaps they were about twenty years old - wanted to stay with me on a terrace to have some coffee and talk, I thought it was curious, girls who wanted to see me and talk to me, talk about what? I remember that there were several girls, all of the same age, about three or four Moroccan girls! They invited me discreetly for coffee, one of them, looking quite good, offered to marry me! The girl gave the impression of being a nice person, from a good family and customs, she seemed serious, honest and sincere; but I was young and I was not prepared for it, besides I had my friend who wanted to come and visit me in Morocco - I do not remember if that was before or after her arrival. Now, after more than forty years, although my memory works quite well, I really do not know how to realize this moment in my memory forty years ago. I remember the coffee terrace, covered in dirt, a bit secluded and next to the street, where we could talk quietly away from the crowd, anyway, my response was categorically no! Apparently, I was a different kind of guy or one attractive to her, for the girl I seemed to be different from the typical Moroccan man she knew, a person to be trusted by her, she thought that next to me she could be happy and respected as a woman; but I had no intention of staying in Morocco, nor could I imagine, she even wanted to introduce me to her parents! It is fair to tell you that, apart from the two policemen who crossed my path and who were unpleasant and disastrous, people were normal and they will continue to be good people, as everywhere in the world.

I also remember two Moroccan men with whom I sometimes chatted near the hotel in Casablanca, where I stayed for a long time. Just a couple of days before I went to Brazil, they invited me to their house for dinner, that was part of their hospitality to a foreigner, since I inspired them confidence. They considered me a brother, because the Arabs, when they cross, ask and say to each other "*Al Akh Arabi?*" (i.e., "Is the brother Arab?"). It is something wonderful and curious that does not exist in Western culture, the Arabs are brothers and that is something very beautiful, I believe it should be so in all cultures, in the end we are all brothers or cousins human beings, we are all descendants of Adam and Eve. Another nice word in Arabic is "*Al Salamu Alayqum*" ("peace is upon you"), so peace is a way of greeting, which is to make peace from the beginning as a condition and basis of understanding between people who greet each other. Everyone, both the four girls and the two men, were Muslims and knew that I was a Christian; this attitude seemed something wonderful to me: even knowing that I was and I am a Christian, they accepted me, admired me and loved me. I think we have to learn, we Christians, many things from Muslims, from their noble heart. Perhaps they also know, deep down, in their intuition or in their unconscious, that Jesus Christ is a true teacher and that he is the Savior. Jesus Christ said, "I leave your peace to you, I give you my peace", the culture of peace of Jesus Christ is the same throughout the Christian Middle East and the Muslim world.

How do we place the American continent in front of Africa, Europe or Asia?

We can say that Africa is the land where the first man was born, Africa is the cradle and roots of humanity, it is an immense continent, rich in many aspects, with its people full of energy, spirituality and enthusiasm and its resources are inexhaustible. Africa has given much to the world and will continue to give off its spirit, its ancestral cultures, its immense natural resources, its people and its populations, which are the African ones. Africa is an inexhaustible source of energy and willingness to want to learn everything and undertake everything.

Asia and the Middle East are the lands of antiquity and civilizations. There, in the Middle East, appeared the prophecies, there was the Jewish people who were chosen by God and led from Egypt to Jerusalem (Israel). God had a plan for the Jewish people that did not come to fruition! There, in Israel, also lived other people such as the Philistines, the Phoenicians, the Moabites and other ancient peoples, whose descendants are none other than the Arab Palestinians of today: they are Christians and Muslims who continue to live in Palestine. Middle East is the land of the mystic and of spirituality, there came the prophets who announced the coming of the Messiah. Then Jesus Christ, the Nazarene, was born in Bethlehem and with him began the Christian era for more than 2,000 years.

In the Mediterranean area, almost all the civilizations of the world were born, there are the roots of the languages of the Mediterranean. In Byblos (in Arabic, *Jubayl*), in Phenicia (now is Lebanon), is where the first Phoenician alphabet appeared, from there it was transferred to the Greeks and then to all Mediterranean civilizations: first to Rome and from

Rome to Northern Europe, France, Germany and England and from Greece to Bulgaria to Kiev, and from Kiev to the Slavic countries. Kiev - now the capital of Ukraine - was the cradle of Russian civilization and culture since the 11th century AC, it was called the Rus of Kiev and is the mother of Russian cities.

The Arabs developed the Phoenician alphabet in another alphabetic language, which is the Arabic language. Then, it came the Islam with his Prophet Mohammed, who lived in Mecca and Medina in the seventh century AC, since then the Muslim era begins, which is called "the century of Islam". With Islam, a great civilization was born and a great empire, which flourished in a great civilization; in this age of prosperity, there were great thinkers, philosophers, scientists, doctors, geometers, mathematicians, astronomers, writers and artists, and so on. The Arab Empire expanded from Damascus, Baghdad, to Al-Andalus (in Spain), and the Muslim Empire lasted several centuries.

Europe is the old continent, which is the cradle of modern civilization. Europe has its roots in the Greek mythology of the island of Crete, where it began with the Ancient Greece and Rome. In Northern Europe, there was a great development from the twelfth century, when Arabs and Jews in Al-Andalus translated the books of science, mathematics, physics, chemistry, medicine, literature, and philosophy from Arabic and Greek books into Latin. From there began the great development in France, England and Germany, etc., which reached its peak from the sixteenth century after the discovery of America and the colonialism of black Africa, where black slaves came to work forced in the new colonial lands of North America and South America.

America is a land of emigration, the same happens with the fifth continent, which is Oceania: Australia and New Zealand. This fifth continent was a huge prison only for Englishmen, criminals and bandits exiled to the Australian continent, those founded Australia and New Zealand. This was the general panorama of world history until the eighteenth century, when great industrialization began in Northern Europe, when they exploited the metals and coal of their own mines and when they invented machinery and industrialization in general. There it came another phase of economic growth, when all the favourable factors benefited both Northern Europe and Italy.

Thus, America is a land of emigrants, there emigrated white European, Middle Eastern, Jewish and Arab - especially Lebanese, Syrians and Palestinians men - in the eighteenth and nineteenth centuries. Slaves from Black Africa - or as they now call it "Sub-Saharan Africa" - from which they came, for many centuries, from the sixteenth century to the nineteenth century, brought as human commodities by the hand of English, French, Portuguese, Dutch, Swedish And Danish people, collaborating with nomadic Arabs from the interior of the African desert, who had caravans, were partly Arab nomads from the African Sahara.

Then it came the abolition of slavery in the early nineteenth century, but the independent state of Congo was owned by Leopold II, who entered the Congo hypocritically and enslaved the country until 1908. That is, a hundred years after the abolition of slavery, Leopoldo II continued to enslave blacks from the Belgian Congo and to do all kinds of atrocities: execution, mutilation, torture, etc.

From all this we can conclude that the wealth of the great powers - or, the industrial *boom* in the colonizing countries of Northern Europe, such as England, France, Portugal, Spain, Holland, etc. - has been at the cost of enslaving Africans of black race and also exploiting resources in those countries. To end with the lie of Belgium, with their famous Leopold II, still present in the praise of the Belgians who consider him "*le Roi bâtisseur*" ("the king builder").

What conclusion can we draw from all this? That almost all the great European powers became rich at the expense of the exploitation of new colonial lands and slavery. Even in the ancient Russia of the tsars there was also equal slavery, but it was composed by white peasants who work for the rich free of charge and as if they were their property, that is why the Bolshevik communist revolution came in 1917.

Even though the great Master came, Jesus Christ, the Saviour, and all those great nations considered themselves Christians, none of these nations acted according to the teaching of Jesus Christ and the Apostles. Proof of this, are the injustices and wars that have not stopped since the world exists.

Now, thank God there is peace in Europe, the only focus of war is in Eastern Ukraine. The wars are now where there is more poverty and strategic interests, oil and wealth: in Palestine, Syria, Iraq and Libya, etc.

The indigenous race of the American continent was largely exterminated; there are very few indigenous people who live in nature reserves. All the states of South America are governed by the descendants of immigrants, especially from Europe, the Middle East and Asia. Now Brazil has the first president of Lebanese origin in its history: Michel Temer, which is not bad. Just as the United States of America (USA) had, in January 2017, President Barak

Obama, who is practically the first African-American president of the United States.

Brazil is a different country from Latin America, they call it "the giant of Latin America", and it is the most populous and most industrialized country and undoubtedly the richest and most beautiful of all the countries of South America.

Now we get back to my trip to Santa Catarina (Brazil). When I was a kid, at school in Beirut I heard a lot about this country, Brazil, where there is now a large Lebanese colony. The country was attractive to me, I heard about Brazil's coffee, Brazil's sugar, and other things like the cashew or the chestnuts of Pará, which come from the state of Mato Groso, exist only in Brazil and other typical products from this country.

As soon as I arrived in Brazil, at the airport of Viracopos, in the interior of the State of *São Paolo*, my endless adventure began. Viracopos is the international airport of Campinas, one hundred kilometers from *São Paolo*. I arrived without a visa, now looking at the seals of my passport, I see that it was the nineteenth of November 1976, on a Friday, I actually left Casablanca on the eighteenth of November, most surely in the afternoon, I think the plane stopped in Rio de Janeiro at dawn. I arrived in Viracopos on the nineteenth of November, early in the morning, about eight o'clock in the morning. The emigration director of the Viracopos airport asked me if I had a visa, I said no, that I did not, but that I had friends in the country and someone was waiting for me. He said to me: "I'll give you an hour: or you can enter the country, or I'll return you on the same plane that you came, returning this afternoon from Montevideo, Uruguay." Indeed, in an hour I was able to enter, my friend's father Annette had a cousin who was governor of Santa Catarina, he called her cousin and told him the story: that I actually had a visa but that it was not on my passport. Then he called the chief of the federal police, who gave the order that I could immediately enter Brazil. My passport was confiscated and held and I was given a white paper, like a *laissez passer*, that is, a permit to enter.

Then, after a couple of months, they returned my passport with a visa for three months.

So I entered Brazil. We went to sleep one night in *São Paolo*, we were then invited to the house of the aunt of Annette in *São Paolo*. There, I remember that they invited a friend of the family, a Lebanese so I could talk to him, since I understood myself in French with Annette and I did not speak Portuguese yet, I just knew a few words, such as "*bom dia*","*tudo bem*", etc. The man was nice, a Lebanese Christian, most of the Lebanese immigrants in Brazil were Christians, he reassured me and said: "You have the cheese and the knife, cut and eat!" He wanted to say with that: you are a lucky man, you have fallen into a good family, be calm and happy, everything will go well for you! I did not understand at first what he wanted to tell me, but yes, more or less! Annette's aunt prepared us a delicious pizza, we ate it and we went to sleep at a hotel.

The next day, we travelled with the bus to Itajaí, passing through the city of Curitiba. The distance is more than six hundred kilometers, it takes perhaps a whole day to arrive, we left at night and arrive the next day early in the morning. Armando, Annette's father, was waiting for our arrival; it was a large family of Catholic tradition formed by the father, the mother and eight children - four boys and four girls. The father was of German origin with a mixture of French, his grandparents - or great-grandparents - arrived more than a hundred years ago to Brazil from Germany; the mother was of Italian origin, mixed with Portuguese. They worked in agriculture, they cultivated sugar cane; it was a very hard life, cut the cane with a large knife, machete type, that work was done by the workers. Sometimes, there were snakes coming out of the sugar cane forest, it was a dangerous job. Then, they extracted the juice of the sugar cane with a manual press of three cylinders; then, later, they used an electric machine. I think they sold the juice to the sugar factory or refinery; it was hard work from that time, in a country of emigration like Brazil.

I was the guest in the Schmidt family: they treated me wonderfully well, as if I were a member of the family, one more son. I am very grateful to God and to such a good and kind and generous family. I was planning to set up a small whiskey factory there and Annette's father, who was retired, introduced me to all the people and supported me, took me to places where they built copper stills to start my small factory. My project was possible to do in Santa Catarina, at that time the industry was not so developed in 1976. The majority of the people in Santa Catarina were of European origin: German, Polish, Italian and Portuguese.

Santa Catarina is the penultimate state located in the south of Brazil, further south is the last state in the south of Brazil: Rio Grande do Sul, with its capital Porto Alegre. There, in the south of Brazil, few *morenos* or *mulattos* were seen, the mulattos are a mixture of Portuguese, African and indigenous; they were found rather in the northern states of Brazil: in Rio de Janeiro, *São Paolo* and, above all, in the northern states of Brazil such as Espíritu Santo or San Salvador de Bahia States, etc.

When I arrived and met Annette's older brother, he began to speak to me in French, he had studied French at school, and he knew how to speak quite well, I said to him: "*Fala, por favor, conmigo português*" with the accent of Santa Catarina. Thus, after two months, I spoke quite well the *brasileiro*, as I frequented the father of Annette, who only spoke with me Brazilian Portuguese and took me with him wherever he went.

There, just after arriving, a few weeks later, we spent Christmas as a family, the funny thing is that in December we were in summer! It was not like Christmas is usually celebrated in the Northern Hemisphere, Brazil is in the Southern Hemisphere of the Earth, like all countries in South America, Christmas is spent in summer, wearing shorts and enjoying the outdoors. The family was very Catholic, all of them - the eight children, together with the parents at the parents' house - gathered to celebrate Christmas Eve and exchange Christmas gifts for everyone. On Christmas Eve religious Christmas songs were sung. On Christmas Day -the twenty-fifth of December 1976- all the children were present as well, everyone ate at the same table, the typical food of Brazil is beans and rice, these two dishes or products must be present and can never be missing on a Brazilian table; «*Feijaom*» and «*arroch*», as they are pronounced there in Santa Catarina. They also ate the "*camarão*"- that is, the small prawns typical of Brazil - and the beef of Brazil, which is good and tasty, besides the typical Brazilian palm that is cooked there as here we cook the mushrooms, with cream sauce; in the end

I came to speak Brazilian with a Santa Catarina accent, typical of Santa Catarina.

Southern Brazil is very rich in sugar cane and pineapple, which they called "*abacaxi.*"

We visited the famous city of Florianópolis, capital of Santa Catarina, where we visited Annette's sister and her older brother several times. He had a very nice and rustic house on the edge of the sea. Florianópolis is a very beautiful city.

I also traveled with Annette in Brasilia, the capital of Brazil, inland, more than a thousand kilometers away from the two great capitals, Rio de Janeiro and São Paolo, where she worked and she was a official in the Ministry of Agriculture. We also visited some of his friends. Once I found the French newspaper *Le Monde* in a kiosk in Brasilia, I bought it with joy to know the news of the world and Europe, it was old two or three days ago, but I did not care! How long it took to get from France! I wanted to know what was going on in the world. There in Brasilia, I felt that I was really at the end of the world!

Once, it occurred to me an idea before Christmas: I wanted to do an experiment in the house of Annette's parents, which was a large two-storey chalet, I think built of wood. I began to ferment pineapple juice into a closed bottle, as if it were to make a sparkling wine; when it began to ferment, I added a little sugar and closed the bottle with cork attached with a wire made by hand, similar to the bottle cork of cava, and put it in the refrigerator to be slowly fermenting. The result was optimal, we opened it at Christmas and it was a fermented pineapple wine, gasified like the cava, of an incredibly good taste and texture, they called it "*abacaxi* champagne", that is, "pineapple champagne". Armando, Annette's older brother, who is an agronomist, an understanding man, very educated, nice and humble - like the whole family, they were very good people - he told me verbatim: "If you get to make *abacaxi* champagne in Brazil , you will become a millionaire!"

In the end, I could not stay in Brazil: my mother needed me; she moved heaven and earth to make me return to Beirut. In the end, I had to return on January 14, 1977 to Beirut through Damascus, very sad and discontented!

This morning, reflecting on this chapter, I realize the importance of this trip to Santa Catarina in Brazil in 1976 and the importance of my mother's decision to make me return to Lebanon. If it were not so, I would have stayed in Brazil, maybe I would now be a millionaire, a great industrialist, but in the end perhaps I would be also unhappy.

After returning to Lebanon, as I was rebellious, stubborn or perhaps rather intuitive, I knew what was expecting me. I returned from Lebanon four years later, in June 1981, and this time for ever, never to return!

After sixteen years of absence, in 1997 I made my first visit to Lebanon. Now I go more often, every two years or so, like a tourist visiting his country home!

If I had not returned to Lebanon in January 1977, I would not have been later in Spain, Germany, Europe, Arabia, Sub-Saharan Africa, or Ukraine. I could not have learned the four languages I was lacking: Spanish, German, Italian, and Norwegian. I would not have made the trips of my dreams across the world and, above all, to sub-Saharan Africa and, without stopping, from 1976 until 2017 - time passed more than forty years. I could not have travelled to the thirty or forty countries of the world I now know, nor could I have seen and experienced so many wonderful things, like my dream of Madrid. I would not have known in Madrid my dear friend Germán Ubillos, the great writer who is supporting me - he and his family - in the writing of this book. Nor could I have seen and been on the island of Crete, which inspired me so much and continues to inspire me with its magnetism, giving me enough spiritual light to be able to write this book on life, addressed to humanity.

That is the story and consequences of my trip to Santa Catarina, Brazil, in 1976-1977.

Chapter 17: Work on yourself and let the work do its job

Work is very important; or rather, fundamental.

Without work, no goal can be achieved. People who are unemployed or without any activity feel depressed and useless.

Always, it is necessary to do something useful, even if one is retired or very old and while the physical and mental state allows it. You cannot be vegetating like plants or living like animals: eating, drinking and sleeping.

You have to do something, where you feel useful, for yourself and for the others.

Working on oneself consists in having a discipline and constancy in the action of observing, learning, creating, inventing and undertaking something new every day.

Working on oneself consists of being the teacher of oneself and, at the same time, the worker who is the accomplice, that is, we will have at least two characters or two actors within the same person: one is the primary - the one who observes, thinks, calculates, works, invents, creates something new every day - and the other is the secondary - who works, executes and does the final work.

After each completed work, the question comes: Did I do it right or did I do it wrong?

Working on oneself: In German, "*Arbeite an dir selbst*" is a phrase I heard many times in my six-year stay in Germany - between 1992 and 1998 -. The philosophy of work, in Germany, is one of the most developed in the world; that is why Germany is the most industrialized country in Europe and the fourth in the world after the United States, China and Japan. In Spain, more hours are worked and the working day is considerably longer, but in Germany the profitability of work is higher, even if fewer hours are worked; but in Spain people live better and enjoy more of their free time than in Germany. I learned a lot from the Germans and from their philosophy of work, but I prefer to live in Spain: in Spain one lives and they let you live...

Working on oneself is to work on our mistakes and our weaknesses, it is also to realize our lack of knowledge and try to learn what we lack in some matter; it is also to correct our failures and overcome our weaknesses. All this in the intellectual, technical, artistic, psychological and spiritual fields; that is to say, it consists in working on oneself to improve your

216

interior and your capacity for intellectual, manual, artistic and spiritual work.

Letting work do its job is letting others do their job as well.

We cannot do the job of everyone, but we can work as a team.

You have to like your job, ideally your work creates you an illusion, as they say in English: "*My job is my hobby!*".

If so, work is all joy and satisfaction and one never gets tired of a job, although a work can last a long time and sometimes it must be worked to the point of exhaustion!

But we need to breathe, a pause can serve for an optimum moment for meditation and reflection, it may also serve as inspiration. Things look better from afar, as a maths teacher told us when we were young at school in Beirut: "Stay away from the tree to see it better"; Therefore, the trips are very good, if not ultra-necessary.

Politicians travel a lot because of the nature of their job and that helps them to work better and have a better performance and always be fit, because they also take care, eat well and practice a sport.

Now, if we want to evolve, travelling will be necessary to discover the world and learn from the many things we see: new cities we visit, new people we meet and observe, new fascinating landscapes, new customs of life, new airs and new foods, new languages we listen to, new music, new beautiful and attractive people, new ways of living and new emotions. As a result, new ideas about how to plan our life back home will be born within us.

All this with the work of learning, practicing, observing, dialoguing, concluding, inventing, creating, undertaking, travelling, enjoying and letting others work.

My father used to say to me many times: "Work is for donkeys," he meant with that, that routine work tires the spirit, work has to have soul and spirit, it has to be inventive and creative, it cannot be just a routine! If so, it will be destructive and depressing at the same time.

Work can become a *hobby*. Take the examples of Jacques Cousteau - the explorer of the seabed or the East Asian voyages - and the famous Venetian traveller and explorer, Marco Polo; these works never tire, they are works full of joy, illusion and passion.

A policeman, a fireman, a detective, a teacher, a nurse, a bricklayer, an electrician, a carpenter, a painter, a singer or a musician... can enjoy their work because they have to improvise every situation and seek solutions to new and innovative problems that can be presented to them on a daily basis; just as a gardener may be in love with his work, a cook, a waiter, etc. However, people who want to get far in life cannot always stay in the same job, they have to evolve and jump like birds from one branch to another, so they learn many more things with life experience. They will forge their own destiny until someday they will be able to fly in truth and joy like the birds, within their imagination, seeing the fruits of their work! They will be, supposedly, on a plane on a business trip or to attend an event!

That is why it is necessary to continuously learn new things. The school of life is endless; it ends with the end of life, that is, with the death of the individual - the inevitable destiny of all human beings. The struggle is necessary and is vital for a long life full of joys; sorrows are unfortunately also things present in life, often inevitable, but the less they last, the better!

The miracle of daily life is explained as a grace of God and of divine creation, it is the one that makes us capable of rising after every storm we live in the family, in our sentimental life, in our professional life and in the job position, also in the state of our health and of our soul.

A divorce can be hard and difficult to overcome, but once we overcome it, it may have been necessary to move on to another stage of life, perhaps more interesting than the first one, where one can do better and get to know oneself better.

Thus, it is not always necessary for a profession to be for life, just as a marriage is not obligatory for a lifetime; that depends on each person and each case. There are no rules or statistics, everything is possible in autodidact people lives, including changes in the workplace or place of residence and sometimes there can be sudden changes in sentimental life. These changes perhaps are necessary for evolution, if not essential, and we see them frequently in the lives of great artists, movie stars, athletes, politicians, etc.

Any change can always hurt at first, but once the situation is over, many are grateful for the fate that has freed them from union with unfit people, blocking their lives and their evolution. The same thing can happen in the couple, as in the workplace or in the city where one lives, even in the country where one lives!

An individual will have to feel good about himself and will not have to change his personality or character for anyone or anything, but try to evolve in the best possible way to optimize the performance of his work and his relationships with his family and social environment.

A change, in general, usually hurts at first, but then it can bear fruit.

It is like pulling a tree out of a dry, arid land and planting it again in a fertile land with plenty of sun and water; that same tree that was struggling to survive and about to die, will now be able to flourish and bear wonderful and kind fruits.

Life naturally contains ruptures and changes; the human being is prepared to be able to live those changes, his nature allows it.

Therefore, many people lose their work and have joy, because it has served as experience for the next job, which is better than the previous one. I remember very well moments of my life: when I was young, when I lost a job, I was happy and invited some colleagues - the two or three favourites - to get dinner and celebrate the new phase of life in freedom and a new beginning. The same thing can happen in sentimental life: a breakup can be positive for one or the other, if both are strong even for the two. But what happens is that the stronger person will suffer less and will quickly rise from his fall and feel better over time, while the weaker person may suffer a setback and could not be able to rise or could fall into depression and despair; but, as a rule, every human being will rise, this is the secret and wonder of divine creation.

Letting work do its thing also means being patient enough for the work to bring its fruits, that is why time is the main and fundamental factor, everything is a matter of time, time is the determinant that governs the course of life.

He who sows, gathers; The one who sows the most, the more he can gather; so it is necessary to fight on several fronts at the same time, to make the work of a team one, counting on the support of its collaborators, being oneself the universal collaborator for everybody, the key piece of the gear.

Thus, working with intelligence, practice, experience and patience can make you go far, as far as you could not imagine, as far as your illusion can go!

Work has to be honest and sincere; it must be done with joy and passion. It is always good to keep something for yourself and not giving out everything, but give and receive; if you give it all, you may be plucked! But that will depend on your creative ability to regenerate and reborn from your own ashes, like the phoenix. If you are an inventor - that is, a genius - you will be continuously inventing new systems and strategies; even if you give it all today, others will not be able to copy you, because they simply will not be able to follow your evolutionary rhythm and stay with their mouths open, knock out, they will not be able to fight against the great phenomenon and strategist you are!

An intelligent and skillful man must be able to win all the battles of life.

In order not to remain stuck, you will have to improve your system every day and have new ideas every day on how to make your work better and more effective so that it gives more and better results.

Thus, evolution may be geometric rather than arithmetic.

The geometric evolution has a hundred times greater growth than the arithmetic evolution.

The poor in spirit save money for tomorrow; on the other hand, the creative man invests more and more energy and money every day in his intellect and in his database, he is not afraid and he knows how to lose to win, because his capital is intellectual, he grows much faster and constantly, compared to the small capital of the saver, who is afraid to invest money and energy.

Intellectual capital is the most important thing and can be translated into economic capital.

Therein lies the secret of the great triumphers -the authentic autodidacts- who learn from themselves, from their own experience, every day more, work on themselves and let work do its job.

Chapter 18: My job as alchemist goldsmith, Beirut 1979-1981

When I returned to Lebanon – my homeland - by force in January 1977 from my first trip to Brazil, after the insistence of my mother, I was very unhappy and I saw no reason to return to the place from which I had gone forever. I remember that, on my arrival, I think it was a Sunday at noon, I was coming from Damascus by taxi-service car, I had to cross the Becca valley and the high mountains with snow from Dahr El-Baydar. The Syrian taxis were old American cars, as they are in Havana, Cuba, they were big and bulky, I remember that they were green; they were also all colours. Beirut airport was closed to air traffic because of the war; I had to come by Damascus airport and sleep one night there in a hotel. Not to be alone, I called a faithful friend of the University of Leuven, named Antoine Siage, who was glad to know that I was in Damascus and invited me to his house to introduce me to his mother and his wife. Then he invited me to get some dinner at a typical restaurant with *meze* of over twenty dishes of starters. The meeting was cordial and friendly, we talked about everything from the memories of the university and the friends of Belgium.

Arriving home in Beirut, I thought I would first greet my family and seeing a panorama I did not expect and as I found it, I felt a sense of distance. As soon as I put the suitcases on the floor and before opening them, I immediately wanted to go back to my beloved Brazil, I saw no reason to stay in Lebanon for another minute, even though it was my homeland that I abandoned for almost two years, although I loved Lebanon as it was before the war, when I could travel in times of peace. Suddenly, everything had changed, I was deprived of all freedom of movement and I had to live as a prisoner in a large prison, this small country, which had become even smaller than it was before by the divisions of the Civil War. I came from Brazil, from the giant country of South America, where there was peace and where I could travel thousands of miles in every way being in Brazil, while in Lebanon in 1977 you could not do even a hundred kilometers without going through hundreds of controls! Lebanon has an area of approximately 10,450 km^2 and Brazil has eight and a half million km^2, that is, it is eight hundred times larger in area; the population at that time was forty times larger. Apart from being deprived of freedom, horizon and perspectives, I could not bear the time that was wasted in vain; time had for me gold value! But, seeing that there was no other way out, I was discontented and began to think what I could do.

Being busy is a good therapy to combat the empty spaces of time. Since I had no clear prospects either, they all spoke of a war that could last ten or twenty years!

Learning is a good occupation, when one is still young, usually has a huge thirst to learn a lot of new and useful things. The brain of a young man is like a sponge, it absorbs everything: knowledge, techniques and memories that are etched in his mind as photographs. However, we who are more mature or older, we tend to order things in our minds, we want to make a synthesis that comes from our memories of the past, from which we could draw also philosophical conclusions that come from our long life experience. So we can understand why things happened in such a way! It will be because God wanted it that way! Perhaps it was necessary, so that we could go even further, than was logically foreseen. All that has been possible through the different stages and schools of our life and also thanks to the will and miracles of God, who put us directly in front of those new paths that we have taken.

The only thing that concerned me at that time was learning more and more, doing many experiments and forging an intellectual and technical capital out of the ordinary to be able someday to have wings and fly, and so leave again from Lebanon! Learning something new was like a drug that could help me forget the ordeal of forced living in a country where I no longer wanted to be, a country that belonged to my past. After having travelled over so much of the world, I could not be in such a small and isolated place, I needed freedom and space, I needed long sea coasts and roads of thousands of kilometers, to be able to manufacture and to sell in a great country like Brazil. I dreamed of Spain, which I only saw three days in September 1976, it was an unforgettable dream; moreover, at that time, Lebanon was a totally insecure country, with no clear future! When I was living in Beirut in those four years (from 1977 to 1981), I saw no future, it was easy to guess the sad and negative future, seeing the lost people around me, talking more about war than about peace. For me, a civil war is one of the most absurd and horrifying things that could happen, I could not forgive or understand what had happened, how could it be that within a single town, with a history of coexistence of more than five thousand years, this incomprehensible human tragedy could happen! Where there were friends who have grown up together, who have played together, and who have studied together in the same school and shared the same desk, people who had to fight with criminal and destructive weapons because of religion or political parties or because of the influence that came from outside Lebanon!

What is a religion? Who knows what a religion means? I see it, rather in the case of Lebanon, as a family tradition, where individuals were obliged to be part of it and to follow it blindly as if it were a tradition, by the commitment and the teaching of the parents. Like a political party, families generally condition the political orientations of all members of a family, unless there are rebels and exceptions, since I was one of those rebels, the exception to the rule!

I remember reading an article from the French newspaper *Le Monde* when I was studying at the University of Louvain, Belgium, in 1974-76. I was sitting in the cafe on a sunny day, at noon, I had asked for a *lait russe*, that is, Russian milk! Hot milk with an envelope of black tea, typical of Russia! I do not know if this custom is followed in Russia. I carefully read an article about Islam, the article's analyst said that Islam is the most modern political party in the world! Because it gave answers to almost all questions and all the questions and concerns of the Muslim believing man, whether spiritual or social matters; while the Christian faith is a totally free faith, which consists in practically following the teaching of Jesus Christ and his Apostles, it is a matter of faith, but it does not condition the social and political behavior of a believing person, where there is a free field for each

Christian to act as he pleases and as his heart feels and with all freedom. But there are also Christian parties as there were in history and there are armed Christians in Lebanon. Those, in my opinion, are not true Christians in the sense of the word; they are, rather, partisans of a political armed Christian party!

Christ was not a guerrilla, he was a king and He said, "My kingdom is not of this world," so I did not understand why there must be a war between Christians and Muslims. Some of my best friends were Muslims and I could not carry a weapon against my friend and my Muslim brother, proof of this, in the Quran there is a *Surat* dedicated to Mary and her Son, Jesus, "*Surah of Maryam and her son, Isa*", that is of Mary and Jesus, where they glorify Mary and Jesus.

So what is wrong with being a Muslim or being a Christian? The one who has been born a Muslim is obviously educated in that religion and can practice it with all freedom and dignity, just as a Christian can practice his Christian faith in the same way; thus, coexistence is totally possible while respecting each other and respecting all the ethics and established laws of social coexistence. Now Lebanon, after forty-two years of uncertainty since the outbreak of the Civil War in 1974, has again a strong and courageous president who has just been elected. I wish for Lebanon and for the Lebanese people, with all my heart, a splendid future of peace, stability and prosperity. Lebanon is more than a country, as Pope John Paul II said: "Lebanon is more than a country, it is a message".

I, personally, saw all those who spoke of the politics of this time of the late seventies as if they were half crazy. That was not my world; I had nothing to do with that drama of Lebanon - implied, rather, of the regional conflicts and interests of the great powers. All the problems of the region and the political garbage of the Arab countries went to Lebanon and in Beirut in the seventies and eighties, all the armed bands or political agents had their headquarters in Lebanon, where they circulated freely; these conditions made Lebanon a vulnerable, explosive and uncontrolled country. The danger also came, in large part, from its two neighbors, two warlike and conflicting countries: Israel and Syria. Both of them were envious of Lebanon on their own way and the two countries interfered negatively in the internal affairs of Lebanon. In addition to all the problems of the Arab countries, conflicts have now returned to their countries of origin and in Lebanon there are 1.5 million Syrian refugees. The Lebanese have enough problems with that, those emigrants will have to return, soon, to their country of origin, when the war in Syria ends to rebuild their country with order and serenity.

I wanted to leave the country as soon as possible, but it was not possible to return to Brazil, the Brazil I knew had already been lost to me. I lost contact with my friend from the Schmidt family of Santa Catarina, I had to rebuild another future and learn more. Then it came the opportunity that was hard for me to take at the beginning, but then I was seduced by the brilliant noble metal that is gold: I made the decision to learn the goldsmith's trade by setting up a small goldsmith's workshop in a room inside the family factory of Liqueurs in Beirut.

Gold is a metal that attracted me a lot, all the beautiful girls painted their blond hair, similar to gold, they also carried gold jewellry. I used to associate both of them with colour and I found it very attractive!

Apart from that, the idea of gold is that of capital, which one can put in a small briefcase; gold is very valuable and does not take up so much space.

War and instability made that noble metal a haven for capital. So the opportunity came to set up that workshop together with a friend who claimed to be an expert in goldsmithing; he had learned from another goldsmith and he only knew the technique of making copy jewels by centrifugation system. So we bought some used machinery from a workshop of a retired old jeweller and started making jewellry.

We made rubber moulds to make wax copies of the original piece. Then the pieces were glued with warm wax on a wax trunk and looked like a wax tree. Then, this tree entered a metal cylinder of iron, the cylinder was filled with plaster; The cylinder with plaster and wax went to the emptying machine, *Vaccum System*, to suck the air into the cast. Then it went to the oven; the plaster was cooked in the furnace and became hard as stone, the wax was burned and evaporated, there was an empty space where the wax tree was before. Then, the newly heated hot cylinder was placed inside the centrifuge horizontally; in front of the cylinder was placed, inside a small clay funnel container, enough gold to melt with the fire of a torch. Once the gold reached the melting temperature and liquid was made at about 1,065 degrees, the centrifuge was operated; the centrifugal physical force pushed the gold that penetrated the empty space of the horizontal cylinder of plaster.

Then the hot cylinder was put in cold water and the hot plaster and was dissolved in the water and made a funny noise. There was only the golden tree that has the same shape as the previous wax tree, which had been burned and evaporated.

The same technique is applied more minimally in denture laboratories to make dental gold crowns or nickel-chromium palladium alloy, and other metals such as cobalt, etc.

That way I learned a lot of technique and art at the same time. Then, the pieces were cut, licked and welded together to make rings, earrings, pendants, bracelets, etc.

Afterwards, they were polished by hand in the engine polisher. In the end, once the jewel was polished, diamonds and carved gemstones were placed like sapphires, rubies and emeralds.

I liked this job very much because it contained many technical phases, art, science, mathematics, physics and chemistry.

The part that I liked the most was mathematics and chemistry, as well as the beauty and perfection of jewellry, a jewel must be perfect to see with the magnifying glass!

I had enough chemical knowledge, but the working conditions were more alchemical than really chemical! They were limited to studies and experiments related to the noble metal, which is gold. The goldsmiths spoke of alchemy and they said that there were some who were able to transform lead into gold or egg yolk into gold, they spoke of other lies as well. Thus I concluded that the alchemists are, more or less, great charlatans, because they pretend to know what they do not really know and believe what they dream!

Goldsmiths have a more alchemical than chemical occupation; they only know techniques and no chemistry and they are not so mathematical, although they know how to calculate in their own way, they know only the practical part. I applied my mathematical knowledge in goldsmithing and some of my chemical studies, which was a subject I liked a lot along with mathematics. Thus, once there was a lot of gold that had to clean or purify and draw from it the pure gold twenty-four carats. I then dissolved all the old jewels into highly concentrated nitric acid, which I boiled in a Pyrex glass. Non-gold alloying metals were dissolved or ionized, the gold remained intact and turned dark red as if it were copper. Then, after about an hour, I had, on the one hand, the pure gold and, on the other hand, all the other metals ionized and dissolved within the acid solution. Within this solution there were other metals such as silver, which is also a noble metal and of a certain value; then came the question: how to get the silver from this acidic solution?

The goldsmiths did not teach the others, they were a little hypocritical in this sense, each one kept his secret to himself. They thought they were intelligent, the intelligent should not be afraid to divulge a secret because he knows that the next day he will invent something new, another secret that the others do not know yet. There is the test of the intelligent and the unintelligent, or, rather, the difference between who is really a genius and who is not!

The goldsmiths of that time - and perhaps now, too - are clever artists who know how to make a living with their craft. I thought about it, I remembered the example of the electronegativity I learned in high school: if we put a zinc plate in a solution of copper sulfate, the copper will emerge on the zinc plate and it will be deposited in the form of metal.

I applied the same principle, I looked in Mendeleyev's Table, I found that copper has more electronegativity than zinc, silver more electronegativity than copper. The same in this acidic solution had silver nitrate, because if I put a plate of copper the ionized silver should be deposited in the form of metal on the copper plate and, indeed, it was that way and it was the perfect solution to the problem! And I said to myself, "Eureka, Eureka!" Bravo, Bravísimo!

So I invented something that was already invented and collected all the silver on the copper plate. Then the silver is melted with the fire as the gold melts with a torch and into a funnel, and so I was able to obtain a bar of silver and another bar of pure gold.

Once, a charlatan came to my goldsmith's workshop, he had a sample of very dark fine earth dust that he wanted to sell me, he said that there was gold in this earth dust. As in Beirut there was a civil war in the centre of Beirut, right in the goldsmiths' market there was the line of demarcation, and there, for more than a hundred years or even more, were the goldsmiths' shops and workshops of Beirut, which was called "*Souk Al Sayagin*" in Arabic, sounds something like "the Albaicin neighbourhood of Granada", but it has a totally different meaning!

There, in the washbasins, the goldsmiths washed their hands and washed their utensils, even their beards contained gold; this dry earth possibly came from earth dust and from the drains of the market of goldsmiths, kept from many years ago. There was perhaps some gold, but too little, the only method of seeking the gold inside this earth dust was to put it inside a rolling screen filled with water and put inside a certain amount of mercury that is a liquid metal. The mercury looks for gold and silver and makes an amalgam with those two noble metals; then the amalgamated mercury is collected, placed in an iron pot and heated underneath with a fire, the mercury is burned and evaporated, it is very toxic, alloyed gold and silver are deposited. The result I think was a gram, more or less, per kilogram or, perhaps, much less, perhaps a gram for ten kilograms, I do not remember exactly. Anyway, it was a very little gold content and it was not worth extracting!

So were some stories of my career as an alchemist goldsmith. I met, through this handcraft, many interesting people and learned a very old job that has served me for other future careers.

Now the alchemist goldsmith trade is a third-world trade, no one buys gold because it is very expensive, only on great occasions they buy wedding rings, etc., people can barely pay their bills of all kinds. The gold of today is the gold of truth, which is the Gospel of Jesus Christ, and also having golden ideas, which are worth much more than gold! I honestly won with iron and aluminum, relatively more money than with gold, with which I learned a lot, but I did not earn any money, on the contrary, I invested more than I earned. It is easy to see how much iron or aluminum is used in the world, compared to what is used in gold, they are used millions of times more! The gold business has become insignificant, it is only a shelter metal and stock market value, but the goldsmith's trade is beautiful, working this noble metal brings much satisfaction and joy to the artist who is the goldsmith, to work the iron or the copper or aluminum is not the same nor can it be compared!

In the end, I left everything in Beirut: the liquor factory and goldsmith's shop, and left them for my brother André. On the day of my birthday, I wanted to invite some friends on April 2, 1981, on this day or I believe that one day before it was April 1, 1981, the

Syrian army attacked, many bombs fell on the Christian neighborhood of Beirut, Achrafieh. The Syrian army played as a referee, first helping Christians against the armed Palestinians in Lebanon, to save them from the fall; then, after a while, they attacked the armed Christians, thus weakening the two sides, so that all depended on Syria and its power. In the end, Syria had to leave Lebanon after the tragic death of the Prime Minister Rafiq Hariri, who was killed in a major explosion by a tremendous bombing where twenty-one innocent civilians were killed; then there was a popular revolt and the Syrian army had to leave Lebanon. So the country was free of the Syrians in early 2005, but I could not wait so long! Neither did the problems end in 2005, now in 2017 we hope that the era for Lebanon of order and stability will begin.

As a result of this attack, I decided to leave forever and it was so: after two months, on June 6, 1981, I left for Brazil, Saõ Paolo, with a «*one way ticket*» via Copenhagen, to never return; now I visit the family from time to time as a tourist. I remember that day, when I left the entrance of the building: it was noon, many bombs fell again in the neighborhood where I lived, I could hardly leave to travel to the airport, but thanks to my brother André, who is very brave, he called a taxi and I went with my hand over my heart until I got to Beirut airport. There, doing the check-in, I happened to meet a friend from the school who worked at the airport; my bags weighed 35 kilos, I had excess baggage, but he let me through as he was my friend. So I left Lebanon forever.

That was the story of my job as an alchemist goldsmith.

Chapter 19: Religions, believers and atheists

This is a very important chapter, very difficult to be able to analyze in depth, to debate and to count, it requires a lot of attention and patience.

The problem that is present today, between those who believe in God and those who do not believe in God, is practically the same that existed in the eighteenth century or even before, for some three hundred and fifty years at the time the famous French philosopher, writer and lawyer Voltaire. Now we are the same, but the conditions, context and panorama of our present time are totally different: we are overwhelmed and saturated with the material and psychological problems that arise from daily stress. That forces us to put aside our spiritual part and forget that we are also spirit!

All this comes from our living conditions, which every day require more sacrifices and adaptation from us to the continuous modernization of the world by new political and intellectual currents, new economic conditions, new social degenerations of all kinds and current wars, where weapons of mass destruction are being used. The situation of the world is much more complex and much more serious than four centuries ago!

Atheists do not believe in God or the Holy Scriptures, they do not believe in the direct influence of God in our life, since the creation of the universe, nor do they believe in God's plan for the future and His possible intervention in our daily lives.

There are now many more religions than before, many of which are commonly called "religious sects." There are also the currents of atheistic convictions, which come from the past and above all from modernization. These atheistic currents are, rather, materialistic or scientific, as they define themselves the atheists; they are based on ethics, science at the service of man and human rights.

To introduce you in this special context, I invite you to read carefully an extract from one of Voltaire's best books, known as "the atheist philosopher". The date of publication is 1763. In chapter XXIII, there is a beautiful prayer to God that can be found on the Internet.

Voltaire was not a true atheist, nor was he an agnostic; he was rather a convinced believer and in his own way: he was addressing to a more tolerant, more sensible God than the God who taught the Catholic Church.

Voltaire was a very critical French philosopher with the Catholic Church, the only predominant Church of that time.

The same thing was the German theologian and Catholic friar Martin Luther, who in Germany was a new reformer of Christianity in Germany in the 16th century. The work of Martin Luther revolutionized the Christian world and put the Catholic Church in question. Since then, the Catholic Church has had to undertake a number of reforms and continues to undertake continually, to this day, to catch up and give a positive response to its faithful followers, Catholic Christians!

The problem of before and now remains the same: many Christians in past centuries were disappointed by the Catholic Church. Some, like the Protestants, tried to return to the roots of the teaching of the original Gospel; others, very disappointed with the Catholic Church, no longer wanted to look for more and moved away from the Christian faith and God, thinking that the Catholic Church was the only representative of God or the Christian faith on earth.

We all know that the first Church of Jesus Christ and of the Apostles was one Church, there was only the Church of Jesus Christ instituted by the Apostles, according to the teaching and the Gospel of Jesus Christ, it had no other names. Then came differences and conflicts between the main churches, which were the great Christian communities: each one wanted to impose more on the others, by their influence and power. After the Great Schism of the East and the West, in 1054, the churches divided themselves between Roman Catholics of Rome and Orthodox Greeks of Constantinople because the Orthodox did not want to accept the leadership of the Roman Catholic Church and the Papacy and by other differences of interpretation and practice of the Christian faith.

Then came Protestantism in the sixteenth and seventeenth centuries, which today is the Evangelical Church and other churches that generated from it. Then a multitude and a myriad of churches were born: some, parallel to these churches with different rites; others, totally different; some may be considered ideal or true Christian churches; others may be considered benign, which often create confusion; others may be considered as evil, destructive and even dangerously spiritually speaking!

Each one of us, Christians who have received the Holy Spirit, if we get to know any of these churches or Christian sects, we can judge ourselves according to our own *feeling* or by the sense of smell and spiritual sensitivity. We have to be very careful with the spirits of all these unknown congregations, who call themselves churches of Christ and try to analyze this spirit, stranger and unknown.

We will be able to notice if it is a spirit of peace, a spirit of mercy, of consolation, of blessing..., or if it is a spirit of confusion and charlatanism. All these sensations can be perceived by the soul, it can recognize whether the spirit is good or bad, if the spirit that is manifested is the spirit of God or the Holy Spirit, or else it is another spirit! We may also notice in our interior whether it produces a permanent spiritual discomfort or if we feel some weariness or disturbance in our soul; that we can notice in our dreams or the way we wake up in the morning or after a night's sleep or a nap in the afternoon is when the soul can manifest better than ever. Sometimes we can also lose love, fear and respect for God: this alarming case is a clear proof that these congregations we have just met or visited are true sects of the devil or of Satan; we will have to leave immediately, change course and pray fervently to God, asking for forgiveness and comfort, and God will forgive us and comfort us.

To avoid these terrible situations, it is better not to take the Eucharist, or the sacred bread, or the blessed water, by other spirits that serve us these unknown priests; it is better to wait until we know and we are absolutely sure that the spirit that is manifested from that altar is really the true spirit of God. And if we feel after a time that this spirit is really good and is giving us spiritual peace, then we can take confidence and receive the Eucharist and the Sacraments.

On the other hand, there are non-Christian and monotheistic beliefs or religions, some that recognize and respect Jesus Christ and the Gospel, such as Islam. Islam has several ramifications, although the Holy Book for them is the Koran, unique book sacred to all Muslims. Another belief is Judaism of the Jews, who believe in the Old Testament: the Torah, the Jews are still waiting for the coming of the Messiah.

There are also other religions other than the monotheists who have other spiritual philosophies, such as Buddhist, Hindu, etc., who believe in reincarnation. There are also pagan beliefs of the inhabitants of the countryside; some of them are monotheistic and endless beliefs around the world.

I remember an Arab proverb that says, "Believe in the stone and you will be saved," it means that man needs to believe in something, whatever it is, as long as he can believe; there were civilizations that worshiped the Sun, others worshiped the stone statues that represented the gods.

The apostle Paul said to the Athenians, "And when Paul was in the midst of the Areopagus, he said, "Men of the Athenians, I see you as more superstitious, because by seeing your sanctuaries, I also found an altar on which was inscribed: To the

God not known'. The one therefore, which ye honour without knowing him, this I declare unto you. The God who made the world and all the things that are in it, this, as Lord of heaven and earth, does not dwell in temples made with hands, nor is he honoured with the hands of men, as if he needed something; for he giveth to all life and breath, and all things"(Acts 17: 22-25).

It is not enough to believe only in oneself, in a stone statue or in matter, in money, in power, in our work and profession, in our family or in some special people that we love and respect, or in some dominant political leader, or systems that give us security, such as the banking system, health insurance and social security. All this is necessary in our modern life, but it is not enough: without the Spirit of God and the help of God, man is lost and disoriented.

All these systems are vulnerable and offer a relative security, which reassures us to a certain extent, always offer us a material or financial solution. We cannot live with the idea that "as long as I live, I am someone and if I ever stop living, I will be nobody or nothing!"

It is necessary to know that, besides matter, there is the soul!

The secular system or French secularism also comes, to a large extent, from Voltaire and the French Revolution. French secularism has been good up to a certain point, particularly to free itself from the domination of the Catholic Church, the only one predominant at that time. However, French secularism was not the good solution, because in the end, the system had its great failures!

There was also in the history of the Greek Orthodox Church a great Cretan philosopher and writer, who was a controversial atheist and called Nikos Kazantsakis, from the island of Crete, they called him "the antichrist". One of his most famous works is the book *Alexis Zorbas*, which made the film *Zorba, the Greek*.

When Kazantsakis was born on the island of Crete, Crete was under the Turkish-Ottoman rule. He had greatly suffered under the rule of the Ottomans and was seeking answers to his questions and spiritual doubts, his conflicts between his body and his soul, answers he could not receive from the Greek Orthodox Church of that time. Kazantzakis was influenced by the atheist German philosopher, Nietzsche.

The Vatican had banned the publication of his famous book *The Last Temptation of Christ*.

The German philosopher, Friedrich Nietzsche, had a great influence on the philosophy and thoughts of Kazantsakis, who adopted Nietzsche's concepts of atheism and superman "*Der Übermensch*"; but, on the other hand, Kazantzakis had his spiritual preoccupations and sought union with God. For this reason, he retired from society and went to live for six months in an Orthodox monastery.

What synthesis can we make of all that? What are the conclusions?

Believing helps us to live with respect, love and fear of God, the Creator; it teaches us to have love for our neighbour, it produces us inner peace and so we can have a harmonious relationship with God, the Father, from which we come and to whom we will one day return.

The French secular system has not worked, not to say that it has been a total failure; it is shown by recent developments in recent years. In the suburbs of the marginalized, children of immigrants and marginalized classes who burn and continue to burn vehicles every year, thus expressing their anger against the system through social frustration, they manifest themselves and they break everything in their path. Now, some of them, maddened, have followed Satan's calls and horribly murdered innocent people, children, women, old men, and men in cold blood. All this barbarity is done under the motto of religious freedom and freedom of expression!

The French secular system has, in my opinion, generated more atheism, more spiritual doubts and more spiritual degeneration among citizens because of their dissatisfaction and disorientation. It is clear that it has not worked; many French are spiritually lost and, like them, so are societies throughout Europe and the world.

In August of 2016, I met a nice couple of Frenchmen of my age on the beach of Gouves, on the island of Crete, some twenty kilometers from Heraclion. When I spoke to them about this sensitive topic, they gave me the reason: the French lay system did not work, but the funny thing is that they do not worry too much and they do not seek solutions or seek to meet God!

In my case analysis, I see that they are doing very well materially and that is why they do not worry, they have not learned since childhood to worry about anything, they only care about their financial well-being and, perhaps, their health and not being alone, that is all! I, personally, see it degrading, it seems pure selfishness to me. Apart from loving oneself, as is normal, and loving one another, it is necessary to love and seek the truth, to seek God, because God is love and God is truth!

It is necessary that we think from now on and that we are gradually inventing a new system, a wiser, more sensitive, more spiritual and more valid system than secularism: a system that can serve us as a new philosophical basis of ethics with God for our present time and for the future that we see coming. Once we found this socio-spiritual system, we can apply it in education for all citizens, big and small, so we could also educate children spiritually from childhood!

The problem of belief in God and of spirituality is a problem of our present time which extends to the whole world and, above all, to the civilized world.

Voltaire's lesson remains the best: a God of tolerance and love for all human beings.

This God is none other than the one taught by the apostle Paul, "the unknown God" of which the Gospel of Jesus Christ speaks to us.

Chapter 20: My trip to Saõ Paulo, Brazil, in 1981

The trip from Beirut to Saõ Paulo was quite entertaining; we left on June 5, 1981 with a flight from the SAS (Scandinavian Airlines) via Copenhagen. We arrived in Copenhagen in Denmark in the afternoon, we got a transit visa and slept one night in a good hotel. There were other Lebanese who made the same route Beirut-Saõ Paulo. I think the flight from Copenhagen was in the afternoon and had a stopover the next day in Rio de Janeiro. We arrived, at noon, at the old airport in the city of Saõ Paulo, it is a small airport, too small for the considerable traffic that this great capital has, the airport is built on a plateau or a hill and has a very short landing area.

Saõ Paulo is the economic capital of Brazil. The state of Saõ Paulo at that time had more than twenty million inhabitants and the city of Saõ Paulo had approximately twelve million inhabitants. Saõ Paulo was the fourth most populous city in the world, the first most populated city in the world is Tokyo, the second one is Mexico! These data have changed from that time, now the state has double of inhabitants, and Saõ Paulo happened to be the sixth greater city of the world; those changes came in the face of the growing demography of cities in the Far East.

There, in Saõ Paulo, the children of my father's friend, Georges Maini, also called Abu Eli, that is, "Eli's father," who is his eldest son, were waiting for me. Eli and his sister Leila, who is a little older than him, were waiting for me at my arrival.

I was staying at the Maini family home, where Georges' parents, his wife, three sons and two daughters lived as well. The older sister who is called Nadia and the younger brothers Pierre and Nabil, I believe there also lived the grandmother, the mother of Georges. I was invited for almost a month, every member of the Maini family treated me very well and I was always welcome, they were very good friends of my father, who had passed away five years before, in August 1976. Eli took me with him every day to his cowboy factory, and introduced me to his trusted friends and acquaintances to relate to good people who could be useful to me and so that I could start my path in this great country. Eli was helping me a lot!

Afterwards, I wanted to have my independence and open my own way. I then looked for a place where I could live and found an apartment; I think I found it through the newspaper advertisements with the help of Leila. It was an aparthotel on *Rua* Bella Cintra, which is a central street of Saõ Paulo, perpendicular to Paulista Avenue, which is a famous main avenue of Saõ Paulo where there are the great buildings of the ministries, banks and offices of the large companies, etc. Bella Cintra Street was parallel to the *Rua* Agusta, which is very famous for its discos and nightlife; if you go down the *Rua* Agusta in the direction of the city centre of Saõ Paulo, you will arrive directly at the famous Republic Square named *Plaza de la República*, which they say does not exist anymore, maybe it has another name!

I was looking for a job, but I did not know how and where to look and find, I knew how to do many things. I also wanted to do my paperwork to stay in Brazil, it was apparently quite complicated, but it was also possible in spite of everything! Everything was possible in Brazil, as they say in Brazilian «*tudo tem o seu jeito*», that is, "everything has its way or its way of doing it". They also said that, in Brazil, you could make the dead walk! That is, they meant that everything was possible in this fantastic country!

Once, I was introduced to an elderly Lebanese couple who knew people who could help me and make me a birth certificate as if I had been born in a town in the interior of Brazil and where witnesses could testify that they knew me and that I was the son of some peasants, I do not know what, blah, blah, blah... on condition of paying a lot of money for it. I said no! I thought it was risky! For being rather fanciful and not serious!

Another way to stay in the country, a more realistic and direct way, was to marry a girl, the daughter of a Brazilian Lebanese that was born there. Once, a friend who worked in banking in Beirut, gave me, before leaving Beirut, the address and telephone number of his uncle, who was single and lived in Saõ Paulo for many years so that I could contact and meet him, as it could be helpful. So one day I remembered it, I called him and I made an appointment with him. He was very nice to me, it is always like this when one comes from afar, the compatriots take care of him, I remember he took me to the market, it was Saturday, we talked a little and had coffee or something. Then he called me and we met another Saturday or Sunday and he invited me to the house of a Lebanese friend of his, who immigrated to Brazil many years before. I was invited to eat typical Lebanese food at their house; I remember they made a dish that I really like, which is the raw kibbi. The kibbi is a typical Lebanese dish, is made with burgul, which is semi-cooked wheat semolina, broken and without the leaf, to that is added ground onion, salt and pepper; then it is mixed with the burgul dipped in water. Once the burgul has absorbed enough water and mixing it well with the onion and is quite tender, you add the ground quality raw meat; usually it is sirloin of lamb, although it may be perfectly made with a sirloin of beef or good meat without fat and without nerve, like the meat used to make tartar steak. Once everything is well mixed, you can eat it raw; you could also add on top of it some peppermint leaves and virgin olive oil. It is eaten with Lebanese bread, accompanied by red wine or better still Lebanese arak, dry anise with water and ice, similar to dry Spanish Machaquito anise but it is better a good arak from Lebanon! Others add fried minced meat with onions and pine nuts. You can also make it in the oven: in a tray, there are placed two layers of raw kibbi, in the middle you put fried minced meat with onions and pine nuts, top and bottom the tray is spread with butter and goes into the oven, it is called baked kibbi , or in Arabic, *'Kibbi bil Forn'*.

Next to the kibbi, you can eat humus or mutabal. Mutabal, also called "*Baba Ganoush*", is similar to Lebanese hummus, but instead of chickpeas, you use roasted, ground and peeled eggplant.

Hummus is very easy to make: to the cooked chickpeas are added sesame paste called tahini, lemon juice, crushed garlic and little salt. All is passed through the mill or the blender until it is fine and in sufficient proportions until you get the correct flavour. It is served in a dish on which is adorned with grains of pomegranate, paprika, ground cumin, parsley leaves and virgin olive oil.

They also prepared tabulé, which is a dish that cannot miss on a Lebanese table. It is made with burgul, fresh tomato, white onion or red onion, parsley, peppermint; all chopped very very fine with salt, pepper, paprika, virgin olive oil and lemon juice. The tabulé is eaten with leaves of lettuce and is a very healthy dish, as it contains many natural vitamins.

The food was delicious. Apparently the father liked me very well, he showed me his factory, which was a small workshop inside his house, where they made children's clothes and introduced me to his wife and daughter, who studied, I think, Pharmacy. There, in Brazil, the Lebanese people seek to marry their daughters with boys from Lebanon, but my goal was not to marry anyone, I was a free man and I was looking to find myself; I looked to find the three great secrets of life: God, myself and true love.

The first Lebanese who arrived in Brazil in the 19th century, when Lebanon and Syria were under Turkish-Ottoman rule, were called Turks because they came with a Turkish passport; later, they were called Syrian-Lebanese. They sold fabrics and went from house to house, in the villages, to sell things they had in their suitcase. It was a very hard beginning for a newly arrived emigrant in a large country like Brazil. Then, once they had made some capital, they developed their stores; later, they established their factories of confection and their factories of fabrics.

In Saõ Paulo there is a street of Lebanese business shops called *rúa veinticinco de marzo*, March 25th street, it is a very long street, it is like a big famous market that is full of clothes shops, garment factories and fabrics; Lebanese businesses on both sides of the street. Now it still exists and it is still very famous.

Saõ Paulo is the second largest city in South America and the largest in Brazil, Saõ Paulo's GDP is more than 12% of Brazil's GDP, Brazil is undoubtedly a country with future! However, Brazil had long suffered from a serious economic and social problem: inflation, injustice, lies and corruption.

Once, I found in a public place - I do not remember where, perhaps in a telephone booth or a bank - a gentleman older than me. He was a Frenchman who was quite old, had white hair, looked like a knowledgeable and experienced man, had lived in Brazil for many years and worked at Unesco. He told me that Brazil needed a revolution and the revolution would one day be made by women, because women are the ones who raise the children and have the responsibility of the house. They are the ones who are most concerned about the future of the children and the country, while men do not have time to think. They, in general, take care of other tasks: first, of course, their work and, in their free time, they follow the tendencies of the country, that is, the five things that make up the social life of Brazil - or the five drugs of the Brazilians to distract themselves and forget their reality -: football, carnival, samba, mulatas and finally cachaza, which is Brazil's sugar cane schnapps.

After more than thirty-five years, after leaving São Paulo, Brazil has tremendously grown and it has experienced great progress in all fields and economic aspects, in modernization, technology, industrialization... In Brazil, everything is manufactured, even planes that are imported to Spain and Europe. However, Brazil has not been able to solve structural, fundamental and social problems such as poverty and social differences are growing: the poor are always more, the rich are getting richer and the middle class is constantly deteriorating; this is due to financial burdens and inflation, and people are becoming impoverished. The country is much more indebted and corruption is at its highest level and all of this has reached its extreme in recent years, when the last presidents of Brazil came to be in the spotlight of justice.

The current president of Brazil is of Lebanese origin, he is the son of Lebanese emigrants from São Paulo, his name is Michel Temer. There are several Brazilian politicians of Lebanese origin; in my time, I heard about Paulo Maluf, a Senator from São Paulo, of Lebanese origin.

I hope that this new president, the son of Lebanese emigrants who contributed for more than a century to the economic construction of Brazil, can give the Brazilian people from his experience and his spirit to the good of this great country. I hope that this great country of dreams will soon become a healthy and healed country of its socio-economic diseases and be put in the good way of stability, as it deserves!

Leila, the daughter of Georges Maini, was trying to help me, look for work through her contacts and friends. Once, I found a technician job at the Vermouth factory of the Italian brand Cinzano, but I said no, I did not want to! I did not like this job! The reason was that I did not want to work as an employee. My father used to say to me when I was a little boy: "You must own your own business, never work for others," that was imprinted in my mind! I do not know if it was good or bad. And Leila said to me, "But do you think the sky will open and close only for you?"

I had no immediate answer, inside I said yes! In fact, now, after thirty-five years and since 1981, I do not regret having taken that negative decision: I have worked very few years in my life as an employee, but I have always been free traveling as a *freelancer* and doing my job my way. If I had taken that opportunity, I would be in Brazil now, where I did not have to be!

Now, after passing through the long schools of life, largely in Spain and less in Germany, and with journeys that I made through half the world, I can say that heavens open and close every day for me; not only for me, but for all who trust in God and pray every day, so that the beloved God enlightens his way and covers them with his grace and protects them with his angels.

Life is a continuous struggle and without God the human being is lost; if one comes to think that God does not exist, he is totally mistaken. Normally, atheists become depressed and sometimes aggressive because they remain without a valid argument and have no other position. They themselves are not convinced of their position because they know and intuit that in the end they go in the wrong direction; in spite of this they continue with their wrong position, they do not want to recognize God. Perhaps, out of pride, for having a hard head, for being omnipotent and even arrogant, in the end many of them are conducive to suicide!

God is life and light. If one believes in God and asks for His help through prayer, God manifests Himself in His life and gives him help, gives him His angels and His mercy, and gives him eternal life. God gives light in the way of those who believe and trust in Him.

Once, I went to the Leilao, that is, the place of sales by auction. The bank offered lots of described jewellry, those lots of jewellry came from people who had fallen into financial misery and had deposited their jewellry as collateral for the bank to lend them money in return. What had happened, as can often happen, is that these debtors had not been able to return that money, and since they had a small salary, they had not been able to work miracles. A salary is not a stretchable gum; if a salary is not enough to pay the bills for food, rent, water, electricity, etc., and above comes inflation, how is it possible to return the credit to the bank? The client asked it to fill a hole, but now he will need another credit to pay the bank credit and thus he will lose his deposit, otherwise he would be continually in an endless vicious circle!

The bet is made like this: anyone who wants can put in a sealed envelope a paper with the lot number and the amount of money that he will be willing to pay for this lot and from a minimum amount stipulated by the bank. Then, when opening the envelopes, the lot will be given to the highest bidder, to whom had bet the largest amount of money. In this case, it was me! So they gave me the lot for which I bet; apparently I gave a reasonable price, the highest of all, or perhaps no one was interested in having this lot, just me!

I do not know how much the amount I paid, perhaps the equivalent in Brazilian cruzeiros to about five hundred or a thousand American dollars, I do not remember exactly. The lot was about ten or twelve rings of gold with stones, which could be sold with luck for twice its cost, that is, for a thousand or two thousand dollars, more or less!

Then they introduced me to a Greek compatriot who knew many people and some friends of him, some Lebanese who had a small liquor factory in Rio de Janeiro, to meet them and to work with them. In passing, I told him about my concern, about my lot of jewellry, and he said to me suddenly: "Give me those jewels, I can sell them to the neighbouring girls who work in the offices where I work, and I do not want anything in exchange, because you are a Greek compatriot like me!" I trusted him and gave him the jewels. He had a bit of the physical appearance of the Jewish man of Morocco, Mr. Albert Saúl, even though he was Greek! Then time passed, and as I heard nothing about him, I began to worry; in the end, I called him several times and I could not find him. In the end, I managed to find him and we met and he invited me to take breakfast, it was hot milk with French baguette bread and I went so far as to say that if he did not pay me, I would be totally ruined and I would have nothing else to live for! It seems that I had very little money left over from savings. In the end, he felt sorry for me and paid me, he was not really serious! It made me feel scared, I suffered a little, the situation was critical, but I think in the end I was right! Adventures are like that, hard and bitter!

Afterwards, I had a job as a French language teacher at a language academy run by a South African lady, I think she was of Dutch origin; she was an elegant, beautiful and intelligent lady about forty years old. I began to give the first classes of French, with much energy, enthusiasm and passion, putting all my capacity and knowledge of French in the service of the students, I taught French in the most practical and simple way. They were afternoon classes, after working hours; there were lessons for grown-ups, clerks, or students, between eighteen and maybe thirty years or so. I remember that the students were attentive, they listened well to the class, I controlled them, I did not allow any of them to be distracted, I gave much importance to the pronunciation of the French language, language that I mastered and that it is still after Spanish one of my preferred languages, the one that I mostly use in my work. In fact, I only see the news in French on channel France 24 at night and I see the news of the world and France that interest me. As I did my studies in French and up to high school, and then I was in the university in Belgium, I also see every evening Africa News *Le Journal d'Afrique* from Monday to Friday, I also read the news on *Google Actualités*, Google news in French.

Once, a student girl and I – I think one of the youngest, who always met me on the bus on her way home, she was a pretty girl, I think she was about eighteen or twenty years old - we talked about many things and came to tell me about her private life, she told me that she had a boyfriend, with whom she had just broke up. One day, she invited me to her birthday at her house, where she lived with her parents and siblings. I remember that she was a very nice girl, white, blond, slender, sensitive, cheerful of character, very polite. I gladly accepted the invitation and brought her a present: a bottle of Cointreau, a French orange liqueur that Leila advised me to take there, since it was fashionable at that time. Her father, a young man about forty or forty-five years old or so, became interested in me; I think her ex-boyfriend was also invited to her birthday. She was interested in me, but I said no! That she should not be interested in me, but that she should return with her boyfriend and not abandon him!

I do not know if that advice was a mistake or a success. I think it was rather a success; if not, I would now be where I would not have to be and I would not be here in Spain writing this book, counting my long stay in Saõ Paulo.

After giving French classes for two weeks, it was time to talk to the director of the academy about how much she would pay me. The South African lady paid me a miserly amount of money, perhaps the equivalent of today to one or two euros for the teaching hour, which I considered miserable as a payment and I had to leave that job. I told her that I was sorry, that I could not go on and that I had other commitments.

In the *rua* Bella Cintra apartment I met many interesting people. To begin with, the owner of the hotel: a Jew who, I remember, was bald, was about fifty years old, I think he came from afar, from Canada, to Brazil to start a business in Saõ Paulo, he wanted to make a fortune in Brazil. Jews think, in general, that they are the most intelligent in the world!

I do not think that's true, the Jews were the people chosen by God and they still have a special place for God because of their history. However, now and since the coming of the Messiah, Jesus Christ, the people chosen by God is the one who follows Jesus Christ and His Apostles, and believe that Jesus Christ is the Saviour, and expect His coming with the first resurrection and prepare for it, when He will come as a lightning to take His people from the earth and from eternity to the heavenly Jerusalem.

It is true that the Jewish *lobby* dominates the great money capitals in the world and the Jews help one another among them. Once, when I lived in Germany, a German friend told me an anecdote, he was an expert man, an insurance salesman, very intelligent, he knew a lot of people and he liked to say jokes, he had a great sense of humour and he said: "For one Jew, ten Germans. For a Lebanese, ten Jews." I was very amused by his anecdote and he left me feeling pensive!

Indeed, the two peoples, the Jewish people and the Lebanese people, have something in common: the two peoples are merchants and traders, but who is smarter? It is a difficult question to answer, the Jews help each other, the Lebanese sympathize with each other, but they do not necessarily help each other! Perhaps they support each other, in countries of emigration such as sub-Saharan Africa or Brazil, where there are large colonies of Lebanese, they support each other in the work! But what I saw, as a rule, is that they are families that group together and live in clans.

In addition, I am an atypical person, I am not conventional, as my friend the writer, novelist and playwright of Madrid, Germán Ubillos. I do not consider myself a typical Lebanese, although I have roots from Lebanon and others from Greece, I also now have new roots for living so many years in Spain, I also have something that I learned when I lived in Germany and other cultures I met, I also love countries like Brazil and Ukraine, and especially France, although there I have not lived, I was only of passage. Perhaps, because of the permanent cultural contact, I am at the end as Socrates said: *"I am not an Athenian or a Greek, but a citizen of the world."*

Now what is clear is that we must all learn from everyone, no one should feel superior or inferior to anyone, every human being is a universe and must learn from others, regardless of race, ethnicity, origin or religion.

There, in the *rua* Bella Cintra Hotel, I met several interesting people, including a lady of Lebanese origin who was blond, which was probably dyed, was quite pretty and attractive despite her age, was around forty-five or fifty she was interested in me and wanted to help me with her contacts, she was from Rio de Janeiro, I think she had two daughters, she came to Saõ Paulo to make a living with what the Lebanese businessmen gave her, who apparently had extra-marital relations with her! She lived and could support her family in Rio de Janeiro and send her daughters to good schools!

So hard is life in Brazil, there are unfortunately many women who were forced to sell their dignity to survive, as it is now in our time. I think those things are still the same and they have not changed in our time almost all over the planet Earth.

Once she introduced me to some Lebanese businessmen. I went out with them on a night of revelry, always the same story, night life, businessmen with beautiful girls, Russian, Brazilian, etc., and lots of vodka and lots of *whiskey*! This world did not interest me, they drank and the next day they did not remember, they forgot what they said the night before! I stayed one night with them and never again!

In the end, I realized one thing: that Lebanese emigrants in Brazil, now that they are Brazilian citizens, learn, study in the great schools and universities, work hard, amass fortunes, eat, drink, sleep and live their traditions.

I felt like a foreigner in this world, I wanted to be something more, a different personage, I wanted to learn and to leave one day my seal in the world, like, for example, through this book that I am writing!

<u>My father told me</u>: "Banks are full of money, why worry about money so much, if you could win it with your genius! You can make a lot of money, you do not have to suffer so much and sell your soul to earn the money, and you are worth much more than money!" So the money did not attract me so much and it still does not attract me, I like to earn it, like everyone else, and I also like to spend it and save something for tomorrow, for hard times, but money is not everything in life, there are things that are worth much more than money, there is something very important, which is the satisfaction of the soul and the full realization of the spirit.

It is very important to get to feel like a true child of God, to know that God loves us, that there are people who can love us and pray for us. That is the synthesis of happiness, which I perceive.

There, at the hotel, I finally met a Brazilian gentleman named Chavas and we sympathized. This Chavas was a businessman who had no idea of business, he dreamed of becoming a senator, I do not know if he achieved that in the end! He thought that business was about having a gold ring on his hand with a gemstone like a ruby, to wear a suit and wear a tie around his neck. He lived in an apartment room with his young wife, he was a few years older than me, perhaps thirty or thirty-five.

He asked me to go with him one day and to introduce myself to several influential people he knew in the Government of Saõ Paulo. Once, I came to shake hands with the famous senator and governor of Saõ Paulo, Mr. Paulo Maluf in a celebration, with a cocktail. They said that the pockets of his jacket were sewn so that no one would stick a piece of paper or leave anything in his pockets.

Chavas and I did several trips, we went to visit some factories of cachaza in the interior of the state of Saõ Paulo.

We travelled together to several places far and near. First, we visited a famous and large factory of

Brazilian *whiskey*. The director of that factory was called Mr. Calatayud, said that his surname was of Spanish origin; indeed, there is a town in the province of Zaragoza, in Spain, Calatayud. When I looked for it on the Internet, I found that the name is of Arab origin! "The castle of Ayub" is of origin of Valencia. In Arabic, *Calaat* means "castle" and *Ayud* would come from *Ayub*, the name of Job in Arabic.

We always rented a car and made a long trip. We had to sleep a couple of nights in Rio de Janeiro, where we visited, in Rio, the *Pão de Açúcar* and the immense statue of Jesus Christ, the Corcovado, a marvel of nature and unique monument in the world! We also visited Germany in Brazil! Something incredible! About a hundred and thirty kilometers away from Rio de Janeiro, towards the interior, in the mountains at a thousand meters above sea level, there is a small town founded and inhabited only by Swiss and German people, called Novo Friburgo. There, the atmosphere, the nature, the houses, the trees, the rain... they are as if it were Germany or the black forest, an impressive spectacle and landscape. Thus I met many wonderful and unforgettable things thanks to the friend Chavas.

We also sometimes ate the *feijoada*, which is the typical Brazilian dish. In many countries, this is the typical dish of the poor people; it became famous and became the typical dish of the country that also the rich people eat.

The *feijoada* was the dish of black slaves who worked the lands of the rich Portuguese. The owners gave the slaves the parts of the pig that they did not eat, such as the feet, head and tail. They, the slaves, put salt on it and dried the flesh in the sun. Later, they cooked this dried meat with black beans, which are called *feijao preto*. Once well cooked, it is put down in the *farofa* dish, which is manioc flour fried with butter, which gives a consistency to the broth of the beans. Next to it, they put white rice and orange slices, so we return to the *feijao* and rice, which cannot miss on a Brazilian table.

Feijoada is accompanied by the *caipirinha*, which are pieces of lime crushed with sugar and ice, to which cachaza is added in abundance, which is sugar cane brandy from Brazil.

Rio de Janeiro was, at that time, a city of madness, there were six lanes on downtown highways and no one respected any driving rule, it was total chaos! I think it is still like that.

In the end, I had a great idea, because I liked the fresh and natural juice of the sugar cane, its taste is very rich, but it does not have enough acidity. Therefore, to make Brazilian *cachaça*, you must ferment the must or juice of pressed sugar cane, so that the sugar is transformed into alcohol. The yeast could not act, it needs a sufficiently acidic environment;

therefore, sulfuric acid is added to lower the PH, so they could be fermented and then distilled.

My idea, which did not come to fruition, was to make a fermented drink based on the sugarcane must, adding another natural fruit that is acidic to get the pH down and a new fermented drink from an exquisite flavour, which could become a popular drink in the world and could compete with beer. I was thinking of a fermented and sparkling drink, such as beer or cider, I had a lot of tests in my little studio in the *rua* Bella Cintra Hotel, I had specific ideas but I was not sure if my ideas were going to work, I needed time and dedication and supposed a good laboratory, of which I could not achieve.

In the end and for many reasons, I became physically and spiritually tired of Brazil and Saõ Paulo. My body, my mind and my soul were restless. Saõ Paulo was and is a large industrial city, there was a lot of pollution and my eyes hurt, there was also noise pollution from the noise of the city and the factories. All this set of negative conditions and annoyances were like an unbearable cocktail of chaos for me. There were also scary things, like the macumba, which is a fetishistic ritual of Brazilian blacks, which they also call black magic. In my opinion, it is a demonic spiritual practice of indigenous beliefs and witchcraft, since they tied a black tie on a power station, next to you could see feathers of a cock and rooster's blood, something that scared the soul and terrified me, and it gave me chills to see it!

I remembered the Spain of my dreams and, as I had on my passport, a visa of 90 days to enter to Spain, I decided to go and leave everything behind! So I bought a one way ticket with the Iberia airline. It was one day, on November 17, 1981, when I traveled to the unknown, to Madrid. I knew that Spain was going to be the right place, where I could live in peace. And so I left Brazil forever, to never return. Here I am, after thirty-five years, writing my book for the joy and satisfaction of all!

This was the story of my trip to Saõ Paulo in 1981.

Chapter 21: Action-reaction

Without action, there is no reaction.

Without personal initiative, we can expect nothing from the universe or our environment. If we really want to see the fruits of our work, whether intellectual, practical, artistic or labour, we must know how to move the sky so that those valuable fruits can fall, which are the result of our efforts and sacrifices throughout our whole life!

If we want to move forward in life, it is necessary that we have ideas, our intelligence and imagination, accompanied by our restlessness, would undoubtedly help us to find them.

Apart from having the good ideas for each day and every moment, it is necessary to take them to the practice, from there comes the action that emanates from the necessity of the realization of the human being. We also need the action that comes from our personal initiative; we need to work on ourselves, to find oneself, and to find the truth of things in life. We must not fear the difficulties that will stand in our way, no matter how great they may be, nor the long time that we would need to reach our goals, which are summarized in the perfection of the masterpiece we are building. We must always think that the great day is near; the phases and the passage of time to reach this great day will have to be motivation, encouragement, pleasure and joy for us, in the action of struggle and fulfillment.

Action is born of motivation and the need of wanting to realize an idea, so we often ask ourselves: "What should I do?" Wanting to take action is a natural desire to improve our condition of life on earth and to move forward with the project of building our person from inside and outward, towards the world that expects something good from us.

To carry out a project, we must work on ourselves and work on our idea, refine everything that is possible, step by step, until we put it into practice. We will have to make the necessary and appropriate investigations in a suitable place and environment: perhaps in a laboratory, a workshop, our office..., using the appropriate tools that are within our reach, such as a pencil, a pen, a notebook, a brush and a canvas, a computer... or in nature and outdoors, where we would be performing and sculpting our universal work of art.

The action is the fact to set in motion a system based on logic, which comes from an intuition, a vision. For this, we would need to move on to research, which can demonstrate to us throughout its process if our ideas are really valid and coherent, that our project is viable or is not viable. Then, in this particular case, we will have failed because we have taken the wrong course. With this disappointment, we should not become sad or lose hope, as it would serve us as an experience to avoid falling into the same error, on our next attempt or project that we want to undertake.

When we carry out research work, we will need to have at our disposal the basic tools and the necessary means to carry out our work or action, such as, for example, a mobile phone (which is nowadays ultra-necessary to communicate with others), a computer with internet to investigate, as if we were on a library, but now it is almost no longer necessary. We have at our disposal all the information we want to research, we can write our essays and save them in the folders that we open inside the computer. We will also need a vehicle in good condition to be able to travel, such as a bicycle, perhaps a bike is better, and, much better, a car with four wheels. We need to have good physical health, enough money in our pocket and in the bank account that will allow us to face a multitude of expenses that would derive from the cost of living and the work to be done, thus we could pay all the expenses of the investigations that we carry out and what it entails with it in trips and displacements. In addition, it is imperative to be spiritually prepared and to have intellectual capital and sufficient experience, maturity and wisdom; without these conditions, the work of action cannot bring great results, it will be a frustrated attempt that will be repeated many times throughout our life until we achieve true success.

If we feel really ready, we would also need to have someone on our side who can help us and support our daily struggle, who could be our partner, a relative, a friend, a *manager*, an expert who really loves us and listens, who would be attentive to our actions and who could support us morally and give some useful advice from time to time. Thus and in this way, we could achieve our goal and the reaction can be positive; our project can be carried out on its preliminary, advanced and final stages.

Our project may be an invention that we are trying to realize, that we have already been able to qualify it theoretically and we have only to put it into practice, we have the conviction that it is necessary for the society, which could have a good acceptance, a book that we want to write and publish, which could charm and persuade people, who would probably enjoy reading it and learn a lot of things from the wisdom it throws from its content and spiritual strength.

If we achieve great success, we will automatically become the creators of our inventions, our ideas, our products or our books and wisdom, and we could become famous; we will also be sellers or leaders of our own ideas.

A seller is an inventor who needs to create the product in order to offer it and sell it to the public. The product is the idea; the action is the fact of offering the product in an intelligent way to consumers and customers who might need it. The products are born of the need that comes from the intelligence, from the perception and the creativity of the human creator.

An industrial engineer needs to manufacture the product he has conceived, invented, and made. The product has to be good and at a minimum cost so that he can offer it to the market with a good value for money and that is, above all, useful and attractive enough.

A scientific researcher has an idea, which is the way he should undertake in his research, making the necessary tests. At this point, the action that will accompany him throughout the investigation process begins.

A farmer works the soil and plants the seeds. After a while, these seeds will begin to germinate, grow and bear fruit; the fruits and the harvest are the reaction of the action of the farmer, who has worked the land and sown it.

The reactions can be different: success or failure!

In the case of the farmer: A year of drought, without enough rain, a cold winter year with violent winds and hurricanes or frost is undoubtedly a nefarious year. That will result in a bad harvest and, if the weather has been favourable (with sunshine, abundant water and gentle wind), then they give an excellent and kind harvest.

In the case of the industrial engineer: It would be the acceptance or rejection of the product in the market. If the customer or dealer says, "Yes, I'm interested, I'm going to study it," or he says, "No, I'm not interested, I do not think it's interesting because it's not competitive in price or it's not useful for the customer for many reasons."

A salesman, at the beginning of his action, needs the luck of the beginner; this luck will give him the courage to follow his action of struggle. Without this stimulation, he will get tired of fighting and will end up abandoning his sales management for lack of courage; the business will be in this case destined to failure. We all know that luck does not fall from the sky, you have to look for it with daily struggle, patience and perseverance, but the luck factor has always existed, it is the fact of offering the good product at the right moment, it is like wanting to sell something that is missing really in the market and people are looking for it for a long time, it is like wanting to sell water in the desert or to sell bread to the hungry and abandoned to their fate, they would give everything for it!

Thus, if the seller has the luck of the beginner and succeeds in convincing the first customers, he will have possibility of success, everything will depend on whether the final consumers get to buy the product in the stores or at the points of sale. And, if the product really likes and convinces them, then they will repeat and there will come the great success or the positive reaction of the action.

A researcher needs to see light in his path or, as they say, "see light at the end of the tunnel" when he realizes that the road he is transiting is really the correct route and that his invention or his search are evolving positively and going on the good sense, so that the dream becomes a reality. Then, he may have the strength to pursue his research or to write his book of life to the end!

I remember that, when I arrived in Madrid at the end of 1981, I rented a modern studio for that time that was not cheap at all. The rent was about just over thirty thousand *pesetas* a month, a little less than the minimum salary at that time, which was hovering forty thousand *pesetas*. The studio was a large room facing Conde Duque Street, in the Argüelles neighbourhood, near Plaza de España and Calle Princesa. This relatively large room served for everything: it was at the same time a living room, an office, a dining room and also a bedroom at night. In the room, there was a worn blue armchair, and a glass round table with three metal chairs that were lined with wood, that was all the studio furniture.

On the right side of the room, looking out onto the street, there was a wall of cupboards and below, under the cupboards, there were drawers. From the middle of the wall, came down two narrow beds about seventy centimeters wide, as if they were wardrobes. On the back, there was an American kitchen with a refrigerator, sink and two electric plates, the kitchen was closed like a cupboard, it had two white lacquered metal folding doors, there was no washing machine, there was no place to put it! Behind the kitchen, there was a full bathroom that had its entrance when entering the studio from the hallway.

On the round glass table that was positioned at the end, next to the windows facing the street, there was an old-fashioned disk telephone. So in summary, in this large room with three walls, and a wall of windows facing the street and with a small work table and a telephone, I had to look for my life, as it is said in the street language. That is, with what little I had, I had to solve the problems of every day, to give meaning to my life and to live as a citizen, which was not easy!

At that time, there was no internet, no mobile, no fax, there were only letters that could be mailed and there was also the telex, which could be sent from the post and telegrams office in Cibeles, where there was a burofax (which they formerly called "tele-copying"). However, the fax was not used in business, because nobody had a fax, only some large multinationals, the fax became popular at the business level from the nineties, before the telex was used!

When I came to Spain, they called me "el portugués", I did not take long to learn Spanish without school, I learned Spanish speaking to the people and reading newspapers. It was not easy for a foreigner to open a single path in a large country like Spain when he did not speak the language correctly and did not know anyone, but, with the help of God, everything was possible, little by little, wanting to work with the infinite actions I undertook day after day, trusting in God and not losing hope!

I said to myself: "I need to do something to get a reaction. No action, no reaction!

Without work and without personal initiative, there can be no result, nor is there a loaf of bread for each day!

Now, after more than thirty-five years, I am naturally much better and I am very satisfied, but I am still the same and with the same philosophy: every day

I need to do so many actions that are necessary to advance, just as I need more action, ideas and divine light now to be able to write these words, which I am writing in this book of my life.

An autodidact person is a hyperactive person, is always doing something, he can never be still, that is where his need to move to action comes from, from his permanent and untiring restlessness. Action must always be good and never go against God and His commandments, or against people or nature, which are the creatures of God.

Action has to be an action for good, have good foundations and good philosophical thoughts.

There is also the action of evil, this action obeys the spirits of evil and consists in doing the will of Satan, who is the prince of darkness and evil.

We always have to make sure that our action is good and constructive for the good in general, that action can undoubtedly produce feelings of joy and personal satisfaction.

There are also many actions that we undertake and must undertake that are non-profit: actions to help people in need, actions of material help, intellectual aid and spiritual help..., which we can offer for free to others, those who need it. The reactions will be so positive that they will benefit these people and bring them joy and happiness.

Good, generous and uninteresting action has its reward and comes back to itself after a while, even if it has been a short or long time. It is like a bummer that we throw and come back to us sooner or later, it brings us back with good, spiritual abundance and happiness; the universe or God returns good with good.

The action of evil also returns, sooner or later, as a bummer. The one who has committed it will one day, sooner or later, receive a negative reward from Satan that will let him fall like a tomato that crushes and shatters after having supported it for a certain time. I have seen many people do harm and have ended very badly here on earth; so lies, hypocrisy and evil are actions that return to the human being by the law of God and by the law of the universe. God does justice in heaven as on earth, there are of course the laws of men, which only apply when there is a complaint or an apparent evil action that is detected, but God sees everything, the apparent and the hidden, the visible and invisible, God sees within each one of us, God does his justice in heaven and on earth.

There is also the spiritual action of spiritually helping people in need, it would be necessary to intercede before God and pray for these people who need our prayers for God to listen to us and help them. It would also be good to give them a testimony of faith, telling what we have seen and what we have experienced, it would be good if we could teach them the good way of faith in God and his son, Jesus Christ, so that they may follow the teaching of Jesus and his Apostles. These teachings are found in the Gospel of Jesus Christ.

Our positive actions in the world and throughout our lives will undoubtedly have as a reaction, a better world in which we could all live better.

Chapter 22: My Dream of Madrid, December 1981

In this chapter, we will talk about many important things at once. First, we will talk about how the beloved God communicates with us, human beings, how He talks to us through signs, through dreams, through messages..., which come from the hand or the lips of other persons. Also through real consequences and events, things that we call by ignorance "pure coincidence"; but they are not coincidences, but they are real messages of God that come from His will, wanting to help us on our way to the eternal glory. These phenomena can occur if we have faith in Him, if we are really restless, worried, if we pray and we look for His help, the beloved God hears our prayers and reaches out to us.

God sends us messages for our sake, many times they are signs that teach His great power and glory to those who believe in Him to make us sure He exists and that He is at our side. Through these signs, He expresses to us His great love and mercy, untiring and eternal towards us.

God sent messages to the prophets Abraham, Moses, Elijah and other prophets. There were prophecies that came from God to the prophets who announced the coming of the Messiah, the Lord Jesus Christ, who came and had to suffer and die on the cross to pay for our sins, but rose on the third day and are alive among us forever. Jesus Christ is the Saviour; he who believes in Him has eternal life.

We, the believers, who are not prophets, continue to receive messages from God of different scope, form and dimension.

It is a mistake to think that messages are an exclusive thing or monopoly of the prophets or priests, or of those who have a high ecclesiastical or religious ministry, whether those are true servants of God, put by the will of God, or false prophets or priests, appointed by the will of men, who do not really follow the spirit of God, but serve other unknown spirits, or Satan himself! There are servants of all kinds: true and false, rare and evil.

All of us who deeply believe and recognize God in our lives and in front of others can be somehow priests or servants of God. Those servants are the saints, those who leave everything and follow God and His son, Jesus Christ, those who preach the Gospel of Jesus Christ, those who have the light of the Holy

Spirit and know how to differentiate between good and evil.

<u>Who is able to say,</u> "This is holy and this other is not holy. "? Normally no one, only the beloved God, He is the only one who will be able to answer these questions!

<u>We, too, could in some circumstances say</u>: "This person is really a Saint!" It is as when the Roman soldiers saw that, after the death of Jesus Christ on the cross, the veil of the temple was torn in two! Then the centurion and those who stood there said, "This was truly as he said: the Messiah, the true son of God."

Matthew 27: 50-54.

50 And when Jesus had cried out again in a loud voice, he gave up his spirit.

51 At that moment the curtain of the temple was torn in two from top to bottom. The earth shook, the rocks split 52 and the tombs broke open. The bodies of many holy people who had died were raised to life. 53 They came out of the tombs after Jesus' resurrection and went into the holy city and appeared to many people.

54 When the centurion and those with him who were guarding Jesus saw the earthquake and all that had happened, they were terrified, and exclaimed, "Surely he was the Son of God!"

<u>The messages may come in different ways</u>:

A shocking dream that we have lived while sleeping can condition our whole life and can give us confidence and satisfaction to know that God loves us and gives us divine peace, that is, peace with God that comes from Heaven.

All this philosophical development of evidence is based on personal experiences.

I wanted to write, at the beginning, only the chapter with the title *My Dream of Madrid, December 1981*, but then, things happened for almost a month. A holy person also died at the end of 2016, she is our friend and sister Magda, of our Christian community of Denia. We have known Magda for more than twenty-five years, she loved us very much, my son Alexandros and me, she cared a lot for us, she knew we needed her moral and spiritual help, she prayed a lot for us. I felt, the day after knowing her death, a great force entered inside of me to keep continue writing my book of life, since then my friend Germán Ubillos, the great writer from Madrid, tells me that, when reading my new chapters, he saw and perceived light within my words! I think it will be the light of the love of this holy woman who wants to help me from above, from heaven.

I compared this new situation with the dream I had in December 1981 in Madrid of another holy woman who had gone to Eternity almost forty years before, I believe that in 1979, when she died in an attack in Beirut, where there were many cars stopped by traffic, during the Lebanon war, in a Christian neighborhood of Beirut that is called Achrafieh. A bomb exploded with a great explosive charge and 70 people died, according to what they told me, including Heleni, my father's cousin, who we saw from afar and greeted us on our pilgrimage trip to Jerusalem in Easter year 1973.

From these two situations I deduce the following: that every person who dies and goes to eternity - because the body dies but the soul eternally lives-, if this person is really a saint, it will go directly to Paradise, like the other saints and prophets. God hears them in a special way and, if this Holy person knows us well and truly loves us, it can intervene from Eternity for us here on earth, it cannot intervene negatively! Paradise is in the hands of God.

In Eternity, there are no fleshly temptations or material richness, there are no marital pairs either, and there is no envy or no desire for power, no carnal or material desire!

Eternity is the life of the soul, near or far from God. If it turns away from God, it suffers the heat of the fire of hell for the sins committed, according to their importance and gravity, with which the soul will have gone to Eternity and have not been forgiven by God. If the soul is closer to God, it will be in a place of happiness and rest, closer to Paradise, awaiting the coming of Jesus Christ, who will come as a lightning to gather His people from the earth and the spheres of Eternity towards the Heavenly Jerusalem when the time comes, on the day of the First Resurrection, the day and hour that only God the Father knows.

Now let us return to the main theme, which is *My Dream of Madrid, December 1981.*

There begins the first revelation or sign of God that I had in Spain, which happened in the dream, in a decisive and very restless phase of my life.

I had just arrived in Spain on October 18, 1981; I did not know well the country or its mentality, I did not speak well the language. I did not trust people very much, so I needed the presence and the follow-up of a lawyer during the negotiations and the signing of a commercial collaboration contract with the company with which I wanted to work.

Everything in Spain seemed to be going very slowly and they said to me: "The things of the palace go slowly!" And repeated: "Tomorrow" and "Do not worry!" They also said: "We are on it!" Tomorrow could be tomorrow or the day after tomorrow, within a week or within a month!

I remember that I was a little afraid of this new mentality, which was not very clear to me. Now I am used to waiting and that helps me in my rhythm of life and in my work, it helps me to do many things at the same time. I see it more as a positive thing than a negative one, as the English say "*take it easy*", and in Spanish "*¡tómatelo con calma y no te perturbes el alma!*" My word!

Before, when I was very young, the time seemed very long, I was very impatient, even with more reason, as if I depended only on one thing and a single result!

Another phenomenon of the Spanish mentality is when they say: "Do not worry". I was told by a Lebanese friend: «When in Spain they say" Do not worry ", that is when you must start worrying». Maybe he talked about negative experiences that he had, as undoubtedly there are too!

I did not know who to believe: my own feeling or the others. It seemed to me that the world would end tomorrow; I was waiting and they told me, "Tomorrow and tomorrow!" Until one night I called my friend Ángel Rodríguez saying that I could not sleep, that I was too worried, then he affectionately said to me: "My son Vango, do not worry, leave everything in my hands." The next day or later I think we signed the contract and I calmed down. However, that was the beginning, with that it ended nothing, but began the hard and thorny road; it was still missing the great work and the school of thirty-five years of struggle, which still continues, as is normal in the life of each human being.

I remember the days before signing the contract, which I believe was signed in early February. I now remember the date, it was an unforgettable date: 02-22-1982, a curious date of the fatal and hard month of February!

It happened at the end of December 1981, a few days before Christmas. I was sleeping in a deep sleep, this holy woman came in my dream, it was Heleni, the one who died, she wore a long dress of fine linen almost transparent white snowy, she came from afar, I recognized her right away by her face and by her voice, she looked like an angel. I was standing and had a great rusting iron cane in my right hand, it looked like a shepherd's staff, but it was made of iron. Heleni made me the sign of the cross from afar, a tremendous force entered my heart, and I saw before me an immense light and splendour, the rusty iron rod transformed into pure gold, which shined divinely, and she told me textually: **"Stay here, everything will go well for you."**

After this dream, when I awoke, I had great consolation, confidence and security in God, in myself and in the future that awaited me. This promise could not fail and based on it I continued my fight, day after day, until the end and I stayed in Spain five years until the time came when I felt prepared and I was convinced that it was time to leave Spain, at the end of 1986, when I met my German ex-wife Susanne. We met in early 1986 and we were later together, she became pregnant with my son Alexandros. After a few months, we got married in Madrid, on November 18, 1986; more than thirty people were invited to our wedding. My friend Rafael took us in his new red car to the courthouse in Madrid and he made me a friend's gift, a nice Seiko brand watch, which showed the position and movement of the moon. Many friends were present at the wedding: friends of Susanne and her parents, who came from Germany; my Spanish friends, Germán, Ernesto; the Greeks, Dimitri, Vasilis, Nicos the Cretan; a crowd of people, Marisa Montalvo (my generous neighbor of C/Conde Duque who was in charge of preparing the buffet and drinks for the wedding), a multitude of Lebanese friends, among them my friend Elie Saad and his future wife. It was a wedding made out of nothing and it came out perfectly. Twelve years later, at the end of 1998, Susanne and I got separated by circumstances of life, as can happen in the best families, I continue to pray for Susanne and her parents every day for God to keep them and give them protection, joy and happiness.

Now we are also near Christmas, thirty-five years have passed since that dream of Madrid of 1981 that gave me confidence to continue trusting in God and I still trust in Him, in His promise and in His mercy.

Here the story of God's messages does not end. God appeared many times, once in a special way through the witness of faith, received from the hand of a servant of the New Apostolic Church. A deacon I met in Germany, in the city of Braunschweig, I think it was late August of 1987, that day it rained a lot in the afternoon. He then took me in his car to the house of Susanne's grandmother, Emma Gehrmann, who had her house where we lived, in a village in Braunschweig called Stiddien, which he knew very well because his father, he and his brothers had built the roof of Emma's house, *Oma Emma*, as they say in German, and we became friends with time.

There in Germany my life was quite hard and sad, I did not live up to my ideas and the education I had received from my parents. There I felt like a slave, depending on the German social system, I did not know well the language, so I could only access to manual jobs. First, I worked in the kitchen of a Greek café, the owners were a Greek family, the eldest son who owned the business was an architect with academic studies, he was a very bad person, his father had abandoned his mother with the three children and it seems that he did a lot of damage since he was little. I think his name was Michalis, and he would say to me: "Here in Germany, if you do not spit blood, you do not get money for your work!" This boy was very bad, he seems to have a hatred towards the German people, I believe and I am convinced that he should thank the Germans, since they did not abandon him and gave him social assistance, security, studies and work to him and his family. The culprits of his misery and his psychological complexes are not the Germans, but his own father. I wanted to finish this job as soon as possible, in the end God helped, it was very cold in February 1987, it was -25 degrees at night and I got sick because I worked there from six in the afternoon until midnight, after my school of German. He threw me out of work and paid me very badly, and he owed me a large part of the salary, and in the end I told him that one day he would fall on his head, because of the bad person he is, he would surely receive from life what he deserves!

Later, in the month of August of the same year of 1987, I found work in an Italian restaurant, it was called Restaurante Guido, it was located in a street of pedestrians. I was the *grillman*, that is, the steakhouse man, I grilled hamburgers and sausages, hot dogs and Texas steaks, it was a more entertaining job for the public and at night, before I left, I had to do the inventory as if I were an accountant, count the sausages, hamburgers, steaks that remained... This work was insignificant for me, knowing of my technical and intellectual abilities, I was a technical investigator in my father's factory, I had to work like a simple worker! I remembered the famous parable of the Gospel, the prodigal son, the son who went away from his house and then returned to his father to apologize, but my father had already died in 1976, more than ten years ago! I did not know where to return, when I entered this work, I said to myself: "I enter this door and go out a month with a job as chief export in Spain," and that was possible with the help of God!

I started buying the newspaper *El País* on Mondays, it was the Sunday newspaper, inside was the work notices, inside pages of salmon colour. I sent several letters each week with my curriculum, until I sent fifty-four letters. After seven or eight weeks, came a couple of positive responses from interested companies that could offer me a job, there were some interest in Madrid of a leather jewellery factory and others interested in Valencia in a wine factory.

The family of the deacon of the New Apostolic Church prayed much for us, so that I could find a job, and God listened to the prayers of those faithful.

I travelled to Madrid with a direct flight from Düsseldorf to Alicante, I arrived in Alicante in the afternoon, I first took the airport bus to the Renfe station of Alicante, there I took the train that left very late, almost at midnight, the trip lasted perhaps about eight to nine hours, it took an entire night to get to Madrid. The next day, early in the morning, I was going to an interview in Madrid with the company Matute, a fashion jewellery factory, I do not know if the company still exists, I do not think so. Valencia was far away for me, I remember the owners, Javier and his brother Mariano, the one who interviewed me was a Catalan of Andalusian origin, very funny, his name was Fidel Lopez Salvador; they were all very nice and very kind to me. Fidel had interviewed almost a hundred people for this position of export manager, in the end they chose two people: a Frenchman to sell the jewellery in France and me to sell the jewellery in Germany. Thus I obtained my first job in Spain and I left the slavery of Germany to be free forever.

I remember that I came to Spain in October 1987, just when my son Alexandros had just been born, he was only about five months old. I moved heaven and earth to find a job worthy for a young family; I had a little money for a few days, something like twenty thousand *pesetas*, not even enough to pay for the hotel. First, my friend Marisa Montalvo offered me her home in Navacerrada to sleep for a couple of nights; then a Lebanese friend of mine, Elie Saad, who was just married, invited me to sleep the last few days in a room in his apartment in Madrid. The Matute family bought me a plane ticket back to Germany, Madrid-Düsseldorf; they gave me money as a fund to travel in Germany and visit clients. They gave me many catalogues and a large box, like a trunk type briefcase, filled with samples of fashion jewellery to show the samples to the customers. I cannot describe how great my joy was.

That and much more I can tell you about the daily miracles that I lived and I continue living after my dream of Madrid, in December of 1981.

Chapter 23: The keys to success

<u>What are the keys to success?</u>

- Being intelligent and know how to use intelligence.
- Being constant at work.
- Read and learn.
- Knowing how to listen, which is not easy.
- Thinking in the future.
- Seeing things coming, that is, have spiritual eyes.
- Have good and great ideas according to time.
- Knowing how to do something out of nothing, from a simple idea.
- Having a happy fighting spirit, to know how to lose in order to win.
- Knowing to wait, to be patient and preserve, to be active continuously.
- Knowing how to make yourself loved, to know how to give of oneself, of kindness.
- Knowing how to hit the nail on the head, as told me my dear friend from Granada in Madrid, Ángel Rodríguez. He told me often: "My son, Vango, you have to hit the spot!"

Time has no value, the value can be found in the results. The important thing is to survive the time and to be able to continue the fight until the end, until reaching the goal.

One should never get burned, but be noble like precious metals, which no one can burn.

We should never fall into despair or depression. We should never sell our soul or body, whatever the price is!

We must always have faith in God and His mercy.

The keys to success are also:

Learn every day and every moment of your own mistakes.

Make an assessment at the end of the day, week, month, quarter, six months, year or a phase of your life and ask yourself:

"Where and why I have made a mistake?"

"Why did I have this seemingly nefarious and negative result?"

What did I do wrong? What did I do right?

Doing good things is normal; you should not normally praise yourself for having done good. Good is not a favour to anyone, but it is a duty of man towards the universe and above all towards the neighbour. The one who thinks differently, for example, that doing good is a favour, is the same as if he paid a pending bill as if it were a favour, no sir, it is a duty! These are drastically selfish people because they think that everything is theirs, the country, the people and the family are their property, even the air that others breathe, that is why they become racist, chauvinistic and materialistic. These people are bad and undoubtedly mentally and spiritually ill, they should run to a psychiatrist, who could equally help them, or a priest, who could teach them divine things like the teaching of Jesus Christ and his Apostles, and pray for them. It is our obligation as human beings to have good will and to want to help others with all our heart.

<u>Also ask yourself</u>:

"Could I have done it better? How can I act? How should I think from now on to make things better?"

It is primordial and essential for us to have confidence in ourselves and to be convinced that we can do things better every time.

Life is relatively long, because it gives us endless opportunities, but life is also short, because time passes quickly and opportunities, although they exist, are not often within our reach, do not come every day, not every week, or month, they come when they come and we have to be vigilant, firm and strong in making our decisions. We have to know how to decide quickly, to take this opportunity or not to take it! Because there are opportunities that seem that to us and they really are not. They are rather traps; they may be temptations of the devil, Satan, who wants to sink us even more into difficulties, uncertainty and despair. If we take them, we will be losing a lot of time in our struggle over time, and time will fall on us, we will find ourselves in a worse situation than before, it will take a long time to rise again from that negative experience, although sometimes this is usually necessary because God, who is the king of divine wisdom, wants to teach us new things. That is part of our long school of our life, which will help us to polish facets of our experience.

Negative experiences and failures are good up to a certain extent; we cannot be learning and fail continuously during all our lives, it is necessary to have success from time to time and to succeed. Failures often cause us to retreat rather than move toward our ultimate goal, which is to live in glory with God.

We must not believe what the charlatans tell us or waste our time listening to their lies.

My father said to me: "Do not trust this or that. If they tell you stories, ask them to move their ears to show that what they say is really the truth, only then you can believe them". He wanted to say with this that I should not trust anyone!

I personally say: "Do not trust anyone or yourself, but trust in measure and keep your eyes open. As the Germans say: "*Vertrauen ist gut, kontrolle is besser!*" which means: "Trust is good, control is better!" In other words, you can trust, but you have to be vigilant with yourself and with others.

Our spiritual eyes help us to analyze the spirits and to know who are the spirits we can believe in and who are the spirits we cannot believe in, because in the end everything is spirit!

In addition, there are clues that tell us that a person is lying. Liars often repeat their lies more than once, repeat their words that are full of lies, it is a way to make us believe what they want to tell us to think that what they say is really true, because the liar knows very well that what is told is pure lies. He often repeats his argument so that he himself can believe in his own lie and for us to believe in the story that he is not able to believe because he knows it is a lie, but ends up believing his own lie and expecting the same reaction from us!

In a trial in the court: an innocent and accused convicted usually repeats that he is not guilty or has to do with what the judges are accusing, in this case is likely to be telling the truth, but none of us are judges to judge anyone. Each one has to look at himself in the mirror, see his own faults and ask God to forgive him.

My conclusion: do not believe in anyone, just believe in God, and believe in yourself and the beloved God first. Just as we can be good and upright, there are other people like us who are upright and good before God, and in those righteous people we can undoubtedly believe.

Obviously there are people who are right and worthy of our trust, of whom we can rely 100%, but it is not always the case, that will depend on the situation. We know that in each of us there are two personalities and nobody is perfect; therefore, we have to know what to believe and what not to believe, it is undoubtedly an art and thus we will become experts, over time, based on our mistakes and thus we will learn.

There are things that can be taken as believable or believe in them and other things that cannot be believed, that is where our nose comes in.

<u>To succeed in life and thrive, it is very important</u>:

To be able to understand how the minds of the people around us works, with which we work or deal on specific issues or live situations of life, with which we have family ties or sentimental relationships. We must try to imagine their thoughts and to decipher how they think and how the mechanism of their brain or their mind works and how far they could go in their imagination, how far they could go in their actions, how they could react to such a situation, and so on. Now, by knowing that, we can surely succeed, because we will dominate the psychological situation of other people, who wanted to dominate us. We will be the strongest psychologically rather than the weakest one.

<u>Here are some examples</u>: We must be able to understand a person without having to see it, just listening to it on the telephone is enough. If not, we would be wasting time uselessly, because the voice and

the way of speaking say it all. You can also analyze a person for his writings, his letters, his e-mails; it is like analyzing an artist for his artistic work, his paintings, sculptures, music or written books, etc. In the way of writing you find all the psychology of a person.

I learned something very important from the Germans and, when any of my clients calls me, I say, "What can I do for you?", «*was kann ich für Sie tun?*», «*qu'est- ce que je peux faire pour vous ?*».

Then people immediately realize that you are a serious person and you are a trustworthy person who goes with the truth ahead. That gives a very good image of your personality, and others will think that you are a sincere, open, humble, generous and a good hearted person, that is to the service of the others. That does not mean that he is also the image of an expert and professional in his work, that is, of a person of trust not only for his goodness, but also for his intelligence and professionalism.

I also learned something very important from myself: "You should never ask anyone what they cannot offer you", it would be absurd to ask, because we are not going to get it, we would get nothing and we would end up being ridiculous! It is better not to ask for favours, unless we have no other choice or alternative; it is like going to the mechanic when your vehicle is broken or the doctor when you're sick, you have no choice...

In the school of life, it is necessary not to waste time and not learn useless things that are useless or contribute to contaminate our mind, our thoughts or our feelings; we should not fill our memory with useless things!

It is better to learn a language of the world, as they say in other languages, a living language or language of the world, in French, "*une langue vivante*"; in German, "*Weltsprache*", means "languages of the world", languages that can serve us for something, a living language is a language spoken by millions of individuals and worldwide. Learning a dialect is practically useless and intoxicating for our mind, unless we live in the place where this dialect is spoken and we really need to be able to speak it to communicate with those people!

In order to be successful, it is also very important to get away from the imbeciles as much as possible, the mentally ill, the self-centered, the omnipotent, those who think they know everything and do not really know anything because they still lack a lot of school. Those people who are proud of themselves, who are often chauvinistic, sarcastic, racist and very convinced of themselves lack, in my opinion, of wisdom, philosophy and spiritual sensitivity, are human beasts. They are for me, as for many autodidacts, really imbeciles and you have to get away from them at all costs because they can do us a great moral and spiritual damage. Losing them as friends or as partners is a great gain, because they are capable of disturbing our minds and our souls.

To be successful, you also need to be selective and try to learn difficult things that no one knows or only very few know. Thus we will be among the few who know something very special and very different, thus we will have more chances of success than if we are one like the others or the masses. It is better to be a personage incomparable to the others to belong to a human species really rare and difficult to find.

We conclude that, in order to be successful, it is necessary to be different from others and to forge an intellectual level out of the ordinary, unique and outstanding.

To learn difficult things, you have to be smart. Intelligence is forged from childhood.

There is an Arabic saying that says: "Learning from childhood is like sculpting the stone". Learning when one gets older costs much more and is usually a bit late, not to say too late! If someone who has never learned almost nothing intends to learn English or another language in his fifties, it is really very late, not to say almost impossible!

If you have learned from childhood to fight and use your brain, then you can throughout your life continue to struggle and learn more complex and difficult things, because you already have in yourself the skills, discipline or practice of struggle and learning. You will naturally have an elastic brain and a hero's heart!

A man from Alicante who I knew a while ago, who was older than me, once said to me a few words that remained in my mind, he said: "Do not be afraid of things," in other words, it is necessary to remove the word 'fear' from our dictionary. Whenever we are loyal and prudent and work with conscience and honesty, we should never be afraid of the struggle, no matter how great, to achieve a noble goal, to realize a new project never reached by another human being. Nothing is impossible, we have to try every day and keep looking for it, keep training and work on ourselves. We could undoubtedly find the truth and the path that will take us to the goal, to success, to human glory, practicing a discipline of constant work and fulfilling a series of human, professional and spiritual requirements.

The faster and more constant we are, the further we can get.

That is why it is necessary to teach children how to think fast and quickly solve problems in the mind. The mental calculation for that is very good.

<u>For example, ask a boy or girl questions of arithmetic multiplication</u>: 5 x 5, 8 x 8, 12 x 12, 25 x 25, etc. However, if we ask them a very difficult mental calculation question, for example, 733 x 534, that is really very difficult. If a boy or girl of ten or twelve was able to solve this multiplication in his mind after five or ten minutes, he would really be a genius. I would also need a few minutes to solve it, of course it is not easy, without pen and paper or without a calculator, but you can get mentally calculating putting every part of this simple arithmetic multiplication in memory and mind, then we can mentally do the sum. This is how the intelligent are forged.

Then we move on to the most difficult mathematical equations, from physics, chemistry, etc., to the equations of life, which would be philosophical and wisdom matters, which need a good and profound overview. It needs to have a general knowledge of the world and of life because of living long experiences that made us experts in solving problems of our daily, intellectual and professional life.

If a person is not good at maths, he cannot be an engineer, but he can study a degree course or study law and be a lawyer!

For a businessman, it is important to know how to calculate and know how to give each thing or matter its answer and its value.

For example, how much can cost this car, this merchandise, this product, this building, whatever it is, this bottle of wine, a loaf of bread, the salary of a professional, according to his grade and specialty. It is also important to be able to estimate or value the time needed to finish a job, for example, how many days does it take to make a car according to the class? How long it would take to build this house, this building or this road. Your estimation should always fall close to the truth.

If you are able to estimate and appreciate, you can succeed in business.

If you are able to imagine and solve difficult things, the deepest and most important things, knowing how to solve the difficult equations of life daily, work on yourself and let the work do its job, believe in others and know how to control where they go in your thoughts... if you are able to do things that are bigger than your own person, which are superior to your own capacity for accomplishment and require much more genius and imagination from your part, then you will be able to overcome and your boat will never fall. You will be able to navigate the waters and difficult seas, you will be able to thrive in your life, because you have in yourself all the tools, the knowledge and experience of the great teacher and the keys to success, that will make you become a great hero, a great winner.

These are, in my opinion and my own imagination, the keys to success.

Chapter 24: ¡Eureka, eureka! Madrid, 1985

Here, in this chapter, I will tell you about a great moment of my life: the spring of 1985, when I discovered the magic powder, which I called in Spanish *"El Polvo Mágico"* in the small studio where I lived, in Conde Duque Street, in Madrid.

This was neither my first nor my last invention. At this time, I was doing research and looking for new products. The magic powder, as I came to call it *"El Polvo Mágico"*, was really magical, as the word says, I think it was the most outstanding among all my inventions of this time, perhaps the simplest, but also the most difficult to discover, maybe for how simple it was!

I had already started to invent several things during my long career as an autodidact researcher and I continue to invent solutions to my daily problems, big and small. Like all the autodidact thinkers of this world, we are always restless; we feel the problems and the conflicts skin-deep. We continually seek to find the solutions, apart we have the tendency to want to invent, to look for great solutions to problems that we consider important in our life. We also invent for wanting to realize our dreams.

The inventions are part of the human capacity, they come from the intelligence, the imagination and the realization of the human being, this capacity is given by the Supreme God. The ability to invent is what differentiates the human being from animals.

An animal does not invent, but reacts by its instincts, looking for its vital necessities. A human being, apart from seeking to survive on a daily basis, constantly invents and builds his own future. To do this, he will use his sensitivity, his imagination and his inspiration, which will help him to find the solutions to the daily problems when he detects a failure in his own system. His imagination and intuition, which come from his intelligence, will help him to invent the right solution to every problem, either big or small!

Autodidact thinkers meditate on important problems that are continually occupying the mind and the spirit. It is a normal feeling that we call restlessness, from restlessness comes the need to invent and wanting to seek solutions to strategic or structural problems. The autodidact person is by nature a perfectionist, he is attracted to solve the great equations of life and especially the problems difficult to solve.

The solutions to the great problems that we consider mysterious or impossible to solve are what we call inventions: they are enlightenments of the mind, which usually arise upon awakening after a deep sleep. They may also appear during the dream, when, through inspiration, we find solutions to the problems that occupied our mind for some time. This happened, for example, often to my father, who found during the dream solutions to difficult problems that he was seeking to solve for a long time.

Solutions or inventions can also be born during or after a relaxing and hot bath. When the mind is freed from the pressure of everyday stress, the inspiration is in its optimal state and at its maximum potential.

"Eureka, eureka" are the words that Archimedes said when he left the bathroom when he had to solve a very difficult physical problem. Archimedes was a scientist, mathematician, and physicist; he wanted to determine whether the crown of King Hiero II, whose jeweller had made at Syracuse, was made of pure gold, as the jeweler claimed, or whether it was made of gold mixed with silver. The king had doubts, and so he ordered Archimedes to carry out the necessary investigations, and he hoped for a clear, sure, and quick answer.

Archimedes had to solve this difficult problem with a procedure of physical analysis without being able to break the crown of the king Hiero II, he could obtain it thanks to a new theory that he invented himself. It happened when he was in the bathroom and watched as the water level rose when he immersed himself into the bathtub. He was able to explain the phenomenon and found a new theory of submerged volume that helped him solve this great problem of the king's crown. In addition to that, his invention was so valuable that it remained as a valid physical theory forever, recognized as "the principle of Archimedes". When he found the solution in his mind, he left the bathroom without dressing, as he was, and ran naked through the streets of Syracuse and saying, "Eureka, eureka", in Greek "*evrika, evrika*", and in English: "I have discovered, I have discovered it, "(the literary translation is: "I found it, I found it").

I remember that I went through a similar or comparable situation, but it was something different. I tried to solve a technical problem for many months, it was not physical; maybe it was chemical or rather related with food. I wanted to invent or find a new natural condiment, in the form of powder, which did not yet exist in the market and which could substitute the wood burning coal. I was looking for a powdered seasoning that could replace the wood burning ember and that could give a special flavour to foods like vegetables, fish, chicken and meats when roasted on a cast iron plate. Using this new seasoning, the taste and aroma of grilled roasts should be identical to the taste and aroma of wood-fired grills.

I searched and searched in my mind and I performed countless experiments for months. I found no answer until one day, much later, I found the perfect solution to the problem, which came in a similar way, as it did with Archimedes, during a hot bath. I was taking a hot and relaxing shower in the bathroom of my small studio that I was renting in Calle Conde Duque, in Madrid.

I remember it was at noon, in the spring of 1985, I had several concerns, as I still have now, but in different ways and scope. At that time, I was at the beginning of my path, my career, now I do not think that I am at the end, but I can say that I am on the road to maturity or in the philosophical age of the life of a human being.

By coming to live in a new country and starting a new life from scratch where no one knew me, I needed to have brilliant ideas and bring them to practice, ideas that could surprise by their genius. Perhaps I could attract or persuade the few entrepreneurs I knew who might possibly be interested and invest in my project; so I could perhaps start the new path and restart my career in the food industry, which was my world. I needed to create something out of nothing, something I could invent with my own resources and resources, which were very limited.

Besides, since I lived alone in my studio, I often cooked and I also enjoyed cooking, I remembered my father's distillery. I cooked and researched inside my American kitchen, which was also my only small laboratory, apart from the laboratory of the anise distillery in the town near Madrid called *Chinchón*, which was within my reach from time to time, but only when it came to liquors. I liked to roast thighs or back quarters of chicken, fish fillets or other foods on the electric iron plate. My idea was to reproduce the phenomenon that occurs when roasting with the heat of wood coals, which give a flavour as special and exquisite to roasts as meat, vegetables or fish.

I also remember my first trip to Greece from Spain, by plane from Madrid to Athens, in early August, in 1984, when I travelled all month to visit my uncle Yorgos, who was still living and loved me very much. I made the trip also to catch some air from the lost homeland and return to the sea of the island of Salamis in Greece, where I have memories of my childhood of the summer of 1966 that I spent with my sister Ketty. Apart from seeing my uncle from time to time, I made many trips to Greece, where I had friends who loved me very much and I loved them alike.

Before returning to Spain, I remembered to buy pine resin, the reason was that I wanted to test and try to make *retsina* white wine from Greece in Spain, in a wine factory near Seville of very nice people I knew. I went to the market in Athens, which is called *Ágora* in Greek, and there I asked in the shops where could I find resin of Greek pine. In the end, after going from store to store, I found the only store that had such a product: it was a wholesaler selling condiments at wholesale, including pine resin (what they call *ritini*). He told me that he exported *ritini* to Australia or Canada; I do not know what that was for! Perhaps it served to make *Retsina Wine* there in Australia or Canada, or was used in the pharmaceutical or cosmetic industry; I do not remember exactly what he told me!

On the way back to Madrid, I tried to make *Retsina* in Spain and I made several tests, I remember that it was enough to put a gram of resin of Greek pine to dissolve into a litre of dry white wine. Leaving it to macerate for a time like a week, the result was a white wine *retsina*, of golden color, similar or even better than the Greek *retsina*, depending on the quality of the wine used, since in Spain abound the quality white wines.

Once the test was done, although the result was good for a *retsina*, the flavour was not familiar to the Spaniards, a future market could not be created! The taste of the *retsina* was strange and very strong to the Spaniards! They did not like its taste or smell, so the idea failed; it was not at all interesting for the local market!

After a while, I forgot about the *retsina* and tried to invent the magic powder, but it was really a very difficult problem to solve, because I did several tests and did not come up with the solution. I did not "hit the nail", as my friend Ángel Rodríguez said. Someone said to me, "We must concentrate the smoke!" Another told me another strange thing that has neither feet nor head!

I decided to try with natural essential oils. I decided to abandon the idea of looking for such a product, since I did not see light at the end of the tunnel, and I came to consider that the invention was impossible. But, in reality, nothing is impossible, as Napoleon said:

"The impossible is the ghost of the timid and the refuge of the cowards...

The word "impossible" is not in my vocabulary. "

So, one day, after having totally abandoned the idea of continuing to look, I took a hot shower in my studio in Calle Conde Duque to rest, relax, forget a little about it and regenerate my ideas and thoughts. But in spite of it, my mind was always occupied with the same problem, and suddenly, under the hot shower, the fantastic idea came to my mind, let's see if that idea I had under the shower could be the correct solution to this big problem!

I thought that the resin of the Greek pine could be the solution to what I had been looking for for a long time. Starting from the principle or theory that charcoal coals from pine tree wood or other trees actually contain resins, they are the essential oils that evaporate from the wood through combustion and are within the smoke. That is why the smoke is thick, because it contains those oils; is what also gives this flavour so special and characteristic of the roasted meat with fire wood or charcoal.

Indeed, I did not wait to get dressed, I was euphoric, I could no longer resist the seduction of this brilliant idea. I got out and quickly put the towel around my waist as if I were coming out of a warm Turkish bath or out of a bath in the time of the Romans or the Greeks. I immediately plugged in the iron in the electric kitchen, and once it was quite warm, I took some resin with a knife out of from the pot I had bought from the market in Athens and spread it on the hot iron. The resin began to boil and evaporate, I approached my nose over the vapours to smell them and analyze the aroma, it was really what I was looking for, the smell was the same, the one I was looking for. I immediately jumped for joy, almost touching the ceiling with such joy and I had an unimaginable deep breath and a unique and incomparable pleasure.

I had already found the product in theory, now it had to be put into practice, that is, processed and dosed to make it into powder and that it was a hundred percent natural in the form of condiment such as ground pepper, ground cumin, ginger powder, etc. I was able to do that in a few days, continuously thinking and without stopping, until I could imagine the entire manufacturing process. All that was possible after having done some tests and doing calculations, I finally managed to put in my mind the whole system of manufacturing at the laboratory level and applicable in the industry.

The product was so successful among friends that everyone liked it, until a friend, who was a chef in the restaurant of Galerías Preciados, on the Gran Vía in the center of Madrid, in Plaza del Callao, came to include it in his menu. It was a new dish which he called "beef entrecote to the fire of oak", it was grilled on the griddle, so delicious that the customers believed that it was made to the fire of the coals of oak. It was a grilled steak with a pumice of my new invention, the magic powder, as if they were pepper or salt. The meat was tasty and exquisite, they really liked the customers, who came back to repeat and enjoy it again!

Unfortunately, I did not manufacture it industrially for many reasons: I did not have the means to set up such an industry myself, nor did I seek to contact any manufacturer who could manufacture such a product. At that time, I could not focus on so many things; I had family and responsibilities...

The invention of the magic powder "El Polvo Mágico" stayed like a memory of the past, was one of my best inventions of Madrid...

Chapter 25: Your destiny is in your hands...

How do we manage to live our own destiny?

This has been the question I was always asking myself. I remember a town, here near where I live, about seven kilometers approximately, which is called Alfaz del Pi. The name of this town is of Arab and Roman origin. "Alfaz" is of Arab origin, comes from *Al Fares*, that is, "the knight". "Del Pi" is Roman, Latin or rather Valencian, meaning "of the pine", this is understood as "the knight of the mountain of the pines". There is a great Culture Centre in Spanish *"Casa de Cultura"* in which, in 2004 and 2005, I was aiming for an oil painting course. Each student painted alone and there was an old teacher, I think his name was Juan, he was a great painter; he helped each student to make his drawing or his painting. There I was able to paint my first painting of oil that I dearly keep from that time. At the same time, I studied Norwegian in a course that was for adults on Monday night and for two years.

When I left the *"Casa de Cultura"* that afternoon, I saw two English women waiting for their children to leave the music class or some similar course. When I spoke to them, I learned that they had both married men, apparently Spaniards, and the two were divorced. I remember that I said in English: "*I want to live my destiny!*" Then one of them laughed a little and answered in English: "*We are already living our destiny!*" They said it with a sad and regretful tone, as if their fate had been largely sadness and suffering.

Maybe they had to resist with a man up to a certain point and for a long time because they loved him a lot and then, over time, they realized that he was not the blue prince they dreamed about, the man who could deserve them. In the end, the separated mothers would have to raise their children abandoned by the irresponsible fathers, who possibly would have left with other women, perhaps younger or more beautiful, etc.

That is a typical and tragic thing that can happen and often occurs in almost every country and society in the world. There are also, of course, responsible fathers who would never abandon their children or their wives!

I dreamed of another destiny, a destiny full of joy, I wanted to live the fullness of life, I dreamed of realizing myself as an individual and I believe I have succeeded in a great part, now even more, writing this chapter of my first book of life.

How do we manage to live our destiny with which we have always dreamed?

Of course, nothing falls from the sky, the one who does not seek, does not find! Destiny is not a lottery that can be bought at a kiosk and suddenly win the jackpot prize; it is much more than that: it is a work of illusion and passion of a lifetime, a job of building your destiny step by step, day after day until the end, until you reach the goal.

The one who seeks glory and happiness will be able to find several ways that can lead him to the goal. To be able to reach the goal, you must take all the necessary paths and be prudent when choosing: some of them will be good; others will be more difficult, others will be possibly very hard filled with stones and thorns. All of us who want to get there must pass through the different schools of life, these schools can be academic, technical or practical experience, there are positive schools and other negative schools; we can learn from everything. If we know how to get the positive from the negative, one learns from his own mistakes and we can learn much more from the great masters who teach us from their long experience.

Whenever we are about to make an important decision in life, the time comes to know how to say "yes" when it is yes, and how to say "no" when it is a no.

In my life, I have not always accepted my destiny as presented through the different scenarios and situations that we call the stages of life. Naturally, I had to adapt myself to many situations, but I was quick on taking advantage of the opportunities presented to free myself from dependence on others and make the leap and return to myself. Thus I have accepted my destiny and I have sometimes had to take the roads that were inevitable, sometimes I had to live difficult and bitter moments because they were, in one way or another, mandatory. These are the paths we call "the adventures of life", those that led directly or indirectly and unknowingly to the goals of intermediate phases and in the end I was able to reach the place and the position where I had to be in the phase closest to the finish line.

Not everyone is able to jump from a branch of a tree to another one, we can compare life to a tree, where up, in the highest branches, is our goal, the destination to which we aspire to arrive. That destiny does not necessarily mean to become rich or a millionaire, but to become master of oneself and become a star in society, which others can envy, admire and respect.

There are, fortunately or unfortunately, people who do not have this mental flexibility or who do not have what I call "an elastic brain." They usually accept their fate as it appears, stay in the job (the first, second or third job they find) and stay there until retirement. They are not capable of undertaking more adventures, nor of trying to be reborn from their own ashes like the phoenix, nor to make any leap in overcoming their abilities; they are practically slaves to their own decisions and thoughts. They are slaves because they accepted their destiny as presented and did not know to say "no" when it was no and say "yes" when it was yes, but they have responded to almost everything with a "yes" because they are poor in spirit and they are desperate mentally speaking. A self-confident person should never lose hope of being reborn and improved, he must know how to lose to win and say "yes" when yes and say "no" when is no.

These people are afraid of losing their privileges because they think that if they lose some privileges or a job, they will not be able to recover an equal social position. They are afraid to jump into the void, to adventure, with their breasts and faces uncovered, they are afraid of failure, in the end they will fail, they will also triumph as poor rich and resigned.

Many of them consider that they only serve to work as slaves without challenging a boss; it is true that a boss is always right. If you do not accept the rules of the game, you must leave; these are the only two options: take it as it is or leave it ("*take it or leave it!*").

These people, who represent the majority of society, think that the most important thing is to maintain their heritage or their property, to support the family; they have sacrificed their lives for the good of their children so that they have good studies, futures and properties. They have often rejected God and the building of inner glory and have dedicated themselves to building or collecting property, diplomas, and money in bank accounts; it is a totally correct position and worthy of respect of our materialistic world, suitable for people with a medium mental capacity.

But if it were people with a higher IQ, it would not be the right way to think and act. A man or a woman should, by nature, be bigger and stronger than their own destiny and thus could realize themselves as persons, experience happiness and live the life in its fullness. Happiness is not only that of the children or that of the superiors; happiness must also be selfish, because it is also of oneself, it is a sacred good that each one must get to possess, to live and to enjoy; it is not the monopoly of anybody, nor of a leader, nor of a ruler, is a right of every human being.

If a person feels unhappy, it is their own fault, because he did not know how to build his personality. Happiness is to be able to finish each day with satisfaction after a struggle, or to enjoy a well-deserved vacation, a well-deserved rest, or to see the fruit of one's own work, to live it and to enjoy it.

Happiness is to be able to live the dreams of each one.

I have seen many people dream of having a farm with many fruit trees and many animals like chickens, rabbits, goats, horses and even donkeys.

The animal is undoubtedly a good companion of the man who desires it, but of the animal little can be learned! We could also learn from animals, even from ants and their relentless desire to work.

A dog or a cat usually loves its owner, who considers them to be his property. Although man thinks that he is the master, the owner of animals, animals instinctively consider themselves masters of their master, who looks after them as if they were his children. A dog or cat does not grow mentally; it always remains in the same state of instinct, while a human being learns from another human being, a woman or a man, a child, a girl or the elderly.

We must also know that a human being is more important than many things that are part of his life. It is more important than his profession or his job. It is more important that his own company is even more important than his matrimony.

Socrates said: "*My advice is for you to marry: if you find a good wife you will be happy, otherwise you will become a philosopher.*"

They are difficult concepts to accept or understand when we are young and passionate!

Many people think that with marriage begins and ends life. Yes, the life of responsibility begins before the other person, but it is not the whole life of a human being. Life is much more than a matrimony, although a matrimony could last for a lifetime. The proof of this is widows who do not commit suicide (the male widows do not commit suicide), they usually redo their lives as do the divorced people, who find even easier to rebuild their lives, whether they are men or women.

A technician or a free professional will be able to learn many jobs throughout his professional life, he will be able to found and close many companies, he can be employed, placed and lose many jobs, but a person who wants to succeed in life should never get himself lost! The time will come to lose everything, when the old age comes, what was never expected and what cannot be avoided. At the end of a human's life, death is inevitable, all by luck or unfortunately we must die. Although no one likes and nobody wants to imagine or take it for granted, one day he will lose himself as a person and will gain eternal life. At that moment, he will disappear from the world, from his work, from his direct family, from his friends, who would naturally lose a loved one; only the memories, the properties and the companies will remain, but that option must be the last one, since it is also inevitable.

If you want to know about me when I was young, in my far and near past, losing was often a joy. Although I found it difficult to lose, as everyone, I knew that new doors would open later, as when I heard someone close to me say: "After a door that closes, at least two doors open." Fighters should never grieve for losing a job or for having to close our company created for many years where we have put much of our effort and our illusion.

I remember something I read once when I was very young: a scientist and his disciple, who was much younger than the first, worked together as researchers in a large scientific laboratory. One day, as they watched sadly as the fire consumed mercilessly the building of their laboratory and their offices, the senior scientist said to the younger man: "Now it is burning our successes, along with them it is also burning our mistakes. We could rebuild a new laboratory with more successes and with fewer errors!" With this example I learned that losing is often winning, so it is necessary to know how to lose to win so we can have the opportunity and the illusion to rebuild everything again, getting better and making less mistakes.

Now, if we move this philosophy or way of thinking and seeing things in the family, it would be harder to imagine and accept that one day we could lose a loved person, a great friend and, even more difficult, a relative. There are people who overcome it very hard or it is very difficult for them to lose their parents, their father or their mother by the law of life, even more difficult when it comes to a brother..., these are things we could not imagine, but they also happen by law of life. More difficult would be to lose a daughter or a son, those situations are extremely hard and terrible, many are not able to imagine them and few imagine that they could overcome them. But apparently human beings are endowed with a magical force that helps them to overcome all kinds of situations, bitterness and sadness over time!

We only need to look at the current wars of the 21st century, where many adults, children and the elderly die every day, and many families are sadly destroyed.

It is very painful to lose a family member sooner or later. Another pain is the rupture of the sentimental union, to lose the union with a person whom we have always wanted and suddenly happens the day in which we are forced to abandon. It is easier to overcome this last situation than losing a beloved one, a relative, although the two situations can be equally bitter and painful.

Family, friends or loved ones cannot be recovered or re-created; that is impossible in our lives, but the hope that God left us is that the soul does not die and it will continue to live forever.

With age, man tends to stability and serenity, although the older man tends to work more using experience and philosophy instead of using physical strength. Life asks us more and more until a certain age.

God made man in such a fascinating way that He gave him the necessary strength, physical or spiritual, to face adversity and meet his needs in all phases of his life!

> The wise man is the one who knows how to give the necessary energy at every step of his life, in the construction of his own destiny.

> Our destiny depends entirely on ourselves and is in our hands.

Chapter 26: The «synthesis man»

The "synthesis man" is the man pure of spirit, the distilled and refined man, is the essence of the true man in every sense of the word, is the man who had to learn a lot and go through the long schools of life across the world. He is the one who has learned everything and is able to create something out of nothing or very little because he has incarnated, within his own person, all the necessary faculties to be able to do it.

The "synthesis man" is also the man who has learned to love, to be generous and to give from his great heart everything that can serve to others, knowing that they need it.

The "synthesis man" is the man who can move the heavens so that the divinity can answer his questions and can show him the way to follow, is the thoughtful man who has absolute faith in God. This man is able to incite other people to think and believe, is the man capable of changing his destiny, of teaching others how to do it and help them in a disinterested way.

In order to become the "synthesis man", we must be born for it and possess within ourselves an immense capacity that will allow us to realize it. What is normally considered very difficult in the eyes of others is of course a gift of God that allows us to have brilliant ideas, to be inventive, creative and to realize our great dreams of life starting from nothing, from a simple idea and having a generous heart.

Not everyone is able to create something out of nothing, although we are all born with this gift of God, which will allow us someday to become this man or woman, who is the "synthesis man", the man of the dream and the crown of God's creation.

Everything will depend on the person, his conditions and circumstances, will depend on the history of his family, where one has been born and raised, the education that his parents gave him, the mentality and history of the country where he has born, of the city, of the people, of social class, etc. So there are many parameters and factors that could influence the personality and development of this man or woman. But with daily and constant effort everything will be possible, it is also possible to change his deficit trajectory and be able to overcome its own weaknesses.

Who are the ones that can be considered "synthesis men"? The great philosophers, the great masters, the prophets, the Apostles, the great discoverers, the great scientists, the great poets, the great writers and great artists. The memory of those who stood out in society and in history will remain eternal, engraved in historical and literary books, their work will be present and their reference will always be studied.

I may be mistaken —or we- in our judgment about who will be the true "synthesis man"!

We are not judges, only the Creator, God, is the only true judge who will define, after our death, who is the true "synthesis man". Those who have been chosen are those who will sit at His side at the heavenly banquet. Perhaps some of them have not triumphed in this world, in this life, they have only had to suffer and endure their own limitations; those are the true saints like poor Lazarus and many others, those who have been really good. God sees all that and appreciates it even more!

There is also a large part of the people, let us say the majority, who can be called "the carefree ones" or "the comfortable ones", who had no time to think or meditate. They are those who did not want to learn so much, did not want to know much about the things of life in depth, nor sought beyond what they see with their own eyes or what they perceive by their limited imagination. These people have not wanted to see beyond their environment or the ambit where they were born, they did not care about their spiritual dimension, perhaps they lacked this restlessness, perhaps they did not have an elastic brain, nor a golden heart. Their life consisted in vegetating, eating, drinking, sleeping and living his their traditions, also studying at the big universities, earning a lot of money and getting rich. They always needed to have some security and their back covered. Most of these people always needed to stay in their home country, to which they belonged as citizens, to be always protected and relatively close to their family because they were simply afraid to leave, they did it to not get lost!

The adventure of going to live in distant and unknown lands and never to return to their own land after many years of absence is not a speciality of all human beings. There were great travellers, such as Marco Polo, who opened roads in the East, and other solitary travellers who travelled to discover the world, like Christopher Columbus, who intended to travel to India, etc. All these travellers, who were sure of themselves and convinced of their own ideas, had to rely on themselves and with their own abilities, for they had to overcome the difficulties that laid in their way.

The apostles of Jesus left everything behind and went around the world to preach the Gospel of Jesus Christ. At that time, the Apostles had no endorsement, God was their only endorsement. And of course their faith in God and in Jesus Christ helped them through the Holy Spirit; they are the true saints.

Yesterday I spoke with my dear friend Germán Ubillos. I commented on the idea of including in my book the article he wrote about me in the newspaper La Sierra de Madrid on January 16, 1986, more than thirty years ago, and titled **My friend Wangelis**. I asked him for permission to do it.

Here is his affirmative answer, where he says:
«*Dear Wangelis,*

I have read the article I wrote about you and I find it very beautiful, endearing, emotional and positive, the best of our great old friendship, the wonderful heart and Aries we both have.

It is a great joy to me that you are writing, because I know it will be and it is a great joy for you.

Include the article (already published) in your book and, if you want, you can add, in the margin of the text or afterwards, the note that I am enclosing.

A hug from German."

I thank with all my heart for it my great friend German, who is undoubtedly a true "synthesis man" and who has dedicated his whole life to writing and discovering the wonders of this world. His words express his noble character, humble, generous and affectionate, full of love to others.

Germán is a true friend.

The article *My friend Wangelis* will appear at the end of this chapter. I do not know sincerely if it is convenient to put it here or elsewhere, but why not? So I put it, I hope you like it!

Speaking with my friend Germán, I suddenly remembered an English friend who lived in Madrid, in the neighbourhood of Argüelles, above where I lived, in Calle Conde Duque, was rather close to Alberto Aguilera Street. Her name was Paula, she was a little older than me, she was sincere and very affectionate, I remember her typical English skin, white as snow. We used to talk and have coffee or a glass of wine. She was a little distant but a very good person, communicative and intellectual. She was able to read the hands, so she did it once with my hand and said: "You have received very little from your parents and from life. With that little you have received, you have done much!"

These words stuck in my mind, but they were hidden somewhere in my memory. Speaking to my friend Germán, telling him that I wanted to write this chapter specifically (without the title being decided, I already knew its great lines and was in draft form), then came to my mind the memory of the short conversations with Mrs. Paula of England.

Thus we conclude that we all receive something from the life, love and education of our parents, from the teachings in the different schools. If we want to succeed in life, we should try to do much more than the little we have received!

To do much more means: to bear many fruits of our learning and the opportunities, the paths that life gives us and, if we are convinced, we must take them and not be afraid.

My father told me: "**Go to the world, learn everything**". With these few words and this short sentence, I had to create everything from nothing or very little.

Everything has been possible thanks to God and my confidence in Him and thanks to *My dream of Madrid, in December 1981,* which was the key signal. This signal came at the right moment to give me confidence and give me immense strength to continue the fight with dignity until the end, until the promises had been fulfilled with the passage of time.

I invite you to read, at the end of this chapter, the article by Germán Ubillos Orsolich, *My Friend Wangelis*, dated on January 18, 1986.

The article talks about me and describes how I was more than thirty years ago.

Of course, I do not pretend to be the "synthesis man" or to be a hero, but it is my dream to become one, just as it could be the dream of many autodidact thinkers, like some readers who are reading this chapter and wanting to triumph in life, to overcome their own weaknesses and one day reach the glory. I think that is the dream of every human being, because nobody wants to be mediocre, we all want to succeed, but each in his own way and according to his own possibilities.

We all receive something from our parents, some support, although often is not enough. Therefore, we should contribute with something and much more of our part, our spirit.

I remember that when I arrived in Madrid at the end of 1981, I was negotiating with two companies from Chinchón: one belonging to the Rumasa group and the other belonging to the González Byass group, which still exists. I remember that they compared Gonzalez Byass with an elephant that is going slow, heavy and sure. Instead, they compared Rumasa to a tiger, which is rather aggressive, jumps and runs much faster.

The interlocutor, manager of the distillery of Chinchón, of the group González Byass spoke French. As I did not speak Spanish well and he did not understand Portuguese either, we understood in a common language that was French, he had learned French in school and me too.

In the end, after he showed me his distillery at Chinchón and when he learned of my project (I wanted to produce arak of Lebanon in his factory), he said clearly: "But you intend to sell me the label you have in your hand for your arak Al Bacha!" I said: "yes, why not? Where is the problem?"

This label represented my project! Although it was a simple piece of paper, he was not convinced by my idea or project!

In the end, I was able to work with the other Chinchón distillery, which belonged to the Rumasa group. They did accept my project and were convinced of it, and with them I began to work little by little. After a year of starting work, on February 23, 1983, the Rumasa group was expropriated, so all the work and the illusion were in vain! However, this event was not bad, because in the end I could learn from my own mistakes, my disappointments and my failures, from my positive and negative experiences!

Failures are good, belong to the school of life. Without them, the school of life falls short and insufficient.

Who has passed all the exams and was able to win, first, at all stages of his life? Normally, no one!

But there are also excellent children in school, who were lucky enough to live in places where there is peace and their parents were always by their side supporting them and giving them their experience. Children who never had a failure, who then triumphed in their university career, were placed in excellent jobs, married happily and love their partner. But who knows, some day later failures and disappointments may come, it would not be bad, rather, they will be necessary, they will help to grow!

Failures can be professional and even sentimental.

From the failures, the experiences that lead us through the difficult paths are born; this is how we would become true adventurous masters and we could become great professionals.

When we have an ambitious project that convinces us and stimulates us, the project becomes a dream and the will is automatically born, which allows us, together with trust, to believe in ourselves and in our project. In this way we can, through daily effort, realize our dream and leave our masterpiece well finished.

Many times, even absurd, for the simple fact of believing in our project that fills us with enthusiasm and passion, we jump into adventure and jump into the void, we make the "**leap of faith.**" Even if we fail, we must know how to draw conclusions.

If the project that we propose is very little or nothing attractive, even if it has no value in the eyes of others, it will depend on our personality and our will to be able to see its true value and believe in it, to realize it and to carry it out, is like bring a boat to good port.

Usually, a salesman sells himself more than his own project, people buy more the salesman than the product itself.

It only takes the product to be good enough or, better yet, to be excellent, then it will succeed for sure. If not, it will be a pure failure!

The "synthesis man" is the man who performs at every level, who adapts to all circumstances. He is a great life artist; he is a man capable of doing masterpieces.

If we want to incarnate this "synthesis man", we will have to learn many things at once: not only to become a great businessman, an artist, a philosopher, a scientist, a writer or a politician... more than that, we must become worthy before God.

That is why it is first necessary to believe and trust in God. He will guide us and give us the strength and patience that are necessary to be able to forge our future and learn from our mistakes until one day we realize our dreams in life.

This is the "synthesis man". It could be you, it could be me and all those who want to make their big dreams come true.

Mi amigo Wangelis

Apareció en mi vida con la mediación de una máquina tragamonedas. Acaban de tocarle, con gran estruendo, cinco mil pesetas y me invitó a desayunar en el mesón que tengo bajo mi apartamento.

Al principio ofrecí esa resistencia hacia la amistad que mostramos los castellanos, sobre todo si el interlocutor es excesivamente afectivo y locuaz, pero debo reconocer que ganó mi confianza a pulso.

Es un ser generoso y su corazón es de oro, pero posee una fantasía que a veces me preocupa ya que se cree las historias que inventa y temo termine como aquel Alonso Quijano, caballero manchego y sublime paranoico.

Fabrica productos alimenticios, mejor dicho los inventa, inventa sus fórmulas que luego patenta con el objeto de venderlos en el extranjero sobre todo en el próximo oriente. Así, como un Leonardo de Vinci culinario, ha inventado la mantequilla de leche de oveja y de cabra destinada a los países árabes o el fuertísimo anisado «Arak al Bachá», o los polvos de resina para asar la carne que después de espolvoreada sabrá a carne asada a la brasa de leños de pino. La verdad es que hasta ahora ha ganado muy poco dinero con sus inventos y no sé si acabará millonario o teniendo que regresar a su país cargado de deudas.

Es libanés aunque de madre griega. Su país lleva en guerra diez años y él odia la guerra, le espanta, es grandullón y pacífico, como un enorme oso de peluche de ojos saltones y bondadosos.

Al principio no comprendía su manera de pensar, de razonar, era una extraña mezcla de árabe y oriental con aditamentos belgas, pues allí estudió, pero ahora dialogamos ya perfectamente y debo de confesar que enriquece mi vida, me da él a mí, espiritualmente, mucho más de lo que yo pueda ofrecerle. Es vital y sensual, vive al día y no sabe si el mes que viene tendrá para comer o para pagar su apartamento, pero ama la vida y lucha con tenacidad, sabe siete lenguas y posee cuando habla un gracioso seseo extranjero. Es muy sentimental y sensible y Aries, como yo, creo que nos parecemos y a veces nos enfadamos pero pronto se nos pasa y nos tendemos la mano. Yo soy más intelectual, más ilustrado, él ha vivido en muchos países, en Brasil, es un niño grande de cien experiencias con algo de fenicio, de comerciante nato.

Creo que lo más tremendo de la vida es la monotonía por eso Wangelis ha traído sal y aire puro a mis relaciones sociales. Las cenas en su apartamento tomando ensaladas de repollo o salsa de puré de garbanzos y obleas de pan ázimo son pintorescas, pintorescas como el edificio que habita donde los ocupantes de cada «estudio» van y vienen a su antojo y se reunen y entran y salen. Allí conocí a Silvie, la modelo francesa, a Marisa, la filósofa, a Carol la locutora de radio, a Paco el fotógrafo y sus bellísimas adolescentes, a Nikos, Dimitri y Vasilis, los griegos, una verdadera lluvia policroma que expande el alma; las charletas y tertulias son deliciosas, igual hablan en francés, inglés, árabe, griego o turco, y uno se siente querido y valorado. Todo eso y mucho más me ha traído Wangelis, mi amigo libanés.

Cuando ve a una chica guapa me dice al oído «se come, se come», con su acento extranjero, otras veces sonríe y dice «primero se adoran y después se sacrifican», hay en sus dichos algo de maya o azteca, hasta de antropofagia brasileña. Yo me río y disfruto con esta lluvia exótica y vivificante, pienso que muchos españoles deberíamos aprender de Wangelis, ese milagro cotidiano hecho de alegría, fantasía y riesgo.

Germán UBILLOS
ORSOLICH

My friend Wangelis

He appeared in my life with the mediation of a slot machine. He just won five thousand pesetas, with a great rumble, and he invited me to have breakfast at the inn that I have under my apartment.

At the beginning I offered this resistance to the friendship shown by the Castilians, especially if the interlocutor is excessively affectionate and talkative, but I must admit that he earned my confidence to pulse.

He is a generous being and his heart is golden pure, but he has a fantasy that sometimes worries me because he believes the stories he invents and I fear he would end up like that Alonso Quijano, a man from La Mancha and a sublime paranoid.

He manufactures foodstuffs, rather he invents them, he invents its formulas that later patents with the object of selling them abroad, especially in the near east. Thus, as a culinary Leonardo de Vinci, he invented sheep's milk and goat's milk butter destined for the Arab countries or the very strong aniseed licor "Arak al Bachá", or the resin powders to roast the meat that after being sprinkled will have the taste of meat roasted using pine logs.

The truth is that until now he has made very little money with his inventions and I do not know if he will end up as a millionaire or if he will have to return to his country loaded with debts.

He is a Lebanese, but his mother is Greek. His country has been at war for ten years and he hates war, he is frightened about it, he is big and peaceful, like a huge teddy bear with bulging and kind eyes.

At first I did not understand his way of thinking, of reasoning, it was a strange mixture of Arabic and Oriental with Belgian additions, as he studied there, but now we are already perfectly talking and I must confess that he enriches my life, he gives me, spiritually, a lot more than I can offer to him. He is vital and sensual, lives up to date and does not know if next month he will have enough money to eat or to pay for his apartment, but loves life and struggle with tenacity, he knows seven languages and when he speaks he has a funny foreign accent. He is very sentimental and sensitive. Aries, like me, I think we look alike and sometimes we get angry but soon it passes by and we reach out. I am more intellectual, more enlightened, he has lived in many countries, in Brazil, is a big child of a hundred experiences with something of Phoenician, of born merchant.

I think the most tremendous thing in life is the monotony that is why Wangelis has brought salt and pure air to my social relations. The dinners in his apartment, taking salads of cabbage or sauce of Chickpeas purée and wafers of unleavened bread are picturesque, as picturesque as the building that inhabits where the occupants of each "studio" come and go at will and meet and enter and they leave. There I met Silvie, the French model; Marisa, the philosopher; Carol, the radio announcer; Paco, the photographer and his beautiful teenagers; Nikos, Dimitri and Vasilis, the Greeks; a true polychrome rain that expands the soul; the talks were delicious, they speak French, English, Arabic, Greek or Turkish, and you feel loved and valued.

All this and much more has brought me Wangelis, my Lebanese friend.

When he sees a beautiful girl he tells me in the ear "she can be eaten, she can be eaten", with his foreign accent, sometimes he smiles and says "first they are worshiped and then they are sacrificed", there is in his sayings something of Maya or Aztec, even of Brazilian anthropophagy. I laugh and enjoy this exotic and vivifying rain, I think that many Spaniards should learn from Wangelis, that everyday miracle made of joy, fantasy and risk.

Germán UBILLOS ORSOLICH

Chapter 27: Returning to yourself will keep you young in spirit

It is very important to return to oneself.

It is a necessary therapy that must be constantly practiced and throughout the life of a human being, even the animals return to themselves.

If we look well at domestic animals, they are quite independent. Although they need to be close to their master, they also escape from time to time to return to themselves, to the nature from which they have come and that is their natural environment. They try to return to their wild origin, they seek to find specific herbs necessary for their organism, they instinctively hunt small animals that are part of their original feeding or they simply spin around themselves in the earth to feel totally free in the nature.

The worst thing in life is not being able to live according to your own ideas, with your own nature and not being able to constantly evolve.

The examples I could give are many...

<u>First, we have to observe the degree of satisfaction of individuals.</u>

There is a part of society that are generally people with an average IQ and who, in the end, are not happy or satisfied with themselves for the simple fact that they did not have time to think, to meditate, to look for themselves, to seek God, to seek the true love and thus be able to return to themselves.

They think they have neither soul nor spirit!

They appear to be happy and express it with a false smile that hides behind a deep sadness that comes from their great disconnection with reality.

They are individuals (men and women) who do not know or have not learned to think in depth, they remain in superficiality. I think it is a problem of education that usually comes from the parents, because children often instinctively imitate their parents. If the parents did not have the time to think and did not have the faculties for it, the children usually do the same simply because of pride, for wanting to maintain the family tradition! They fall into a very serious error!

If your father or mother did not know how to do things well in life, why do you want to do the same thing and repeat the same mistake? Normally, if you are intelligent and evolutionary, you should do better and even much better than them!

If your parents were wrong, you should not repeat their mistakes!

It is possible that what I call an elastic brain were missing on the parents or also continues to miss on the children equally, or perhaps both generations have limited imagination! They usually live to work, eat, drink and sleep, earn money and keep it, follow their traditions and they also enjoy life. In addition, they talk about feelings that animals also have: love, affection and family, that's it! They think that philosophy is a waste of time and that God does not exist, they do not overthink about it, their life is transformed into a spiritual vacuum and they live in a totally materialistic world. They lose their spiritual sensibility, they forget that they are spirit and they become obsessed with money, with power, with properties... and they exteriorize it with sarcasm and terrible arrogance. They want to get the world, they want to get the best jobs, they have the clear goal of getting richer and stronger. It is a very serious disease that affects a considerable part of the world society, it is a both psychological and spiritual disease, probably difficult to cure, but of course everything in life has a cure, less death, which has no cure!

On the other hand, there are other kinds of individuals in our society:

Those who are sadly frustrated because they do not get more than they can, think that the foreigner is to blame for their failure, even if it is a countryman newly installed in his country. These people think that he came to take the bread from their mouths, as the Germans say "*Lassen Sie sich nicht die Butter vom Brot nehmen*", which means: "Do not let the butter be removed from your bread!" They put on this long and hard face, they do not know how to greet or smile at another human being who crosses their path, because they themselves are not happy inwardly, that is what I observe in some villages...

Fortunately, on the other hand, there are many free and satisfied people inside of themselves; you can see that from the outside and in the behavior of those people.

I have just given two negative examples: These two groups of individuals represent in their totality (perhaps ten or twenty percent of world society) the negative cases, because they look for the negative within the positive, they have stones in their hearts, stones which prevent them from feeling and believing that there is something beyond what is seen with natural eyes. They have the mind, the eyes and the ears covered, they are usually generally racist, chauvinistic, omnipotent, selfish and materialistic. In my opinion, they are human monsters because of their insensitivity; they are also -and unknowingly- disciples and slaves of the prince of darkness, Satan! They have no respect for God or divinity; they are usually the stupid class of atheists, who are the ignorant. They often do not want to baptize their children, thinking that it is a decision that they should take when they are adults, which in my opinion is a serious mistake! Thus children are raised without God, and when they become adults, it is rare for them to return to God; Satan will have had time to do his work and prevent them from returning to God, from where they have come and where they will one day have to return!

Feelings and spiritual education are forged from childhood. It is the same as if we wanted to school a child from the age of puberty (when he turns fourteen), you cannot teach him practically anything! He will not understand anything, unfortunately it will be too late! The same thing happens with faith in God: it is a feeling that must be cultivated from childhood. Trees cannot grow on their own, they must be attached to a stick or a stick to grow straight, otherwise, they will come out crooked; likewise is in the education of the children, whether educational, civic, scientific, literary, artistic or spiritual; in the same way happens with memory and intelligence, are faculties that must be cultivated from childhood.

Now we move on to the good and positive part of human society:

They are the good ones who are not convinced that God exists, they do not see it manifest in their life, they are also called "agnostics" (those who do not recognize or do not know God), they could also be called "atheists" as they do not have a relationship with God. They are generally good and wonderful people, they are usually respectful, educated, sensitive and intelligent. Those end up eventually returning to belief in God and will one day have faith in His power.

Those good atheists are the great majority of society, taking away believers, who are fewer and fewer. Good atheists do not practice any religion, but they want to baptize their children, they also want them to make the first communion in the Catholic Church, to which most of the Spanish people belong, they are Catholics by tradition, even if they are not practitioners. In Europe, there are countries where most of the inhabitants are Catholics, others are Orthodox, Protestant, Anglican, etc.

Those whom we call "non-practicing Christians" or "average atheists" often have respect for God and the teaching of Jesus Christ, but each one understands God in his own way because they have no time to meditate! The companies where they work as professionals, require a lot of sacrifice and dedication, they have very little time left for themselves, they have only the weekend to rest and vacations to take advantage of and go there somewhere to forget the weight of routine and daily and continuous stress.

To those good and sensitive people whom I address in particular, among others, to tell them not to lose hope in God and in His son, Jesus Christ, and that they should continue to seek God. If they could not find Him in their Catholic, Orthodox, Evangelical, or Anglican Church, they will certainly be able to find

Him somewhere they did not expect or imagine, somewhere holy and humble, just as when the Three Wise Men came to seek the King of the Jews, who was born in Jerusalem and who was Jesus, who was born in Bethlehem, found him in a stable, in a humble place, stood there and worshiped him.

A couple of years ago I was in Vigo, it is a large city of Galicia, which is in northwest Spain, on the Atlantic coast. I was in a hotel with a client of mine from Sub-Saharan Africa, from Benin, who is called Monsieur Yaya, it is an African name of Arab origin; it comes from "Yahya". We were talking, my client and I, as we got off the elevator. As we were very focused on our conversation, we ignored a Galician gentleman who was also in the elevator, and we did not greet him, it was rude of us! The Galician gentleman politely said in a slightly angry tone: "But there is not even a good morning!" Vigo is a civilized city and people greet one another, even if they do not know each other; so we learned this great lesson for the next time: I said "good morning" and I apologized!

On the island of Crete, people greet each other even if they do not know each other and do not put on that stupid face that we see in some isolated villages. On the contrary, you can see the smile on the face of the people; foreigners are always welcome on the island of Crete!

This unsatisfied majority are usually stupid, as my neighbour, Tomas who has recently moved here, in front of my house. He lived before in Benidorm, where he had a business facing the public, a stationer's shop or something like that. Tomas said to me, "Those who do not say hello are really stupid!" I believe that they do not have an elastic brain that allows them to see beyond their nose, they have been unwittingly or almost always slave to their own decisions, they have chosen a job because of obligation or necessity, there was no other option, because it was the only available one and they had to stay in the same job and endure a boss tyrant, the same for a lifetime. I think it is better to be a slave to freedom and constant change, which will certainly give oxygen to our spirit so we can breathe and keep ourselves young in spirit.

Those ignorant people did not look for God either because they considered that simply God does not exist because, in their little brains and imaginations, if God really existed, He should give them everything: money, cars, palaces... even airplanes! They imagine that God should be like a Swiss bank, full of money, that will give them money, health, love and life for all of them. As they have not understood or wanted to understand, since they cannot think of ten things at once, they cannot even think of one thing! Neither could they feel God's love for men; they were only concerned about one thing, or rather three things:

family, money and pride, with which they repair their inferiority complex.

They think that the family is sacred; they do not remember that they were born alone and will someday die alone, although their family has sustained them for many years or supported almost a lifetime. In eternity, there is no family grouping, souls are grouped according to the gravity of the sins committed on earth, there are like large prisons where the prisoners are in large cells according to their category.

Money has been created by man as a reference for change, that is, to exchange money for gold, for silver or for any merchandise: object, food, service, property, to pay taxes, to pay for travel... But money does not serve to pay for freedom and to get out of slavery nor can buy happiness, those two things are won with the mind and heart. Neither can they buy with money the pardon, the love of God, nor the respect of the others.

Pride is useless, it is a mask for the arrogant, who do not want to respect the order of the universe, which has been created by God, do not know that it is necessary to put God and truth above all things in life. Pride is a sign of inferiority complex that is externalized with a feeling of superiority; respect is won with kindness and humility and cannot be demanded. If one is mistaken, he will first have to apologize, acknowledge his error first and be willing to pay damages, so that his conscience will remain calm. Apart from this, he will have to learn from his mistakes, change his posture and evolve as a human being. Thus others will respect him, because they will say: "This man is honest, he has worked on himself and changed for the better, therefore he deserves all respect."

Returning to oneself releases the spirit; that is why the free people in their spiritual consciousness remain young in spirit. If you are free and young in spirit, you can get to perform as a person at any time of life and even in old age.

If you are not free in spirit, you will fail as a free man and working as a slave will burn you. Although you can become rich in money and poor in spirit, it will not serve you, it will not be any triumph, it is necessary that your spiritual life is rich before your material life. However, they could perfectly coexist the two riches provided that, when you are materially richer, you can transmit it spiritually and make more people happy around you with your generosity, your affection, your sacrificed time and your money given. That way you will help more people as you can give more of yourself materially and spiritually.

Noble or precious metals cannot be burned: gold melts with the heat of the fire, but it cannot be burned, while mercury, copper and iron can burn. In other words, metals that easily oxidize can burn and react with the oxygen from the air or with fire; whereas noble and precious metals like silver, gold, platinum... cannot be oxidized or burned.

If you consider yourself precious, you should not let life and your circumstances burn you, nor let others burn for you, for your wrong and unjust position towards others!

You have to be firm in your position, you must remain a young and free man; you can be the example for others to learn from your philosophy.

When you see that you are about to burn, change course, present your resignation at work, and leave a place or a country where you suffer injustice, where you do not feel fulfilled, since suffering is not good, that is the sign that something is wrong in your life.

Stress is not the same as suffering. You can live with stress by having an elastic brain, like an elastic motor that can rotate a thousand revolutions, two thousand revolutions to drive the turbo, and three thousand or four thousand revolutions when necessary!

Your brain is like an engine that produces universal and creative energy, and that helps you to have brilliant ideas in every situation of life; all that will help you get back to yourself.

To return to oneself, one must get away from the routine, since it burns with time, and also move away from imbeciles and hypocrites. Imagine that we were surrounded by imbeciles or hypocrites, our life would look like hell, because you cannot live with the insane or false or liars. It is necessary that we share our life with good, healthy, honest and intelligent people, with them we can live, we will have happiness and freedom of spirit and we will feel young in spirit.

Changing the air helps to return to oneself, as well as occasionally go to see a theatre performance or go to the cinema to watch a movie, or stay with a friend and talk about things that give joy to the heart.

Other ways to get back to oneself are learning a new art, learning a new language, learning how to play a musical instrument, to try to write a book, to paint a picture... All this helps us to return to ourselves and keep our young spirit.

Knowing new people, taking care of others and trying to help them without any personal interest helps without a doubt to return to oneself.

It is also very important to repair one's past: Reconciling oneself with one's past and recognizing one's guilt will help to free oneself from the burdens and guilt of the past.

A vacation helps to get away from the forest and to see it better. When we move away from our world and daily stress, where routine is also, our spirit rests and begins to see things better and as they are. There, in the place of holidays and afar, we began to meditate on the things that weigh us down and to see everything better and more clearly, with a freer and more open philosophical spirit.

From the island of Crete and its capital, Heraklion, I had the idea of writing this book of life, which has returned me to myself.

It is important to return to one's roots, but where they really are, it is in our cultural, ethnic roots, that will certainly help us to identify ourselves. But I believe that every human being is a world, surely we are not a flock of lambs or goats, we humans are something more than that!

To return to oneself is to be born again of water and spirit, is to return to the teaching of Jesus Christ and the Apostles. We need, from time to time, to hear the word of God that comes from a true altar of grace and receive the true sacraments. That will help us to free ourselves from the evil spiritual burdens, it will also help us to free our soul from the burdens of daily life and thus we can return to ourselves or, rather, to return to God, where we come from and where we are going.

Returning to oneself helps to see one's own defects and mistakes, occasionally looking in the mirror to try to do things better and better, to work on oneself and to let the work do its job. In other words, let God do his work in our soul and in our life.

Returning to oneself is to discover oneself.

The "know thyself" is what Socrates practiced in the ancient Greek philosophy. This practice helps us to discover new talents hidden within ourselves that allow us to embark on new paths to achieve ourselves more and more, to go much further, where our imagination can reach, and to realize our great dreams in life.

Returning to oneself is a necessity of the spirit and soul.

Returning to yourself will keep you young in spirit.

Chapter 28: Straddling between Spain and Germany, 1987-1989

Here I am going to talk about a long passage of my life, passed between Spain and Germany, where many things happened. I will tell you about the most outstanding situations and experiences, those that come to my mind and memory, those difficult times of my life, when I was no longer single, but married and father of a son, which I still am.

In October 1987, my son Alexandros had just been born and he was only a few months old. Now, at the date of publication of this book, he will be thirty years old and no longer need me physically and less materially, but I believe he will continue needing me spiritually and emotionally just as before because a father never ceases to be a father. We learn this from our parents and also from the parable of the Prodigal Son, which is told in the Gospel of Jesus Christ. The Prodigal Son returned to his father's house, in this case reference is made to the house of our heavenly father, who is the beloved God the Father to all human beings. Jesus Christ also returned to his father God. We humans have a soul that belongs to God. Therefore, it is our duty to recognize God the Father and return one day to our Heavenly Father with the help of our great brother, our Lord Jesus Christ.

I remember when I returned from Madrid to Düsseldorf, in October 1987, after the trip to Madrid I made from Germany, where I lived by life circumstances. I had traveled to Madrid to meet with the owners of the Matute jewellery factory and the Catalan consultant, Mr. Fidel, who had chosen me from more than a hundred professionals who had applied for that position. I lived since the end of 1986 in Germany, because of my new German family. This was meant to be my first job as a professional, as a representative of the Spanish factory Matute, for the sales of their fashion jewellery products in Germany.

I remember that I had not negotiated any clear or special conditions on my base salary, nor on my commissions for sales, or anything like that! I had preferred to leave these matters after a certain time, once they could see a palpable success in my sales and that the minimum goals marked had been reached, so that those who had employed me could clearly see devotion and professionalism in my work! I remember that they bought me a one-way ticket Madrid-Düsseldorf, they also gave me enough money to provide funds for the expenses of future trips, so that I could visit interested customers in Germany. They also gave me many catalogues and a large box like a trunk type briefcase that was filled with samples of fashion jewelry to show them to customers. I just wanted to work for a Spanish company and nothing more, so that one day, soon, I could go with my head held high to my dear Spain and thus be able to honestly leave the great prison that Germany was for me, where I really felt as a prisoner, just as I felt imprisoned in Lebanon after the civil war broke out in 1974, but those two feelings were different! Places or countries can become large prisons if a person does not feel comfortable or free to perform as a person and live according to his ideas. I was very sad in Germany and I did not see any possibility of evolving under the conditions I had, neither in the short term nor in the long term. My hands were practically tied, without any freedom of action or initiative. I felt like a man trapped in my mind and in my imagination, in my fantasy and my illusion. It was the mood of a prisoner, quite the opposite of a free man!

Now thirty years have passed since that time, which was the most difficult time of my life, when I had to take my first steps as a married man, when I was in charge of a family and a newborn son. Now I feel at last totally free and calm, in every sense of the word, I can plan my time and my future as I see it convenient. I do not have to give an account to anyone, only God and myself, and of course the companies with which I am working and with which I am committed, those who trust me and are hoping to have positive results with my work and my business trips. I also have to give accounts naturally to my wife Marina, who expects a lot from me, even though they are totally different concepts!

I remember thirty years ago, at the end of 1987, when I began my work of introducing Matute fashion jewelry to the German market. The task was not easy, as the German saying goes: "*Aller Anfang ist schwer!*" which means in English: "Every beginning is difficult!" So it is in all principles and in any new sales work, whatever the epoch is! It has always been difficult for all generations, especially in this particular case, when the products I offered to the German market were not attractive enough, and if it was, it was not well presented. I had to rely on my own imagination and imagination to know how to present the product. Using my own ideas and improvisations, I had to think and invent the proper way of presenting the product to the clients to surprise them, seduce them and make them fall in love with the collections of the Matute costume jewelry. With the new ideas, I had to make them see it as a unique opportunity, to take it and not let it escape!

Most of the people who eventually bought wanted to support me in one way or another. That is why they bought what I offered them when they saw the enthusiasm with which I proposed them to see the products and their qualities, they often bought the seller rather than the product. They did not know if they could sell it in their market or not, but it was almost the same for them!

Germany was living in a time of great prosperity, people were earning a lot of money and expenses were not as high as now, nor fixed costs, nor social security for workers, nor direct and indirect taxes. At this time, in the late 1980s, the German entrepreneur who was a bit intelligent, let's say professional enough and who knew how to work and organize, could easily earn a lot of money because fixed expenses were low and taxes too. Right now, in our time, in Europe, the opposite is true: let us win what we win, we have a partner that is the state, whether we want it or not. We have to pay very high direct and indirect taxes and our fixed expenses are also very high; so if we earn as entrepreneurs about five thousand euros gross a month, at the end of the month we maybe will have two thousand euros, which is a misery of money for an entrepreneur with all his work, structure, responsibility and daily sacrifice! The account is easy and depends on what we win and what we spend. Therefore, we will need to earn a lot of money to live well and save for unforeseen expenses and for old age, which is not obvious or easy to get, I would say today is practically impossible !, especially when we look at the global crises, which accumulate over each other...

At that time, there was no war at the gates of Europe, there was still the Soviet Union and the Iron Curtain, the Cold War and the Middle East War and some conflict there, and it was over, there was no more... So nobody spoke about war, Europe lived in peace...

At that time, the use of the fax was not common, the fax only existed in the big companies. Medium-sized companies used the classic and old telex, which in the end was quickly obsolete. It was a telegraphic device of data transmission, it is like a typewriter, after writing a text is saved, is recorded in a perforated band that is sent by a telex line, the recipient will receive the identical text. Those who did not have telexes or faxes used the letters that they sent by mail and they used as support the fixed telephone to speak, to communicate and to confirm, the said word was worth a lot. The mobile phone did not exist either, some rich people had a mobile phone in their car, but it was a strange thing to see, although it existed at the level of millionaire people or big businessmen. Faxing existed in post offices, as well as in large companies.

At first, in my work selling the Matute fashion jewellry, I had to think about how to organize myself. My father taught me and said to me: "Use your brain before using your body," he wanted to say to me: "First think and then act." Unfortunately, many people do it the other way round, first they work on what they have not well thought about, then they think about what they have worked and realize they did it wrong, when it is really too late! This also happens a lot in politics; many politicians make decisions and make big projects with euphoria or personal interest. If they worked thinking with their heads and hearts before moving on to action or executing their projects, they would do useful and wonderful things for their people.

My former German family, I mean my wife and my in-laws at the time, did not have enough experience or enough courage to help me write a text or a letter to clients for the first contact. In Germany, not everyone feels free to have their own initiative, everyone has to respect rules that limit their action and evolution. The Germans have to obey a boss and rules already instituted by the laws, so the personality is not free, is tied and paralyzed because of the system that limits their freedom of action, they almost only receive orders! Protesting a boss automatically means losing the job!

In Germany, there are few Greek Zorbas and, perhaps, there are fewer Greek-Lebanese Wangelis! The Zorbas and Wangelis will have to leave sooner or later to be free and to reach fullness in a free world.

And from there, from the city of Heraklion, from the island of Crete, launch their philosophical message to Germany and to all the peoples of the world!

I wanted to show the variety of Matute products to the customers I was planning to visit and to show them the collection of samples and catalogues. My goal was to send a series of written letters by mail, on the letterhead left by the Matute company. I remember it was a letterhead with a very nice logo, a good DIN A4 white laminated paper, with the bust of Nefertiti up on the letterhead, the famous Pharaonic queen, in turquoise and gold, that gave a sensational image of the product. I remembered the memory of my trip to the island of Salamis in 1966, our visit with my sister Ketty and the Greek couple to the Greco-Roman Museum of Alexandria, Egypt, where I saw many pieces of gold matte jewelry with turquoise gemstones. The letterhead with the Matute logo was very seductive and deceptive at first sight, it was one of my fighting weapons; my business card had the same Nefertiti logo. The collection was really beautiful and extravagant, it was a novelty at the time, the zamak leather and metal costume jewelry remembered the pharaonic era of Ancient Egypt. Zamak is a zinc metal alloy with aluminum, magnesium and copper, is a light alloy, is a cheaper alternative than brass, weighs much less and can melt at less temperature, which makes zamak to be easier to work with automatic machinery and with rubber moulds.

The Matute brothers formerly were craftsmen, they sold their jewelry in the Rastro of Madrid, which is the most important market, held on Sundays in old Madrid, in the neighbourhood of La Latina, near the Plaza Mayor. They manually did everything; they went from being craftsmen to being manufacturers.

I collected from the Chamber of Commerce of the city where I lived, from Braunschweig, some addresses of manufacturers and large jewelry stores in Frankfurt, Hamburg and other big cities in Germany. Then, in order to prepare and write a model letter, I had no choice but to ask my ex-teacher Helga for help. She was very kind to me and wrote me an excellent letter that gave a very good image, so I could send some twenty letters. After a few days came some answers, I had to call the ones I had written one by one; I asked them if they had received my letter, etc. It was an unimaginable job to do today, no one wants to read more letters that come from unknown people, not even e-mails, we eliminate them right away; no one has time to start a conversation over the phone during working hours! At that time, there was no globalization or stress. Helga was my ex-teacher of German for foreigners at the town hall school, which is called the *Volkshochschule*, or "school for adults." She was very appreciative and helped me with interest in writing the letter. My family and I kept with Helga a certain friendship and she came once to visit us and to eat at our house in Stiddien, which is a small village in the west of Braunshweig. Helga was very nice and very cultured, she knew about letters and philology, she was very interested in politics, etc. She was also an inspired artist, an oil painter, I remember that she had done an oil painting of the portrait of my face and bust; I was an interesting person for her to paint, something rare to find. She proposed to give me private lessons in exchange for posing for her, so she could paint my portrait and I accepted. I have never seen the painting finished; I think it was exhibited in an art gallery in the city of Braunschweig.

Helga wrote an excellent text, very well written in German, and I made of it a model letter, like a template that I had to print with a photocopier on Matute letterhead. Then I sent about twenty letters to different recipients, who were distributors of jewelry, fashion, or leather goods. Many of them seriously took my presentation letter of Matute products.

After a while, I had the luck of the beginner, although I was a born salesman, as described by my dear friend, the writer Germán Ubillos, in his article in the newspaper *La Sierra de Madrid*, in January 1986, which you can find in the end of chapter 26, *The synthesis man*. I remember that once when I was very young and when I started selling, I was only about fourteen or fifteen years old, it was the first time I wanted to sell alone the whisky made by my father. The customer in question was a big strong man in his forties, had a food and drink shop or maybe a bar, I do not remember exactly, but I remember very well his bookshelf where he had the bottles, which were placed straight. The man tasted my father's *whisky*, it was not good enough for him; he said he did not like it, that it was not good! I answered and I told him that I did not know the taste of his mouth, my spontaneous response made him very angry, it seemed a great offense to him, a great insult and that I was very rude! He almost got aggressive with me and wanted to kick me out of his store, I had to run away. And I learned from this rather negative experience to treat clients with more courtesy and diplomacy. It was a life lesson for the upcoming sales. I think the art of the good salesman is to know how to present the product and possess the art of creating the interest, so you can introduce the product little by little into the customer's mind. The seller should be indirectly guiding the client on his tasting, giving him more and more valid arguments to convince him, let him decide for himself and support him in his final decision, whatever it may be, because the indecisive client, once convinced of the product, will buy it by himself! And, if the product does not convince him, he will never buy it! Let the customer be free and not pressured to make his own decision and help him, without realizing it, to make the decision that suits the seller!

The beginning of my new job was very difficult; I had to make many trips to different parts of Germany. I traveled first to Hamburg without success; then to Offenbach, which is a small town near Frankfurt, famous for the fair and leather goods industry, but there was no interest by the customer. I remember that he told me about a holiday trip he made to the island of Cyprus and complained that the food did not have the right temperature, what should be hot was cold and vice versa! Since then, I learned that the dishes should have their proper temperature. Afterwards, I went to visit the famous fashion fair in Düsseldorf, called 'Igedo' or *'Collection premiere Düsseldorf*. There all the women were very pretty and very elegant, well dressed, like the men, all chic *à la mode*. But unfortunately I had no success, no one bought me and I could not make good contacts. Someone advised me to go to the Munich fashion fair, which is called "*Modewoche München*", which I believe had its date in February and which I visited after time, at the beginning of next new year 1988. I was constantly struggling until one day suddenly the beginner's luck came when I did not expect it: young clients, who were half crazy, saw the fashion jewellery of Matute. They were blond men with pigtails in their hair, like *hippies*, the two of big stature, they were perhaps brothers, they were distributors of custom jewellry in Frankfurt, they imported from outside, I think from Asia, and they seemed to earn a lot of money. Seeing the Matute fashion jewelry, they went crazy; they liked almost all the jewelry: the earrings, the bracelets, the pendants..., they even liked the leather belts. They made a great request, they faxed me to a fax number that I had to ask Javier, who is one of the Matute brothers and who was the commercial director of the Matute company. Javier gave me the fax number of a friend of hers who had a fax just installed. These customers placed a large order of approximate value 50,000 DM -more or less- I do not remember exactly, they bought everything and hundreds of belts. With this request, the Matute brothers were very happy and thankful for my efforts, so they continued to send me money for my travel expenses; the postman came to our Stiddien house to pay me money for the cash transfer. After this luck, I discovered little by little where I could offer and sell better Matute jewellry: in a town near the town of Kaufbeuren, which is a small town near Augsburg, near Munich from Stuttgart. Next to Kaufbeuren there was a village called Neugablonz, in the Allgäu area of southern Germany. The name of Neugablonz refers to a German city called Gablonz, which was a city in Germany of the Third Reich in the Sudeten. Today it is called Jablonec and it is a small city of the Czech Republic, where the Czech Bohemia crystal that contains lead continues to be manufactured, Jablonec is famous for this industry. The Germans who left Gablonz to southern Germany because of the Sudeten crisis created a new Gablonz, which they called Neugablonz. There, in this small town, they manufacture the same thing they used to make in Bohemia: jewellry with Bohemian glass and other handmade crystals that imitate diamonds and precious stones. The Swarovski is the best known and is exceptionally manufactured in Austria.

In order to sell the Matute jewellry, I made my trips with the famous Intercity train, ICE or Intercity-Express, it was the fastest train of those times, it was about 120 kilometers per hour, and it stopped only in the big cities, from there came the name Intercity. I had a great time traveling on this train, the only sad part was when I got on the train from Braunschweig railway station, which is called in German *Bahnhof* or railway station as RENFE here in Spain. People were getting on the Braunschweig train, which was going to stop first in the city of Göttingen; the second station was in the city of Fulda, a small catholic city of the state of Hessen, which has as capital the city of Frankfurt. The people who came from Braunschweig and traveled to Fulda generally went up early in the morning with long, serious faces, then in Fulda a lot of people got off the train and others came up to go to Stuttgart and Munich. I noticed that these people had a totally different expression, relaxed and much more joyful, already the rays of sun could be felt and the weather became warmer. People would smile and greet me and I could start some conversation with some of them, no matter if they were young or old, people were much more open and relaxed, open to dialogue and conversation. Inside the train, there was a corridor that communicated with the cabins, as if they were rooms with interior doors. In each cabin, there were four to six people; I liked to have conversations with some passengers of different classes. After the stop in Fulda, the Intercity train became joyful; it was for me a place of social relation and dialogue, as was the Agora of Athens for Socrates.

There, in Kaufbeuren, I slept in the Hotel Hasen, which was a central city hotel, the people of the hotel knew me, and there they served very good typical Bavarian food. Once in the evening at the hotel restaurant I met two Jewish men from Lebanon, I talked to them in Lebanese Arabic, they lived in Canada, they could not believe or imagine that I was still with my passport from Lebanon, it seemed very strange and incomprehensible for them! It was really very difficult to travel the world with a Lebanese passport and I think it is the same thing now, although the Lebanese war has ended many years ago. To travel through Europe and other Western destinations, the Lebanese need a visa, now perhaps it is easier with the

Schengen visa, it is valid for all the European Union countries, except the United Kingdom, in addition the latter will soon leave the European Union with the famous Brexit that takes its name from British Exit. I remember that there was always a large colony of Lebanese Jews in Lebanon who lived very comfortably, they mostly had good business and good social and economic positions. When the war broke out in the mid-1970s, Jews mostly had their businesses, schools, synagogues and cultural centers in a central neighbourhood of Beirut called *Wadi Abou Jmil*, which stood just in the line of demarcation of the war of Beirut, where combatants of the two sides fought against each other. Most of the Jews in Beirut had to leave and migrate quickly to various destinations where they had relatives, especially the United States, Canada or Brazil, some of them also went to Berlin, Germany, where there is now a large Jewish colony. According to current statistics, very few Jews currently live in Lebanon, although they were once an integral part of the Lebanese multicultural society; the Hebrew religion is one of the eighteen officially recognized confessions in Lebanon.

In the end I was quite successful selling fashion jewelry, since the manufacturers of Neugablonz liked Matute jewellry very much because it was totally different from what they made. Some of them seemed to find it as a very attractive and extravagant collection, they made orders and they paid them in the bank against delivery of documents or by advance payment. Unfortunately no one repeated, the quality of the samples was good, but then the quality of the delivered goods was not satisfactory and always left something missing. Customers made many complaints. The Matute company had long had a technical breakdown and had called on some Catalan consultants whose job was to tease their clients, who were economically ill patients. The objective of the consultants was the same work as the vultures camouflaged in professionals: they made the most of their money professionally before their impending death, gave them instructions on how to do a new *marketing*, tried to change their personality to make them mad, created a new profile, changed the company logo, made new business cards, a new letterhead, employed new professional directors, took them to expensive international fairs, created a new distribution of franchises, indirectly forced them to request more credits to the banks... All these actions were to keep them excited, hoping that someday everything would work very well! But it was really late and everything went from bad to worse! It could not work because the foundation of the business was already rotten due to the big financial hole. In general, when a company asks the help of consultants is because everything is going really bad, they owe money to all suppliers and banks, they do not know how to bring the business afloat again! The consultants passed astronomical bills for their fees, their minutes and hours of work. Shortly thereafter, the company in full agony entered the state of coma; then came the second phase, which is the official or technical bankruptcy, that is, the competition of creditors, when the company passes into the hands of a manager who is responsible for dismantling it, sell all the property at auction and bury it. All that talking in general!

In the particular case of the Matute company, it is that they could not pay well to the assemblers who worked from their homes and manually assemble the jewelry, the quality failed due to lack of quality in the raw material, the tail was not good, the pieces stuck were detached. In other words, the spirit failed, the fitter worked in disgust because he did not know when he would charge!

The German shopper had to repair the jewellry himself; if he could get it, well, and if not, he should throw it away. Until there was a customer who once sent me a letter complaining about the quality of the products delivered and wrote in large German: "*Arme Spanien*", which translated into English is: "Poor Spain!". That was a big problem and a great embarrassment to me, a cross that I had to carry for many years with all the obsolete companies that I represented and for whom I worked from 1987 until

1995, I was almost ten years suffering with sales! The quality of the products produced was not good enough and did not comply with the *DIN Deutsche Institut für Normung*, which did not require a quality of the other world, simply a product well made, conscientious and professional, that could obey the German quality. It was not pleasant for me, so I could not make a career, for those reasons my school has been very hard and very long! I had to start all over again, from zero!

Afterwards, I remember that we went to the famous Milan fair, I think in the month of January 1988 or so. We were both, my wife Susanne and I, on a train from Braunschweig via Frankfurt and I think via Paris to Milan, in Italy. We had a great time; we sold a lot at the Milan fair. The Matute brothers were very fond of my way of working and my enthusiasm, they promised me that I could come to live soon in Spain and work as export director of their company in Madrid.

I had to wait until my son Alexandros turned one year old. I travelled first by plane, at the end of April, from Berlin to Madrid and I immediately looked for a flat. I preferred to live in an expensive neighbourhood in the north of Madrid. I found a small apartment on General Peron Street, in a large, twenty-six-storey building that was on the corner of Orense Street, near La Castellana, the Congress Palace and the Bernabeu football stadium. I rented a flat with two bedrooms on the fifteenth floor, I remember paying 70,000 pesetas a month for rent, it was a lot of money for renting a flat in Madrid in the late eighties! It would still be expensive now. The funny thing is that my place of work was in the south of Madrid and I lived in the north! I had to cross all of Madrid by metro and by bus to get to my place of work in the park Eugenia de Montijo, near the neighbourhood of Carabanchel. I preferred to live in a place where rich and educated people lived even if I was not rich, but I was very bored living in the dormitory towns of southern Madrid, I needed to interact with people prepared and multicultural from which one could learn something good! As before, when I lived in the neighbourhood of Argüelles, which was just as distinguished and I do not regret!

There, in this great building, we met on the fifth floor a beautiful young woman, very cultured and interesting personage, of German father and Spanish mother, Elena is her name, she worked in a great national company of telephony, Elena was divorced and had two daughters. My son Alex was only a year old and he enjoyed playing with both girls, I think the little girl was two years old and the older one was perhaps about four years old. We became good friends with Elena and her family. On the floor of the twenty-fifth floor lived a lady a little older than I was, a very nice Greek woman named Amalia. Amalia, I think, worked as a telephone operator at the British Center, was married to a Spaniard who later died, unfortunately he smoked a lot of cigarettes and drank lots of cognac! We became close friends with Amalia, who loved us very much and loved our son Alex.

I wanted to find God, I wanted to find myself, I had many concerns and above all problems of instability at all levels; I felt the uncertainty in everything, especially at work and in the financial part. I also had a family conflict that was a current against which it was difficult to fight, it was against my action and intention of wanting to settle in Spain with my new family, and they considered me incapable of achieving it. In addition, Madrid was not the place for me, where logically I should not have returned, perhaps I just wanted to remember my past in Madrid; I was looking for a job in a factory in Madrid, where apparently there are few factories. Most of them are in the large industrialized cities and, above all, in ports, or inland, in Castilla, where I did not like to live either. It was too much for me, I am a man of the sea, and Madrid was the interior itself! But behind every error there is a reason that lies mainly in the will of God, which others call destiny. So my destiny was to be in Madrid at this precise moment to learn things that I needed to learn; to meet people that I had to know and to discover truths that I needed to discover.

There was a brother of the Matute brothers who was very special to me and loved me very much. Thanks to him, I was able to stay in Spain, he did me the papers with the help of a very nice Madrilenian lawyer that he introduced me to. The lawyer did it all in the end for friendship and did not want money, I did not know how to thank him, in the end I had the idea of inviting him to our apartment for dinner and it was a very pleasant meeting. I no longer remember his name; he was a very nice man, a little corpulent, a very good person, sensitive and single, about forty years old or so. He liked the opera a lot; he frequently went to Germany with friends from Madrid, who also were fans to listen to the operas and to attend the concerts of classical music.

Then I got my work and residence permit. The Matute brothers separated and I went with Javier, who took the franchise business that the Catalan consultants left to see if it could work. As the exhibitors were already paid, I proposed to try, although we knew that was almost impossible, so we tried to make the impossible possible! As people thought the great exhibitor was very heavy, was full of jewelry that was worth a lot of money and did not know where to place it, it was a lot of investment, I thought of proposing mini wall displays, which were made of lacquered iron rod of the same light gray colour with hooks. Like the large exhibitors, they were modular systems and could be hooked together and thus could be vertically joined several exhibitors at a time. It was only necessary to make two holes in the wall and put two plastic blocks and place two hooks, to be able to hang them and nothing else. The placement tool was a simple drill! I myself would put them in hairdressing salons; stationery or any business to the public where they could accept it. But unfortunately it was not sold, nobody bought anything! Then we took action to look for regional or provincial distributors, each regional distributor for a province had to buy merchandise valued at 500,000 pesetas, which was the value of the gender at cost. The displays were for free, people bought me from Galicia, La Coruña, Zaragoza, Alicante, Granada. The clients were naive dreamers, they had no idea of the business, some were pensioners, they thought that with this business they were going to earn money to improve their income. However, none could sell anything, all of them failed. The business of the franchise, the brilliant idea of the Catalan consultants was a farce and lasted a few months!

I knew this was going to end soon, so I signed up in the afternoons for an English course for export. It was a course subsidized by the Ministry of Commerce for sales professionals who worked and could attend after the working hours. They were classes that were held near the Paseo del Pintor Rosales, in Madrid, below the central Princesa Street, near where I used to live, near the Plaza de España. There, I met interesting people, I met two German ladies a little older than me who were congenial with me, since we spoke the same language. They were each about fifty, I remember very well that they were called Gerborg and Ingeborg, they are old German names that are no longer in vogue; I have never heard them again! Ingeborg I think she was divorced; she was the older and was small enough of stature. Gerborg was taller and a bit corpulent, a little younger than Ingeborg. First came the two together to our apartment in Madrid and then each of them separately. I agreed with both, more with Ingeborg, since she was more lucid, sensitive, affectionate and with more experience and vision than Gerborg, she imagined me one day living on the Valencian Costa Blanca, where I could have a business of souvenirs for foreign tourists, perhaps on the island of Mallorca! Gerborg was more serious, pragmatic and typically German; she knew what she wanted, she thought of setting up an *Import-Export* business between Germany and Spain. She wanted to export wine and honey from Spain to Germany and import other typical German food products, such as fresh salads packaged in PVC plastic food vats from Germany to Spain, which should be refrigerated. Then I began to think about how I could intelligently start such a business, which is the product that did not occupy space, that could have enough value, that did not need a store or fridge, which she could keep at home at the beginning, that you could bill well and sell it very well. I wanted it to be, as they say in German, "ein marktrenner", which translated into English is "a market leader", a product that could be very useful for the public. Then I thought that the condom could be a good idea and a good product to import from Germany and distribute in Spain.

As I am quick looking for and finding things, I searched and found I do not know how the address and the phone of a great manufacturer of condoms in Germany, I no longer remember the brand. I called and talked to the commercial manager of the German factory, the door was open. This famous brand manufacturer did not yet have an exclusive distributor in Spain; they only had apparently a regional distributor in Barcelona, none in Madrid. I offered the idea to Gerborg; it seemed strange and insulting to work with such a product and for both of us to sell condoms. She told me that I should have consulted her before taking any action or initiative on my own, that the boss was her and that I was the commercial that was under her orders. Later, although I was willing to turn back my extravagant idea, she cut off contact with me, better for me! As they say in French "tant pis!" Or in English "forget it!"

In the building there was a family of neighbours friends of our friend Elena, they were a Basque man, a very nice school teacher who had his own institute, he was married to a woman who I believe was Filipina and had a small son, I no longer remember his name. He was willing to invest with me in this business of importing and distributing condoms, now I think it was a great idea, maybe I should have taken advantage of that opportunity! Condoms in Spain were sold at that time only in pharmacies, I wanted to open the market and expand it. Already there was talk of AIDS in the mid-1980s, in the 1990s millions of condoms were sold in Spain and are still sold everywhere: supermarkets, bars, nightclubs, gas stations, etc. How bad is it to sell such a product, which is very useful for public health? But I did not want to involve a teacher and put him in business, because it was not his world. I was tired of all the bad luck I had! In the end, I felt really tired of a city like Madrid, with no solutions for me, and I started looking for a new way out.

Javier Matute closed his shop and I had the idea of looking for the Catalan consultant of Andalusian origin, Mr. Fidel López Salvador, who had selected me for the first job, to see if I could be selected for another job. I called the phone number I had of his house in Barcelona, I think his mother answered and she gave me his new phone number, he had already left Barcelona and the Catalan consultants, and had settled in Santa Pola, where nobody knew him! I called him and he invited me to visit him at his house in

Santa Pola, I traveled alone by train from Madrid to Alicante, it was the month of May. Fidel came to find me in Alicante. The town of Santa Pola I liked a lot, it was a quiet place at the edge of the sea and was near Alicante, where my soul could rest from the noise of the great city of Madrid. He proposed to me to work with him as a consultant! And he told me: "You're already prepared to be a consultant like me, you can repair sick systems and companies like I know how to do, I'll teach you things. Come with your family here to Santa Pola and leave Madrid, forget about this city! Here, you and I can work very well." I began to think and meditate. In the end, I said, "Okay, I'll think about it and tell you things!"

I remember that, on the way from Madrid to Alicante, I met a nice man on the train, I cannot remember what his name was, perhaps his name was Juan, I'm not sure! This man, a little small in stature, had the appearance of a fighter, was a truck driver and a salesman at the same time, he sold in a small lorry exhibitor lamps of the lamp factory of Alicante, which is called FEFRAN. I told him about the work I was doing in Germany, he told me that his boss, a certain Victor, had long sought a man like me to sell his lamps in Germany and in the Arab countries of the Gulf. I kept his card and we arranged that one day I could go visit the lamp factory and that he was going to introduce me with pleasure to his boss Mr. Victor. He showed me on the train a bunch of catalogues of the lamps he sold in his display truck across Spain. I found it very interesting and I kept his card.

At the end I thought that, since I had few savings, only about three hundred thousand pesetas, I could only live two other months in Madrid. On the other hand, in Santa Pola life was much cheaper, it was practically half, renting a small flat was about thirty-five thousand pesetas a month and with another thirty-five thousand you could feed a family and live. So with three hundred thousand pesetas we could live or survive for almost four months in Santa Pola and spend a divine vacation, a long summer from June to September, instead of just two months in Madrid, in a city made of cement, where ever it is really hot in the summer! So we decided to go to Santa Pola and I called Mr. Fidel, the consultant, to say: "Okay, we're going!" Fidel looked for us, with the help of people he knew from a real estate agent, a good new apartment in a brand new building of light gray colour. The flat was also furnished to be brand new, it was located near the smooth beach named *Playa Lisa* of Santa Pola, had a bedroom, living room and kitchen and balcony and full bathroom, so it was enough for us, two young parents and a small child, Álex, who was only two years old and could sleep on the sofa. Thus, we moved by train from Madrid to Alicante. First, we sent by agency to Santa Pola some furniture belonging to us, and then we three left by train at the end of May 1989 and said goodbye to Madrid. There was a girl, Susanne's friend, who said good-bye to us at Atocha train station, she cried as she said goodbye. Susanne was also crying as she said goodbye to her friend, while Alex and I were happy, no tears...

That way ended our long stay in Madrid and we moved to the Costa Blanca, Santa Pola, to start a new phase of our life and enjoy a long summer of 1989 with beach, sun and sea air.

Chapter 29: Looking for the positive within the negative

This is a very interesting chapter, very important for debating, explaining and understanding.

What is the difference between being positive and being negative?

Being positive is to respect the laws of divinity and nature. Divinity is God, the creator of the universe. Nature has been created by God, this is the wonder of divine creation that we can see; we breathe the fresh air; we feel the smell of its flowers, of its forests and the immense sea. All these things produce different feelings, thoughts and positive meditations: of joy and happiness, but also of stupefaction!

Being positive is to recognize God and to thank Him for all He has given us to live this wonder, this daily miracle that is incarnated within us, that helps us overcome difficulties and obstacles, come from wherever they come. This miracle is manifested in our untiring human creativity, which makes us capable of imagining and conceiving something out of nothing. Everything we do to our measure and according to our human capacities, just as God created this wonderful universe: from nothing and according to His own measure.

A believer in God should, in addition to respecting God, the Creator, love Him with all his heart and respect at the same time the nature, which is the divine masterpiece, and the laws created by God, governing the universe and the life of every creature on earth.

We cannot go against divine laws, since they have been instituted by God and transmitted by His messengers, the true prophets. We can do no harm to animal nature or plant nature, and even less to human nature.

That is why no one has the right to kill, in principle, any animal or to destroy any plant, such as cutting trees or burning forests. But our bodily and human needs force us to plant and harvest grain, seeds, fruits and vegetables to eat, fish to eat and survive, hunt animals from the land, plant trees and raise fish, birds and cattle and sheep to later get milk and eggs. We also do this to sacrifice later the animals that are raised to serve us as nutrition, strength and pleasure for our human body. We could also consciously cut trees we need to build houses and boats, make furniture, etc. All that has been allowed to us by God.

God has created the human being as a supreme creature in His image and likeness; that is why no one has the right to harm any human being. The laws of God do not allow it and our human conscience either, although man has instituted his own laws for the coexistence between men in society and in community.

The human being who commits a crime against the laws instituted by man must pay for it in money or in deprivation of his liberty. But a man can never be sanctioned with the death penalty, that would be a greater and extreme sin by who dictates it and who executes it. We do not believe that it could be forgiven by God, but everything is possible, because the judgment and the forgiveness of sins are things of God.

The divine law is above the law of men.

God is light, God is truth, God is love and hope, God is positivism, God is optimism.

The opposite of God is Satan, who is present and free in the universe now and until the end of the world. Satan is obscurity and darkness; Satan is lies, hatred and despair; Satan is negativism; Satan is pessimism.

He who believes in God is free from the influence of Satan.

That is why "bad" atheists are often depressive and often need sleep pills to sleep.

I distinguish between "bad" atheists: ignorant; and "good" atheists: conscious.

A believer in God cannot and should not fall into depression, neither can nor should commit suicide.

Here is a study that proves it, that I invite you to read on the Internet:

More suicides among atheists and agnostics than among believers. *A study by the universities of Bern and Zurich says that Catholics and Protestants are less prone to suicide than atheists and... Atheists, moreover, have a suicide rate higher than that of any religion.*

How do you look for the positive within the negative? I will give you examples of my personal life, because I have always sought the positive within the negative. As a child, I dreamed of travelling the world and discovering it, as my father told me, who supported me in my ideas and said: "Go to the world, learn everything".

This was when the war broke out in Lebanon in 1974 and my father died in 1976, when he was very young, at the age of fifty-nine. At that moment, I was in Belgium. Suddenly came the key moment and the great opportunity to realize the great dream of my life: to travel the world, to discover it, to seek the truths, to learn the deep things of this world and to discover its great secrets. And that trip is still present, not yet finished...

I lived in Germany for several unhappy years in the late 1990s, even though Germany was (and still is) a perfected country in its system of living, welfare and social rights. In their system of work and rights for all citizens, women and men felt (and continue to feel) safe in Germany. There is a rigorous social and economic security, nobody was hungry and would not be afraid of something, you could make a good living. But in spite of all these qualities of life, I was bored in Germany because the way of life did not fill my aspirations or my ambitions; I did not have enough freedom of spirit! I learned many useful and positive things in Germany: first the German language, it was my dream to learn it and also to know the country closely. Everything I learned has undoubtedly served as the basis or platform for my current future. The order of the Germans is positive and has served me well to develop my inner and outer system, to develop my ideas and my vision of the world.

Germany is a great nation, a nation rich intellectually, socially and humanly speaking. Its system and philosophy are based on work and humanism, and above all on financial enrichment, which comes from the performance of the industry, the worker, the technician and the intellectual.

In contrast, Spain, Greece or other southern European countries are different; especially Spain, which is the one I know and I think it is unique in this respect. Spain is a country where one feels the freedom of the spirit, it is true that there are not all the guarantees offered by the German model of life, but there is what I consider "a freedom in realization". In this way, the citizen can live according to his ideas and realize his dreams; which is not possible in Germany, since his system is very orderly and very rigid. That is why Germany suffers from a disease that I would call "overwork and fatigue of the soul", while in Spain one works at another pace and the soul can breathe. All this despite the fact that workers, professionals or intellectuals work long hours in Spain and gain, perhaps, relatively much less compared to what is earned in Germany, England or Switzerland, where they work fewer hours!

For these reasons, I could not continue living in Germany; my life could not end in this country, however rich and interesting it was. Although I have worked there for a few years, I have traveled a lot and I also earned little money, which is normal, I suffered from monotony and routine. I recognize that I had some joys in Germany, I really liked the landscapes of Bavaria and the education of its people, I felt there that I was in another Germany, as in the city of Cologne, where I felt the development of the human spirit. In Hamburg, I felt the confidence of the people in themselves. Hamburg is a large port city; it has the largest port in Europe. However, unfortunately or unlucky, in the region where I lived, which was an inner part of Germany near the city of Wüzburg, people were rather self-enclosed, they worked, built their houses and saved money, that was not the most important thing for me!

Germany is a great school. But the flying bird, when it finishes its learning and can fly, must go to its world, and I had to go to the world, the one that belonged to me, where much more things awaited me to learn and to discover. In Germany I could not find everything I was looking for!

I met people from northern Italy, from the part of Trento who spoke German and who knew Germany during World War II. They were talking about Germany before and after that war. They said that Germany was much more romantic before the Second World War and before National Socialism, because those two human tragedies disfigured the romantic, sentimental and artistic parts of German culture and made it a more industrial and less romantic country, made of Germany an economic locomotive, a large working machine.

But I say and keep saying, "Work on yourself and let the work do its job." How is it possible that a man like me could live in this Germany, where only talk is about work?! "*Arbeit macht frei*" means "work makes you free," it was a typical saying of the time of National Socialism. Since then, and after World War II, the mentality of work has not changed much, it is still thinking with this same philosophy of work.

I think the following: working too much without being creative would, in the long run, cause mental illness if we become obsessed with work. So we can add: "*Zu viel Arbeit, macht dumm*", which means "a lot of work would make us dumb". How could a person like me endure living in a country where this mentality obsessed with order, discipline and work reigns?! I also have order and discipline, and work day and night, but I do not obsess, I like to live and live at my own pace!

I wanted to discover the world, to invent new things and to realize myself at work and in love.

Thus, when the marital conflict and the moment of separation came to my family, I found the great opportunity and the joy of returning to my beloved Spain. I had it planned for a year or two later, but I had to shorten the time and take the step immediately. That was the other side of the coin, that is, the positive part that I found within the negative situation of the family rupture and the overwhelming lack of freedom in the realization. Despite all the difficulties that awaited me to open a new road in Spain and start a new life almost from scratch, I took advantage of the great opportunity of separation to quickly return to myself and my dear Spain.

We travelled to Spain my son Alexandros and I in the summer of 1998, when he was only eleven years old. Spain was in full economic bubble crisis, but was not yet officially declared, there was a large percentage of unemployed compared to Germany. I did my work in my office by phone and fax, and I could take care of my son's education in our small house in La Nucía, a town near Alicante. From time to time, I travelled to visit my clients in Germany. The work of selling natural stones in Germany was gradually falling and lasted only a few years. I was happy as it was falling, because I saw it coming and I knew that I would move soon to another life and I would be able to live new experiences and discover a new world, another world different from my small world between Spain and Germany!

When Spain went through a great economic crisis from 2006, politicians did not recognize the crisis and people could not believe that there would really be a crisis in Spain. Many people turned away from God and sought material wealth: they bought flats, furniture, villas and luxury cars. They bought everything with loans that the banks gave them for everything they asked for. They also went on vacation and lived above their financial capabilities. Some of the people went crazy and arrogant, omnipotent. I felt the crisis coming and my work was going bad enough, I lived on my savings and I hoped that the big opportunity would come, until it really came!

At the beginning of 2007, the signal from Africa arrived. A day before, I heard a noise; it was as if the roof of the bedroom where I was sleeping was broken, it sounded a real "crack" at dawn. It was a phenomenon of dilation of the ceiling that I have not heard again, it was perhaps because of the abrupt change of temperature between the heat of the day and the cold of the night. I think it was also a sign of God, God speaks through signs with us, human beings; this could be through sudden changes of weather, torrential rains, etc. That precise moment was the dawn of the twelfth of February. I was very afraid of this date, because it was a bad date in my calendar, I was afraid of it, especially in that year that I suffered much uncertainty in my work and my future was uncertain, I had suffered several disappointments on the professional and sentimental spheres. This date of February 12 was always, in previous years, fatal and disastrous for me, I have lived sentimental miseries one after another on this date since 1984. Perhaps it was due to winter, when the nights become so dark and it seems that the winter will never end, the cold grows and the humidity increases. This sad and humid winter weather had a negative impact on my sentimental and working life until, on this 12th of

February 2007, my luck drastically and crucially changed. With this "crash" on the roof that dawn, hope came to completely change my life. That same day in the afternoon they gave me the hopeful news at work and with her began a new stage of my work in Sub-Saharan Africa. A fax came to me sent by my dear friend Joaquin Lambea, who is a granite manufacturer in Extremadura. It was a consultation of granite prices, which came from Paris for a construction site in Cameroon, a sub-Saharan African country. The price inquiry was written in French, so my friend Joaquin put my name, circled it and made me follow this fax so that I could contact the clients of Cameroon, who were in Paris, which I did immediately and there everything started...

With this role, and now, after ten years of continuous and non-stop struggling, I have rebuilt my whole existence again. All this has been possible thanks to the help of God and that of His chosen messenger: my friend Joaquin Lambea, may God keep him and give him blessing, health and joy to him and to all his family. Now, thank God, I have the job of my dreams, I travel all over Sub-Saharan Africa to the west, the centre and the east. There, in those eighteen countries that I visited up to ten years ago, from Senegal and Cape Verde to Uganda and Ethiopia, through many African countries, I learned many things and I continue to learn. I was able to discover this great mysterious and deep world that is Sub-

Saharan Africa, I was able to talk and communicate with these wonderful people who have a great heart and thirst for knowledge. They are good and humble people, open to dialogue, people who have suffered much in their lives because of the occupations and injustices of the colonizers, who came for centuries to exploit the wealth of their countries and to obtain human slaves, wood, gold, diamonds , precious stones, rubber, coffee, cocoa, mining, precious metals, lithium, uranium, etc. Almost all those countries in sub-Saharan Africa now have major political and economic problems, and although they still have riches and natural resources that remain endless, they are classified as the poorest countries in the world! This is because most citizens live below the poverty line. In almost all countries there is a lack of infrastructure, electricity, potable water, sanitation and medical health, social security, education, etc. Virtually everything is missing, the elemental and the fundamental, which is necessary for a modern society. In spite of all these shortcomings and difficulties, in these countries there is also a class of very rich people, but they represent a minimum percentage of society!

All that and much more I could tell you about my life, although there is also a negative part with which I have to live... As we all know, nothing is easy, the road remains hard for everyone... as it is for me. In my present life and for almost more than eight years, I have a daily annoyance of a neighbour who lives in front of my house and who is really insensitive. I call them "the family of annoyance," with which you cannot speak or talk. It is people who do not mind about their conscience; who does not care if they continually annoy their neighbours, they think that at home they can do what they want. I wake up every night with an exaggerated noise from their air conditioners, probably bought from scrap metal. That awakening every night at one, three, five and six in the morning annoys me a lot and makes me suffer, I break the dream and I cannot sleep. In addition, they throw me from time to time the bad air of the smoke of cigarettes that they smoke, smell that I cannot stand with, but I have to live with it. Someday, God will help and that suffering may disappear! I did everything I could to do: I installed new acoustic windows with blinds throughout my little house, on both floors. I managed to reduce the noise by maybe fifty percent, you can sleep better when closing the windows, but they keep waking me up every morning many times and I cannot go back to sleep!

I take advantage of this situation of not being able to sleep and I seek to find the positive within the negative. That is why, just before dawn, I started writing this new chapter, which I consider interesting for readers and for humanity, as they can learn from my experiences and my daily art of knowing…

… how to look for the positive within the negative.

Chapter 30: Trip and stay in Santa Pola, Alicante, Summer of 1989

In early June 1989, my ex-wife Susanne, our son Alexandros, who was only two years old, and I left from Atocha station in Madrid to Alicante by train. We arrived at the Renfe station of Alicante about noon. There, at the station, our consultant friend, Mr. Fidel López Salvador, was waiting for us. He was about fifty years old, he took us in his car, a large automatic beige Volvo, to Santa Pola, I think he took us straight to the flat we had rented. There, the few pieces of furniture that we had sent from Madrid had arrived with a transport agency and were inside the apartment, everything had arrived very well. We signed the contract with the lady of the estate agency, who was a friend of Fidel, and we received the keys of the small apartment, it was all new and was freshly prepared to be rented, it was practically missing nothing.

Before, in our time, Santa Pola was a fishing village, a very quiet place at the edge of the sea to rest and little tourism was seen. Now, it is a tourist place and in the summer is full of people. There, there is a fishing port and fishmongers for the sale of fish to the public, you could buy and eat fresh fish every day. They sold in summer fish of all kinds, like chicharitos, which had a good price, sardinillas, boquerones. Perhaps, they were worth two hundred or three hundred pesetas a kilo, which was very good and affordable in price for us, the newcomers from Madrid, because we had few savings. Blue fresh fish is a natural food, full of phosphorus and omega 3, contains protein and calcium, is ideal to enrich the brain, i.e., expand the imagination and have bright ideas. There were also larger fish that were sold in the fishmongers; they came from fishermen's fish market, such as hake, sea bass, red mullet, wild gilt, sargo and "lechola" as they called it there. Its real name is Lecha; it is a very good blue fish to roast it. There was also naturally higher priced seafood and the vegetables were also fresh and inexpensive, they came from Murcia. The only thing that seemed expensive was the Manchego cheese, perhaps worth at that time more than a thousand pesetas a kilo, which was quite expensive for us.

At first, we had a great time in Santa Pola with Fidel, who was very funny and made endless jokes; he had a great sense of humor. Fidel did paintings, I think with acrylic or watercolour painting, he was a landscape painter and also drew caricatures. This man, in my judgment, was very talented and he was also a genius, I learned a lot from him. Besides, he was a true sybarite, he liked to eat exquisite foods, he knew how to drink and talk. But perhaps he did not want to take things in his life very seriously, his system failed many times! From him, I learned strange words that I almost never heard in Madrid, he said when speaking of some character, that this or that one was a "deep subnormal." I think that these expressions came from their environment, perhaps they were used in Catalonia, where he used to live. I do not know exactly where they came from, but they were very funny to me and we laughed him and I; and that made us good, they say that laughing keeps you young! He also said when he became very serious, "blood, sweat and tears." This saying that is widely used in Spain comes from a speech by British Prime Minister Winston Churchill in 1940 during World War II.

Fidel talked without end, I also talked a lot, but not as much as he, and I listened. He did not smoke cigarettes, he was in this sense a good example for me, since smoking, almost thirty years ago, was still a frequent habit. But in return, he drank a lot of wine. At that time, the wine in one-litre tetrabrik packaging was a novelty. The litre I think it was worth less than fifty pesetas, it was very cheap, it still exists and it is cheap today, it is worth maybe a euro or maybe something less for the litre, according to quality! It has risen a lot since then! But people prefer to drink wine today bottled in glass bottles, and not packed in tetrabrik! He and I drank, between the two of us almost a litre of wine a day; that wine had little graduation, perhaps eleven percent volume of alcohol, and was alike to water. We talked all day; we both had much fantasy, ideas and dreams to perform. When Fidel introduced me to the others, he said that I was his colleague, who was also a consultant like him and that I was Greek, Lebanese, Turkish and Cypriot. That made me seem very funny, so I added two origins to my origins, I gave them salt and pepper. I am really of Greek-Lebanese or largely Greek origin in Asia Minor, which was under the domination of the Turkish-Ottoman Empire, also my grandmother Irini was Greek and was born on the island of Cyprus, so the description was quite correct and successful!

Shortly after having settled in Santa Pola, we received a visit. Elena, our friend and ex-neighbour, who lived on the fifth floor of the building where we lived in Madrid, on Calle General Perón. I think she came with her two daughters, which is normal. The three came to visit us a few days later to our new residence on the Costa Blanca. We arranged to receive them at the Renfe station of Alicante along with Fidel, who took us to Santa Pola in his great automatic car Volvo. We had a very good time the two families together, the beach was very nice. I think I had to sleep during Elena's visit at the apartment that Fidel was renting with my son Alex. Fidel's apartment was on the third floor, it was quite bigger than ours, it had three bedrooms, a large living room and a large kitchen, it had large balconies and terraces overlooking the sea and the mountains. The women and the girls all slept in our small rented apartment which had a bedroom and a living room. Then, one day later, I think it was a Saturday, we made a trip together with the boat from the port of Santa Pola to the island of Tabarca. It was a very beautiful, exciting and pleasant trip, I could feel the sea breeze directly, it was also a great day to travel. I remembered my childhood, from my first trip to the island of Salamis by boat, more than twenty years ago, when we travelled in 1966 from the port of Beirut to Piraeus via the port of Alexandria, so I could return to myself a little. Then, time passed and doubts and worries about our future began to come. As the long summer began to be consumed, I tried to do something, I was looking for some work in the month of August, when everyone was still on vacation, but it was very difficult to do anything. Almost three months had passed since June, suddenly the holidays were almost over; it was early September. I had to find a quick way out of our economic situation, stagnant and critical as the savings were already beginning to wear out little by little! In the end, suddenly there was a nervous atmosphere, I no longer stood well with Fidel, we had two characters incompatible or totally opposite. I already knew that and had noticed it from the beginning, but I had no choice but to take this opportunity and come to live in Santa Pola. Staying in Madrid was very risky, almost certainly a bad option, in the summer Madrid became heavy as it always was in years ago when I lived alone in Madrid, I needed to go on a vacation to Greece to the sea and visit my uncle Yorgo on the island Salamina!

The decision to go to the Spanish Costa Blanca was certainly a very wise decision, because the Costa Blanca lies to the west of the Mediterranean Sea, just in front of the East coast, where I was born in the Middle East, in Lebanon! I had little choice and a single chance to get out of the interior and go back to the sea, where I came from, although I sensed that these differences between Fidel and I would end up separating us one day. He was the typical character who thinks he knows everything, but deep down he was missing a lot of school, like everyone else. Nor did he come to terms with his other colleagues in Santa Pola, with whom he had the project of founding a multiservice society, a company that was to be both a real estate agent and auxiliary services of all kinds, such as cleaning, of reforms, of construction. Founding a multinational without having capital is a crazy project impossible to perform! Fidel imagined and believed in his own illusions, wanted to put to work in this company of the future a whole team of professionals who already had each his work. But a company is not always good; you cannot join so many people under one roof, since each had a different way of thinking from the other. Fidel could not convince them that he wanted to lead everyone because he had neither the experience nor the imagination or coherence necessary to be able to put himself in the place of each and tell each one what he had to do. He had nothing to offer them other than his beautiful and hopeful words. He just wanted to make them work and practically live on them, from the work they could produce within the future big company in a large isolated village like Santa Pola. Perhaps, he thought with the same philosophy where he used to work, in that Catalan consultancy, he sold smoke, illusions and surrealist ideas! In the end, everyone went away from him and me too, because he himself was lost and without horizon, nor had emotional stability and as I knew in the end I think that Mr. Fidel was left alone.

I first tried to look for a job by advertising in the newspaper as a salesman, where Fidel himself helped me, as he was an expert in selecting professionals! I think he did it for the friendship we had and to stay well with me. I admit that Fidel was basically a good person and had a good heart, we did wrong in mixing friendship with the business, and that was the big mistake of us both! "If you want to lose a friend, make a business with him, you will surely lose him!" With

Fidel, I did not do any business, we only talked about future projects and we did not do anything.

The jobs I found with his help in Alicante did not convince me. A position was a seller of ads in a free newspaper, it was not for me!

Afterwards, I remembered the meeting on the train with the salesman and driver of the display truck of the lamp factory in Alicante, Mr. Juan, on my first trip from Madrid to Alicante in May. I immediately called the lamp factory and spoke with Juan, who gave me an appointment for the next day; the day of the visit was Tuesday, September 5, 1989. I could find the exact date of that day on the Internet, because just that day there were large floods throughout the area of Orihuela, Alicante, etc. So I went to visit the lamp factory called Fefran. Mr. Victor, who was the owner of the lamp factory, was really interested in meeting me. After a while, he told me that he had had a dream. He saw in his dream a man who came from afar to visit him, was apparently a foreigner, an interesting man for him. Since that day, Mr. Victor was eagerly awaiting the realization of his dream! Besides, since he heard of Juan, who told him about our meeting on the train in the month of May, he was still waiting with more impatience when I was coming! Perhaps the beloved God had already done the work of preparing the way, possibly he would have sent an angel to

Victor during his dream and perhaps said to him: "A man of my own will come to visit you, wait for him and treat him well, he will be good for you!"

Honestly, I have no other explanation for this story because that is what happened. I do not think it was, as many might say, pure coincidence.

Mr. Victor was a great worker and dreamer at the same time; he was able to construct himself out of nowhere a great empire: his factory and his lamp shops. His story began being really very modest. Some of his acquaintances told me that when Víctor was very young, he began his work by selling pots of clay or pottery in the markets of Alicante, something like that, more or less. Now, he has great lamp shops. His family came from Jaen: his father, his mother and his brothers. I think his father first opened a hardware store in Alicante and from there came the idea of making themselves the lamps they bought from the manufacturers, since they seemed very expensive. Thus came the idea of producing the lamps themselves and of setting up a small factory of lamps one day later.

Victor dreamed of selling his glass lamps in Germany, in Europe and in the Arab countries of the Persian Gulf, where he was already on a trip selling his products. He was accompanied by his own salesman, I think he was an Egyptian, a big man who liked horses, I no longer remember his name, apparently they sold the lamps well in Kuwait and in the Sultanate of Oman! At the time, in the late 1980s, there were few manufacturers who dared to go and sell their products in the Arab countries of the Persian Gulf. That era was golden pure, it was the economic boom of oil-rich Arab countries. At that time, it was very easy to sell anything, because everything was missing!

The meeting with Victor and his employee Juan was very cordial; we perfectly understood each other. I showed him the files I kept from my previous sales work in Germany, when I was selling the Matute brothers' fashion jewelry and he liked the way I worked. Then we talked about working conditions and asked me the following question: "How much do you plan to earn per month?" To which I replied: "I think a reasonable price would be one hundred thousand pesetas of net salary per month, travel expenses paid and five percent commission on sales." He marveled at my answer and asked me: "Why did you ask me just what I could offer you, nothing more or less!"

My response was: "You should never ask anyone what cannot offer you!" It was a phrase that spontaneously came out to me and my argument pleased me! So he said, "Okay, great!" There was a handshake and the deal was done!

Afterwards, he invited me to eat in a good restaurant on the way home, arriving in Santa Pola, as is usual in a hospitable country like Spain. There, we ate grouper, which was served even in good restaurants, now the grouper is a very expensive fish and is no longer served in normal restaurants, you would have to ask for it perhaps on order! I remember that I learned that day the famous Spanish saying "of the earth, the lamb; and the sea, the grouper." The grouper is still found in warm seas like the Mediterranean. I saw it on the island of Crete walking through the Agora of Heraclion; it was very expensive in the fishmongers, it was worth more than thirty euros a kilo! I will taste it this summer because it is a fish I have known since childhood in Lebanon and I really like to remember its unique flavour. The grouper is found in the eastern Mediterranean seas, on the coasts of Turkey, Lebanon and North Africa, and in Tunisia as I have recently heard from a friend.

Just on this day of the visit to the lamp factory, there were intense rainfall and torrential rains, it was the typical cold drop, which comes almost every year at this time. More than two hundred litres of water per square meter fell in Valencia and Alicante. Fortunately, Victor had a Mercedes van with a high chassis and we were able to get there without difficulty, crossing puddles of water, to the street where we had our flat in Santa Pola, near the *Playa Lisa Beach*. There, at home, Victor and Juan were able to meet the whole family, Susanne and Alex, and they were convinced by the familiar panorama and probably the spirit of this family, which was ours. The next day, I could start working. After working a month of trial, in September, we signed the employment contract that Víctor presented along with the application for renewal of my residence permit in the Ministry of Interior. First, I had to travel to Germany in October 1989. We traveled all three of our family members on a plane, loaded with large cardboard boxes that were almost empty because they weighed little. Inside them were the samples of lamps protected with straw, were samples that I had to show to the customers to be able to sell the lamps of the factory Fefran of Alicante in Germany.

Thus, a new dilemma and a great difficulty arose: the lamps were more difficult to sell than the Matute jewellry, from which I knew its ways. Now, I had to learn to sell something new and heavier: selling glass lamps. The question I had to ask myself first was: where and how could I sell the lamps in Germany? They had recently installed a fax machine in the Fefran lamp factory, which was a novelty and a very useful tool for me.

I had to do the work this time: look for addresses in the yellow pages of professionals or stores specializing in lighting and call them one by one to arrange an appointment with them. I travelled first to Hamburg. Everything was difficult; all the doors were closed, until one made an order with me, what a joy! And he said to me in German: "*Ich kaufe die Lampen dir zu Liebe*," which in English means "I buy the lamps for your sake." He wanted to support me, he felt sorry for me, he knew that my job was really difficult, it was not easy for a foreigner, and a beginner like me, to find professionals in Germany who knew what they wanted and who could buy from me lamps made in Spain . It was not something understood!

My ex father-in-law is called Arie, it is a name of Dutch origin, his mother was German and his father Dutch. His wife, my ex mother-in-law, is called Marianne, daughter of *Oma* Emma Gehrmann of Stiddien.

Arie bought a car especially so I could do this new job, it was a good idea and a great support by him. It was a second-hand white Volkswagen Passat car; I think it was an automatic car. Previously, it had been used as a police car; then the second owner would have painted it white. It was worth perhaps three thousand German marks, that is, two hundred and forty thousand pesetas, it was a gasoline-powered car and it was doing quite well. This new work of carrying large samples of lamps could not be made by travelling with the Intercity train, it was necessary to have a vehicle to store the samples inside the trunk. I was traveling all the way to Hamburg, visiting a large furniture house. The purchasing chief was an expert, a very important man; he did not have much time to devote to myself. He told me quickly and verbatim:

"All those collections you have taught me are not interesting to the German market! In other words, they are worthless! Only this collection of rustic cast-brass lamps could possibly be sold with luck, but only in Southern Germany, that is, in the federal states of Bavaria and Baden-Württemberg, try your luck there!"

Thus, I later organized a trip to southern Germany, looking to sell this series of rustic lamps, Gothic type and brass cast. The brass was cast in special moulds of a foundry industry that sold the elements already cast to the lamp factory. They, in turn, put the components of the lamps, such as arms, shafts and decoration pieces inside a very large metal kneader, where all the brass pieces were moved along with stone balls that polished the pieces with water. Once well polished; they were extracted, washed and dried. Then they were patinated with a black or a brown colour, it looked like old brass. Then came the lacquering phase, the lacquer was poured with a handgun on the pieces of coloured brass that passed inside a train, a closed circuit. The pieces were hung with wire and went after the lacquered to a chamber of heat, is a kind of oven where they were dried with hot air. Afterwards, the lamps were mounted, the electricity cables were passed, the bulbs were placed, etc. It was a very interesting industry, laborious and handcrafting. Indeed, as the North German expert said, I was able to sell these lamps to some large furniture houses in southern Germany, which sold them as a complement to their solid and rustic wood furniture, but there were really few sales and there were very few customers who bought. It was no big deal; this job was an almost impossible mission!

There were also quite a few complaints because some glass tulips got broken during transport. Other customers wanted to return the entire lamps even though they did not have a break because they were not happy with the quality!

Besides, I also had a collection of Andalusian lanterns, type lamp or handmade lantern made with lacquered tin sheet. In Germany, they called it "*Andalusische Laternen*" I believe that the art of making these lampposts comes from the time of the Arabs of Al-Ándalus, hence the name. The Germans made them similar to the Spanish ones but with copper plate. Copper is naturally more expensive for the Spanish manufacturer and, apparently, more difficult to handle, so it used tin because it was also much cheaper and welded it with tin solder. The product did not comply with the German DIN, which is the standard of German industrial quality, so it was not valid for the market or for the consumer!

We returned from Germany to Spain at the beginning of December, before Christmas, and we sought with Juan's help a flat to settle in Alicante. We found a large apartment on the eighth floor of a building in an urbanization called *Cabo Huertas*, where there were three large buildings, a large Olympic swimming pool and large terraces. In front, there was the sea, you could walk across the road. It was a very nice place, a spectacular floor with a view to the sea, but there was a big problem: inside the apartment was very cold, you could feel the cold wind in winter that made you tremble. The rooms had no central heating, the windows did not close well and let in a lot of wind, so conditions were still difficult for the three of us, two parents with one child. The salary was just enough to live, the rent I think was about fifty thousand pesetas, there was very little left to live with a hundred thousand pesetas. But Victor left me a car, a red Ford Escort, was not well used, it had a diesel engine, spent very little and was well on the road, this car gave a little joy to our life!

Thus we ended, in 1989, moving from Santa Pola (Alicante) to live a life with more horizons and have better opportunities than before.

Chapter 31: Globalization, the new world order and the climate change

There are three topics that we talk about continuously and we do not get to understand them in depth, they are ambiguous themes for many people. They are really serious problems and very difficult to understand. And they are even harder to solve!

Globalization: Today, globalization is an obvious phenomenon. Before, each country consumed the products that came from their lands, where they were cultivated and locally produced. Each country had its own closed industry and economy, its own currency and people lived relatively in peace. Now and for many years, there is a great competition worldwide, almost all the products are listed on the stock exchange, even basic food such as flour, rice or sugar.

<u>The cost of living depends on many factors:</u> the cost of energy, the price of a barrel of crude oil or petrol, the price of natural gas or electricity, staples such as flour, rice, sugar, the meat, etc. It also depends on the price of communications such as the telephone and Internet, basic services such as insurance, etc. They also depend on the cost of transport, the travel

of passengers by plane, bus, train, etc. Many products fluctuate and are listed on the stock market, just as currencies fluctuate.

The economy of each country directly depends on the balance of payments. If a country has a deficient balance of payments, it will obviously have a lot of debt, as it happens in many countries of the world. It will then depend on the price of money and the interest to be paid each month to lenders, which is generally the world banking. All this financial burden that makes the economy of the countries to be in deficit, is compensated with the taxes that pay the citizens to the financial administration of the country, direct taxes or indirect taxes. They are taxes that the laws of the countries establish for their citizens, who must pay to their financial administrations directly to the importation of the products, like customs duties or like consumption tax on value added, that is called VAT. Taxes are also indirectly paid when you declare your quarterly benefits, and when every citizen makes his annual income tax return, taxes differ and change from one country to another.

Each time, we need to be able to earn more money to meet our monthly expenses, which come from our vital needs of all kinds, both existential and intellectual. These needs are growing according to the evolution of the world, of modernization and the rising cost of living.

More than 2,400 years ago, at the time of when Socrates lived in Athens, and Epimenides, the paradoxical philosopher of the island of Crete at the same time, there was no cost of energy or machinery. There was nothing of all that, the stone was only carved to make houses and monuments; everything was manufactured using the stone and the metal like the iron and the copper. The grain was ground to make bread; the olive was ground with the stone to extract its olive oil. They raised animals for their meat and milk, made fresh cheese of sheep and goats, planted vegetables and cereals. Ships were made with wood from the trees of the forests, jewels were produced with gold and silver, wooden carts were manufactured and pulled by horses or oxen. Shows were made, oil torches were used to illuminate at night. People lived in daylight, and at night people slept, and there was no stress! Socrates made philosophical dialogues in the Agora of Athens, just as Epimenides meditated on the island of Crete. There was no mobile phone, no WhatsApp, no *email*, no internet.

Socrates did not need to work because he thought it was absurd. There were no social security, not health insurance, not income tax or pension rights.

Now, work is a necessity, not to say an obligation. No one forces us to work, it is a personal conduct, it is vital and necessary to work and produce benefits to be able to face the high cost of our life.

Without work one cannot live.

There are some (let's say the majority) who take it seriously, as if it were an obligation or a duty that would bring them joy and satisfaction. Others take it as a hobby: "*My job is my hobby*". Others see work as a daily punishment because they made a bad choice from the beginning, they have become slaves to their own decisions, they cannot leave this prison or that vicious circle that is forced labor and decided by themselves.

That also depends on how each one of us take it: for those who takes it as a punishment, it hurts more and will live ill with it, their life will be a suffering; while the ones who take it as a *hobby* or a funny thing, they will live much better and will have more joy and happiness while working, they will obviously have a longer and more joyful life.

<u>The New World Order:</u> This order is changing as new world powers emerge. As the emerging world now exists, they could be like when we hear about the BRICS: Brazil, Russia, India, China and South Africa. But it is always the same countries that dominate the world, capital and world powers, those who possess the world's wealth, energy reserves, mines and mass destruction weapons factories, advanced technologies... all that has no secrets and can be read in the news. But for mentally strong people, those who do not want to depend on this order, should create their own system and their own personal order and try to be independent as far as possible. Every human being has his own order that lies in his thinking and should not necessarily depend on the currents created by those who want to impose their rules of the game, those who manipulate the world continuously.

For example, not everyone is bound to be on Facebook, it is a personal thing and it is a free decision of each, you can live with it and without it. It also happens that not all of us necessarily have to smoke. Although smoking was fashionable fifty or a hundred years ago, now is the opposite, fortunately is no longer in fashion. Now, it is socially badly seen and at the level of public health because it seriously damages the physical and mental health, and also damages the pocket. Most smokers are aware of the damage caused by tobacco, some of them do not care; they want to continue smoking because they probably need it, have some kind of anxiety or have not yet been able to get out of this habit or addiction, although they know that is useless and harmful! Many of them have switched to electronic cigarettes thinking that it is a new fashion and a new way of life.

Those who have confidence in themselves could dispense with many things that are considered for most first need products, such as, for example, Coca Cola. When I was little, I drank Coca Cola, now I have not had for many years! The same goes for the Red Bull, I've never tried it and I'm not interested; I have enough with a good coffee. So is football or formula one. You could do without them and look for your own *hobby*, fun and satisfaction without following the fashion or the currents of the world. Each one could do what he wanted and make him feel best.

There are people who like football or formula one, or watch for some sport in particular; personally I think it is something passive. I also envy these people and admire them, because I do not have the time to follow these hobbies, although I find them interesting. I tried it once in my life when I was little and, to be honest, I was bored. I have other interests, as can many people who think and feel like me.

There are people, who prefer to walk, meditate, think, paint, listen to music, read, talk about interesting topics such as philosophy, talk to interesting and beautiful people who can inspire us, with whom we could talk about love, spirituality. There are people who like to help other people who suffer, who are excluded from society, try to help migrants who need our moral and material help. Others like to deal with people who have health problems, who suffer from serious illnesses in poor countries, which is the great work of *Médecins Sans*

Frontiéres. There are others who like to invent new and useful things; Instead, others want to write a book that could give them personal satisfaction and make them feel useful and interesting to others.

So the world order, in my opinion, is a relative thing. It is also the order of each of us, which is embodied within our own mental, philosophical and spiritual system. Each one of us should have its own order and thus could influence the world order and the philosophical currents of our time.

Climate change: It is a serious problem. There is talk about this, but very little is done because many countries need energy for their economy and, unfortunately, their industry does not stop polluting the environment. They do not want to make the major technological investments necessary to reduce pollution, so they will continue to pollute the atmosphere and the ozone layer.

There are many poor countries that suffer these serious consequences, especially in sub-Saharan Africa. There, they have drought and lack of rainwater, they cannot plant the land to eat or have water to drink. All this comes as a direct result of industrial pollution, the large industrialized countries and the large industries that pollute the atmosphere of planet Earth and produce global warming that affects poor countries in Africa that now have drought.

There are conscious countries that are working to reduce air pollution. There are others who do not care and keep talking about it more and more, but without doing something that is really tangible!

Climate change is an inevitable phenomenon that will surely lead us to an ecological disaster soon, but each one of us have an obligation to do something on his side so that the situation of the world does not worsen even more! We must try to improve industrial conditions and reduce emissions of toxic gases. The alternative comes undoubtedly by the use of clean and renewable energies, we all know that it is very difficult to realize by the high cost of these energies. We must make each one an effort and participate in the costs so that we can live. Someday and little by little, we will all be together in a better world, cleaner ecologically speaking, a world that is healthy, where we can breathe clean air and drink healthy water, and where we could consume food that is not contaminated.

We must have a general discipline and conscience to pollute every day less, which will be difficult to achieve. But, fighting together with conscience and responsibility and thinking about future generations, I think we could surely come to a positive result.

We must also recognize that apart from our work of collective conscience and from each one of us acting freely and on our own initiative, there is also the work of God and the plan of God. He has in His hands the order of the planet, the universe is directed by the great Universal Creator, who is the Almighty God. He has His plans, we do what we can and what we consider good according to our human capacities, but He knows better the future, the one that is to come.

The thoughts and plans of God are above and beyond the thoughts and plans of the human being...

Therefore, it would be good to meditate and believe in God, the Creator, who gave us a promise of salvation of our soul through the sending of His Son. Jesus Christ came to the world to announce the Gospel, the good news; he had to die crucified and paid with his death our original inherited sin, but then resurrected and with his resurrection gave us hope of eternal life.

Therefore, we must pray to God to enlighten us and guide us on the right path of salvation.

Chapter 32: My trip to Arabia, spring of 1990

At the beginning of 1990, Victor and I began planning my trip to Arabia: it would be a tour of the Arab countries of the Persian Gulf. We scheduled the trip for the month of February. At that time, there was a small grant from ICEX for exporting companies. ICEX is the Spanish Institute of Foreign Trade. This State agency partially compensated for the commercial mission trips made by a representative of the Spanish company or factory wishing to open new markets abroad. In this case, I was the representative of the exporting manufacturer. ICEX subsidized the total value of the airline ticket. At the same time, it helped with the organization of travel and business advice. His team organized visiting schedules in the countries to visit in order to promote the products manufactured by the exporter.

The trip was quite expensive; only the plane ticket from Alicante via Madrid to the capitals of Kuwait, the Sultanate of Oman, the United Arab Emirates (Abu Dhabi and Dubai) and Qatar costed more than three hundred thousand pesetas. The expenses of the trip were for the account of the exporting company

Fefran; these expenses were around six hundred thousand pesetas, almost double the value of the two-ways ticket. It was a long trip with plane trips for a whole month, there were many expenses aside from the plane ticket: many nights in hotels, car rentals; meals; phone calls, faxing costs, taxis and extra expenses!

The trip was made from the twenty-third of February to the twenty-third of March of the year 1990, that is, a whole month.

I left on Friday, February 23, in Alicante, via Madrid, by plane. Apparently, I had a fairly long waiting time in Madrid before taking the flight to Amsterdam and from there to Kuwait. In Madrid, I took the opportunity to visit my friend Elie Saad, who was chief accountant on Kuwait Airways, Kuwait Airlines, and who had their offices on a high floor in the building that was on the corner going from Princesa Street to La Gran Via, just before reaching the Plaza de España. There, her Turkish secretary, whom she had known before and who is married to a Greek, sold her ties in her spare time, so she sold me a tie. Afterwards, I went back to the Barajas airport, from there I travelled to Amsterdam and continued with the connecting flight to Kuwait, I travelled with the airline KLM.

Arriving in Kuwait, very late at night, I took a taxi; it was a large American car, a large white limousine. Upon arrival, I found a driver, a Kuwaiti man in traditional clothes, wearing a white chilaba that was long to the ground, we negotiated the price and he took me to the Holiday Inn hotel.

As soon as I arrived and entered the hotel door with my luggage, I experienced an unforgettable drama: a Kuwaiti policeman who controlled the newly arrived guests stopped me at the entrance of the hotel. He was a big, fat, ugly, unfriendly man, looking at me in a weird way, as if I were something strange. I had, besides my luggage, a pile of cardboard boxes, inside of which were the samples of the lamps! Maybe that made him suspicious. He asked me first for my documents, I showed him my passport and the bills of the lamps, they were samples with no commercial value, but he did not trust me, he searched without stopping inside all the boxes to see if he could find anything else! Amazing! The same scene, the same drama, was repeated again, like what happened to me when I entered Morocco in September 1976, almost fourteen years ago. The Kuwaiti policeman was searching and searching for something more than lamps! I was nervous, because I was tired, I wanted to go to my room, take a shower and rest from that long journey from Alicante to Kuwait, but the man kept insisting and searched for more than an hour until at the end he got tired and left me in peace. What a relief! I assume that imbeciles do not like me, neither the hypocrites, nor the subnormal ones! No one of this kind of people likes me! What are we going to do! I have to live with it! *C'est la vie*!

At last I was able to go to my room in peace! However, the drama continued in Kuwait. In this country, at that time, there was no spiritual peace, something was wrong! I stayed in Kuwait for nine days in total, I thought it would be an interesting country according to what I was told, where I could sell a lot. But they were really many days of stay; I could not trust almost anybody. Despite this, there were good people and bad people, as in every country in the world!

A customer from Kuwait whom I phoned from Alicante before travelling was a really good person. He made me without knowing a letter of invitation for business, thanks to which I applied for a visa at the Kuwait embassy in Madrid. He behaved really well with me, he was an Egyptian from a lamp shop owned by a Kuwaiti. This Egyptian was a good Muslim believer. I remember that when I arrived at his shop, it was noon, the shop was open, there was total silence, no noise was heard and no movement was seen. It was the hour of prayer and this man was kneeling on his prayer carpet, praying at noon, I had to wait, no one touched anything, it was time for the pause; there are no thieves in Kuwait! After meeting and talking, I made a substantial request and paid fifty percent of the value of the order, money sent by bank transfer to the account of the factory of Fefran; I do not remember the exact amount, but it was not much. The order was relatively small, perhaps equivalent to ten thousand US dollars. This request could not be served immediately, since he had to pay the rest against delivery of documents in his bank. Just after a short time, the Gulf War broke out: the invasion of Iraq in early August of the same year, so it happened after my return from Arabia, thank goodness! Thank God, I did not have to live a war, because it seems that I was on dangerous lands!

On the other hand, there was a lamp dealer whom I visited after, he was a very bad person, his employee was also Egyptian. The two (the boss and the employee) were fake men. They liked my collection of Andalusian lampposts very much and said that they were going to make a substantial order for a container and immediately open an irrevocable letter of credit, but it was all falsehood and deception! They used me and they lied. Meanwhile, they had my only sample of Andalusian lantern confiscated in their store. They had it hanging at the entrance to the lamp shop and they did not return it to me until I was leaving Kuwait, that is, eight days later! They used me and took advantage of me. What I discovered later was that they wanted to buy a collection of Andalusian lanterns similar to the ones I offered. They were going to buy them from a large Spanish manufacturer that manufactured quality Andalusian lanterns, copper or brass, that is, much more expensive than mine. That is why they confiscated my sample, so as not to let me offer this same collection to anyone of their competition. They really made me suffer! I learned from them a lesson for life: the one of never trusting anybody more and less of a false riff-raff like them!

Afterwards, I left Kuwait for Muscat, which is the capital of the Sultanate of Oman. Before leaving, at the hotel in Kuwait I had to apply for a visa: It was an invitation letter that made me a Lebanese, he was the director of the Holiday Inn hotel in Kuwait. He asked a favor from another Lebanese director of the Holiday Inn hotel in Muscat who was his friend and recommended me as a VIP, as a client of the Holiday Inn hotel chain. So, I was able to enter Oman. My goal was really to travel from Muscat to another city of Oman called Salalah. Salalah is a city that I liked very much, it is very beautiful, it is endowed with a tropical climate, an oasis in the desert where you can see vegetation and totally green and tropical nature, there were coconut palms, it gave the feeling of being in a privileged place in Africa, still the Arabian Peninsula. This city is located far, about a thousand kilometers southwest of Muscat, closer to the equator, the climate is tropical and very pleasant. I had a great time there in Salalah, the nights were very enjoyable. However, there was unfortunately a serious problem: the client I visited, who was an ex-client of the Fefran factory, was really very sad and dissatisfied with the delivery of lamps he had received two years ago, he was practically desperate, he did not know what to do!

Victor sent me there to visit this client thinking that he was going to make a new order, but it was just the opposite, the client wanted to return all the merchandise he had bought!

He appreciated me very much as a person and he was glad to have met me, but I could not help him. He had many problems with quality and could not sell the lamps to anyone, he told me that he could not sell almost anything, nobody bought anything, he sold very little of the container he had received for more than two years.

Thus, the task of selling lamps that did not have enough quality was a really impossible, sad and painful job.

Then, on March 5, I left Salalah to go to Muscat, and from there to the United Arab Emirates. When arriving at Abu Dhabi airport, the man from the Novotel Hotel was waiting for me with the invitation of the hotel in hand to enter the country. Abu Dhabi is the capital of the United Arab Emirates, although many think that the capital is Dubai! As I was able to feel, a rather serious and demanding spirit prevailed in Abu Dhabi compared with other parts of Arabia, there was also less freedom than in Dubai. The stay at the hotel was interesting, there at the hotel I met a young woman who was about my age, worked at the reception, was quite handsome, a beautiful big girl, a rather typical sub-Saharan Arabian beauty, was originally from Sudan. She told me about her life and her sorrows: she told me that she could not travel by plane alone, she had to be accompanied by one of her brothers or her father, which was normal in those countries, which for us are archaic customs and incomprehensible! The meeting with this woman was very interesting, she was very nice and cheerful, she opened her heart and told me about her sufferings. We were also able to talk about various social and cultural issues in the region and the culture of Arabia. This woman wanted to help me, she went up to the taxi with me and she wanted to tell me where the stores were where I could offer my lamps. But unfortunately, again, the work in Abu Dhabi was not interesting or fruitful, it was almost impossible to sell lamps in this city; there was no reaction, although I visited many interesting customers!

After a couple of days in Abu Dhabi, I decided to go to Dubai. I took a taxi whose driver was an Indian, they said that Indian drivers smelled less than Pakistani drivers because apparently the Indians were cleaner and washed more often than Pakistani. They may be right! But the truth is that all taxi drivers were Indians from India or Pakistani from Pakistan. The distance between Abu Dhabi and Dubai was quite long. At that time, fatal road accidents were very frequent, I saw several accidents on the road, there was no airbag, nor was the seat belt used! We did the 140 kilometers of distance in almost two hours of travel. In Dubai, there was no great success either. It was a busy place for the modernization, which was coming at a high speed. There, in Dubai, I met a young man of my age who was of Palestinian origin, he was the employee of the Spanish embassy in Dubai, he worked in the commercial office of Spain and he was a very nice and extroverted man like me. He was the man of the ICEX, who organized the whole business mission of my trip to Arabia, we talked about my schedule of views in Dubai and about personal, social and political things. I remember that I was critical and I still am, I did not like the character of that famous and controversial former president of Iraq, Saddam Hussein, I did not even like him! At that time, his large photos were displayed in public places in Dubai as if they were commercials. That is why the conversation broke out in the taxi, after passing a banner with the picture of Saddam Hussein on a white horse and a shotgun in his hand as if he were a hero or a historical leader. When I talked about this character that was disgusting, I told him that I didn't like him at all. The young Palestinian replied, "Watch out! Do not speak badly of Saddam here, here in Dubai and in the Emirates everyone wants and applauds him." I was surprised, with my mouth open, and then I had to shut up. That was in the spring of 1990. Shortly afterwards, a few months later, on 2 August 1990, Iraq, which was led by its leader Saddam Hussein, declared war and invaded Kuwait, which was a neighbouring country and was considered as a sister country of the Persian Gulf. After this Gulf War, all the inhabitants of Arabia, the Arabian Peninsula and almost all the world of the Middle East and the West came to hate Saddam Hussein and his regime, as his own people had long hated, which judged him later for crimes against humanity and, above all, for crimes against his own Iraqi people!

Thus, people in general are really naïve; believe what they see and what they hear through the media, they do not know how to analyze the spirit and build their opinion based on it. They lack spiritual eyes, they do not have time or head to think and they do not know how to differentiate the bad from the good, the false from the true. What is also difficult in many situations...

I also went from Dubai to Sharjah by taxi as it is very close. There, I visited a Lebanese shop, there was nothing to do either! Now, they say that the United Arab Emirates is a new world, they are among the richest countries in the world! I have not gone further.

Afterwards, I finished my stay in the United Arab Emirates and traveled to the island of Qatar, which I found to be a more pragmatic, quieter country, a rather quiet and serene little island. At the airport, the car and chauffeur at the Ramada hotel was waiting for me, the hotel's shuttle car was a large Cadillac, a large dark lilac limousine. It was like a president's car, the rear seat was an independent cabin and the passengers sat facing each other as if they were in a meeting. There, at the Ramada hotel, I was able to really relax and unwind a couple of nights, even though I worked during the day. I visited a couple of lamp stores and eventually got lucky, I sold something substantial to a native merchant from Qatar, who made me a good order of expensive gold-plated lamps adorned with Czech lead crystal pendants from Bohemia. It was a great satisfaction that he came to the end of my trip to save my face against Victor, who expected big sales figures!

There, at Ramada Hotel, I occasionally had some fun with a blond, pretty, and friendly German girl. She worked at the reception and was standing, I talked to her in my spare time when entering and leaving the hotel. She looked like my wife, there was nothing special, I could only speak and practice a little of my German. I was a married man and I was not looking for an adventure, although at that time I was a very young man and I was a whole month away from home and away from the family. So it was good to have fun with women from time to time; women teach us very interesting things about life that men cannot teach us. I personally grew up among women, I went to my aunt Maro's house a lot; it is a diminutive Greek name for Maria. There, I had fun with my three cousins: Olga, Renée and Andrée, they all loved me very much, each in her own way. Likewise, Socrates learned much from women when he was a child, his mother was a midwife. Women forge the feeling of the individual from childhood and that is noticeable when you get older, as you can grow without doubt in love to the things of life and to wisdom.

On March 23, 1990, I returned from Doha, via London, with British Airways and arrived to Madrid at midnight. The plane arrived very late and I missed the connecting flight from Madrid to Alicante with Iberia, so I had to sleep one night at the house of some Swiss friends. They were a couple of friends called Carlos and Ursula, who we knew from our stay in Madrid, they were very good friends and very generous, they allowed me to stay that night at their house.

The next day, I traveled from Barajas to Alicante. When I arrived, I found my family very bad, my wife was sick and we had to take her to the hospital. It was the consequence of having left the two of them alone for a long time, a whole month. Apparently, Suzanne caught a cold during the train ride she did with our little son Alex when they were traveling by train from Alicante to Madrid to visit the same family of Swiss friends in Madrid and be there for a few days. Suzanne caught a bad cold that did not heal. After a few days, being admitted to the hospital in Alicante and thanks to God and to the help of the doctors, the illness was cured and she was able to return home. Thus, peace and tranquility reigned again in our family.

After spring, summer came. My work in the lamp factory could not continue; the sales results were not enough compared to the expensive trip I made to Arabia! The one-year labour contract expired at the end of September, Mr. Victor did not want to renew it because he considered the results insufficient, but he did not want to take me down at all! He proposed another new job for me in his company: he proposed to take a lamp truck, van type, and travel all over Spain from city to city and from town to town. It was like carrying a caravan and selling its lamps using, instead of camels through the Arabian desert, a truck type van throughout the national territory of Spain. I immediately told him no! It was a resounding no! I told him that I am an export manager and that I am not a national salesman! He was surprised, he did not expect this answer from me, he thought that with money he could buy everything! But in my case, that was not possible. Not everything is bought with money! In the end, we remained as good friends, but friendship, as it had no basis or foundation, disappeared with time until it disappeared altogether. Now, there are only the memories I write in this chapter...

Despite the great failure of this long trip to Arabia, I was able to make some ideas and reflections...

Speaking of Arabia, we should open our minds.

If we really want to understand the reality of this great people or this great ancestral culture and region of the world that is called Arabia, we should ask ourselves where the inhabitants come from, the Arabs.

The first question we should all ask ourselves is this:

Who are the Muslim Arab peoples?

Muslim Arabs are, without doubt, for us Christians, our cousins, as are the Jews or the Jewish people.

What historical relationship exists between the three peoples who adopted the three great monotheistic religions: Judaism, Christianity and Islam?

If we want to understand these close relations between Jews, Christians and Muslims, we must go back to history and go to the roots of these three peoples, from which the history and civilizations of the Mediterranean were born. Hence the cultures and civilizations of almost all the world have derived, except those of the peoples of Buddhist and Hindu beliefs, which have other origins, beliefs and cultures.

According to the Bible, the three peoples of the monotheistic religions of the Middle East (Judaism, Christianity and Islam) descend from Abraham's lineage and are the religions so-called "Abrahamic".

According to the Old Testament, the prophet Abraham had two sons:

His son Ishmael, along with Hagar. Hagar was his Egyptian slave, with whom Abraham had his first son, Ishmael. From Ishmael the Ishmaelites descended. Muslim Arab peoples consider themselves descendants of Ishmael.

The Jewish people are descended from Isaac, who is the son of Abraham, along with his wife Sarah. He is the son of the promise according to the Old Testament.

Jesus Christ is also a descendant of David, of Isaac, who is the son of Abraham.

Thus, we conclude that the three peoples are first cousins.

Why do these three peoples fight each other? For many centuries and until now, they continue to fight and have great dogmatic differences in their respective religions.

Because there were many historical events: First, with the Christian era and the coming of the Messiah,

Jesus Christ, Jews and Romans persecuted Christians. Later, Rome adopted the Christian religion, just as Greece, Antioch and Palestine had done before. A large part of the Jews were baptized, while others refused and didn't want to be baptized or Christianized and thus remained Jewish.

In the seventh century came Islam with the coming of its prophet, Muhammad, and then came the Islamization of the whole Arab region. There were processes of Islamization in the lands conquered by Muslims: in Asia, in Africa and in Europe. After a few centuries, came the Wars of the Crusades in the middle of the twelfth century. The combatants of the countries of Latin and Christian Europe massively came. The Crusades were driven by the pope of Rome to reconquer Jerusalem and the Holy Land.

We all know that Jerusalem is holy for the three peoples: the Jews, the Christians and the Muslims.

Now, if we want to see it from the historical, cultural and linguistic point of view, the Arab people already existed before Islam. In the time of Jesus Christ, the Christian era began. At that time, there were for many centuries the Jewish, Greek, Roman, Aramaic and Arab peoples and other peoples of history. Neither the Jews nor the Greeks nor the Romans nor the Arameans nor the Arabs were still Christianized until the coming of Christ. Nor were Muslim Arabs and other peoples still Islamized until the arrival of the Prophet Muhammad and Islam.

From the advent of Jesus Christ until the fourth century, the Gospel was preached throughout the Roman and Byzantine Empire to cover both territories (Greek and Roman) in full. Jews, Greeks, Romans, Arabs, Armenians, Arameans, Ethiopians, Copts of Egypt (who are descendants of the Pharaohs) and other peoples were baptized and received the Holy Spirit by the laying on of the hands of the living Apostles. Then their disciples continued to do the same until the great churches of Constantinople and Rome were formed. All of this is written in the New Testament, the Gospel of Jesus Christ, and later in the books of written history.

I am convinced that the three peoples who follow the three main Abrahamic monotheistic religions of the Middle East (those I have quoted) have more reason to live together in harmony and peace, to love one another and to respect one another than to live in war and have discord, as happened so many times in history. Since the coming of Christ and when Islam came, with the Prophet Muhammad, the world is still at war and there is great disagreement between the three great monotheistic religions of the Mediterranean basin.

It is important to observe the daily miracle of Lebanon, where Christians, Muslims and Jews peacefully coexist. There are altogether eighteen different religions and confessions that have lived together in peace and harmony for many decades. Among them are the Jews who lived in peace in Lebanon, they were mostly in Beirut before the Lebanon War. Now, unfortunately, there are few left, since most of them emigrated.

When Pope John Paul II first visited Lebanon in May 1997, he said that Lebanon is **"more than a country, Lebanon is a message"**.

In Sub-Saharan Africa, where I travel often, there are many countries I visited, such as, for example, Senegal, which is Muslim majority and where Christian and Muslim festivals are celebrated for all and alike, all celebrate religious holidays without incident . There is no religious hatred, in Senegal Muslims and Christians marry one another, as in Côte d'Ivoire, Benin. In Ethiopia, I saw Muslims and Christians living in peace and harmony with each other and for many centuries.

Now, in order to understand each other, to respect each other and to love one another, it is necessary to build bridges of brotherhood among the three great peoples who come from the lineage of Abraham, who is the father of the believers. *Ab* in Arabic or Hebrew means "father," *Raham* or *Rahim* means "merciful." Abraham is God's friend and the man God has chosen, is the merciful father from whom the three peoples of the three monotheistic religions descended.

My best friend, and I believe that of all of you, the readers, undoubtedly is the beloved God. He is the only one who will never fail us, is a father present to our side forever to whom we can ask everything in our prayers. To Him we can praise, we can ask and beg, He will listen to us and always give us what is good for us at the right time, when we really need it. He gives us love, peace, hope and mercy.

The Lord had said to Abram, *"Go from your country, your people and your father's household to the land I will show you; I will make you into a great nation, and I will bless you; I will make your name great, and you will be a blessing; and all peoples on earth will be blessed through you"* (Genesis 12, 1-3).

We conclude from this biblical passage and from this divine promise that the three peoples descended from Abraham are truly blessed by God, and the blessing brings peace and life in harmony.

Now, all those ties are good and wonderful. We have many important and fundamental things in common: monotheism, the same prophet Abraham from which we all descend, and that the tongues we speak come from the same Phoenician alphabet.

If we want to translate these realities into our spiritual life with God, we must point out the following:

We Christians have learned something very important and valuable from our great brother and Teacher, the Lord Jesus Christ. We have learned from Him the love of neighbour and forgiveness.

We, as Christians, could undoubtedly teach this doctrine of Christ to our first cousins, Jews and Muslims. Surely, they will not lose anything, but they will gain something more that will add to the valuable teachings they received from their beliefs!

We pray and expect with all our heart that our request for the teaching of love and forgiveness by Christ Jesus to be heard and accepted. Thus and in this way, hatred and rancour may disappear between the three peoples or the three monotheistic religions and will be replaced by love of neighbor and forgiveness.

Jesus Christ said to his disciples:

"*A new commandment I give unto you: That ye love one another; as I have loved you, that you also love one another. By this all will know that you are my disciples, if you have love for one another.* "

We, the true Christians, could undoubtedly identify ourselves with the disciples of Christ, as we have been educated in the doctrine of Jesus Christ and the Apostles.

Jesus Christ came to earth to tell us about God the Father and taught us love for our neighbour and forgiveness, which brings us peace, consolation and blessing.

If we know how to transmit this teaching of love and forgiveness to our children and to our cousins, Jews and Muslims, peace on earth will be undoubtedly a possible project.

Chapter 33: My vision of the world, «Meine Vision für die Welt»

This is a very interesting chapter, so I invite you to help me clarify my own view of the world.

To all of us, both to the readers and to the same author, this world seems to be quite rare, illogical and unfair!

The first questions I want to ask all readers and myself are the following:

Who are we?

Where do we come from?

Where are we going?

What have we accomplished so far?

How far have we come in our analysis and philosophy on the secrets of our existence?

What do we still need to learn?

What is left for us to discover?

What is left for us to invent?

What do we still need to find?

What do we lack to live in terms of joys and amusements?

What do we lack to endure and have to suffer?

I have no doubt that the great truths or the great secrets of life are the three that I summarized at the beginning of this book, in chapter five, which are the following: God, yourself and true love. Personally, I do not think there are other secrets to discover and to find...

I do not know any other secrets: If any of you knew other secrets, I would ask you to please tell me! I would be delighted to hear...

To be able to discover these three truths, live with them and feel them in the depths of our hearts, we must pass each one through the different trials and tribulations that are necessary to mature our soul.

Without suffering, human beings cannot and are not able to learn something new and profound. I do not know anyone who has learned something valuable by laughing and saying, "Ha ha ha" as if it were superficial, or reading or listening to philosophy, with headphones in the ears and listening to pop music or jazz.

Learning is not as the Germans say: "*Butter aufs Brot zu schmieren!*", which means "to spread butter on bread". Learning is much harder than that, it's like sculpturing the stone! It needs time, occupation, reflection, meditation, experience and maturation.

These trials and experiences of recognition of the divine things of our lives undoubtedly require many years of learning, struggles and suffering, given the obstacles we will encounter in our journey, which will prevent us from easily discovering the light of truth. Also for the disappointments that we will have to live. We will even go through moments of joy and rest, where we can live positive emotions, until after a long time reach spiritual maturity and with it to reach the philosophical age. Then, it is possible for us to be prepared and could have at this precise moment spiritual eyes, like those that had the great sages and the great prophets!

This phenomenon may occur when the wisdom and peace of the spirit can coexist together within our mind and spirit, and when the love of God can be poured into our hearts.

It is as beautifully described by the Apostle Paul in his epistle to the Romans...

Acts of the Apostles: Romans 5: 3-8, New International Version.

³ Not only so, but we also glory in our sufferings, because we know that suffering produces perseverance;

⁴ perseverance, character; and character, hope.

⁵ And hope does not put us to shame, because God's love has been poured out into our hearts through the Holy Spirit, who has been given to us.

⁶ You see, at just the right time, when we were still powerless, Christ died for the ungodly.

⁷ Very rarely will anyone die for a righteous person, though for a good person someone might possibly dare to die.

⁸ But God demonstrates his own love for us in this: While we were still sinners, Christ died for us.

If that really happened, then we could have a spiritual sensitivity that would allow us to have a vision that was beyond time and deeper than we could see with our natural eyes. We could then have a clear view of the world. In some moments of peace and inspiration, we could see the world as if we saw a clear landscape on a precise map and in an open book.

The Gospel of Jesus Christ is undoubtedly the book that can help us, inspire, enlighten and fill our spirit of divine wisdom; our soul will have joy and happiness.

466

In order to have spiritual eyes and see things coming, it is necessary for us to have the Holy Spirit acting within us. He will help us to have a spiritual perception of the things that are to come and also to have a deep vision of the present and of the future.

<u>The problem that always prevails:</u> it is that we are human beings and by nature we are weak, vulnerable and mortal.

Socrates said: "I only know that I know nothing!"

It's true, in the end we are great ignorant. Although many times we come to believe that we are important and come to think that we are little gods and we know everything, in fact, our school of life has just begun! We all lack a lot of life school and me too, the one who is writing these words!

I recognize that I am no better than anyone, nor am I the worst. I am aware that I am a human being sensitive to the spirits of God, the spirits of man and the evil spirits that come from Satan, the prince of darkness. I can feel and perceive the presence of spirits and recognize their nature, whether it is good or evil.

Where is Satan? Satan is in the mind of each one of us. Satan acts in our negative part, in our hidden part, that we do not want to recognize nor do we want to show. However, in the end we recognize and admit that we are not perfect and that we have been wrong, one and many times!

We have to admit that we are not always good and that many times we fail, we do nonsense and we are wrong!

Sometimes we are unfair and our judgment is premature!

Sometimes, we are stingy, selfish, we do not want to help or give alms or help the poor, which they really need!

Also, many times we are good, helpful, and generous and have a good heart. That makes the balance between good and evil.

Once you have spiritual eyes, we can see better the problems of this world; we can also see the things that are to come.

<u>What is heard on the news and the media</u> is that the world is going very badly, and worse and worse!

In the 190 countries of the world, there are 48 countries that have dictatorial regimes. That is, in more than a quarter of the countries of the world, they do not have freedom of expression or other freedoms, civil rights or human rights!

The cost of living is getting higher, there is much poverty in the whole world and that is increasing.

There are major epidemics and famines in Africa and in other countries of the world, there are open wars fronts in several corners of the world, there are genetic, epidemic and contagious diseases. There are problems with drug addiction, alcohol! There are people degenerated and lost! There is also much injustice and much terrorism!

Where is the world going? The world is surely going to total chaos; even in Paris, the city of light, there is no longer any security. There, in 2016 and the previous year there were many terrorist attacks, as in other European cities such as Brussels. Previously, there were also major attacks in other cities and countries considered free, secure, democratic and rich.

This morning I began to review this last chapter of my book, today is the twenty-third of March 2017. Just yesterday, in London, there was the dramatic terrorist attack on innocent civilians and against democracy. Yesterday, I wrote to my dear English friend Lin to see if she is safe and sound. Lin is my English friend from Liverpool who lives here, near us, in a town called Alfaz del Pi, where she lives with her husband Steve, who is also English, he is originally from London. They both love me very much and I love them alike. Besides, we see each other often.

Lin is a little younger than me, mother of four children and a young grandmother. Lin has helped me a lot in recent years, since we met by chance or by fate at the end of 2006. Thanks to Lin, her friendship, kindness and moral support, I did not lose the desire to continue fighting or hope in redoing my life until, at the beginning of the year 2007, the twelve of February arrived, it changed in my luck and my life changed for good! Lin and Steve were married in May 2007, here, in the town hall of Alfaz del Pi. We, my wife Marina and I, got married in Ukraine in August 2008, that is, a year later that Lin and Steve infected me with their happiness!

Lin was at the time of the attempt of London only five hundred meters of distance from the place.

Here is her reply by mail, where she tells me in English: "*I am in London at the moment and I was on the London Bridge train, which is the next bridge to Westminster, where the terrorist tragedy happened. Not even half a mile away. I am safe and am staying in Premier Inn until tomorrow. I am shocked but not surprised about the attack and just hope and pray for the victims and their families*".

Apart from our immense sadness over this great tragedy and apart from the fact that we must all pray for the souls of the victims and their families, what can we conclude?

What happened is something unfortunately not unexpected or surprising! It would be that many people were afraid and knew that something bad could

470

happen at any moment! In fact, the terrorist alert was in London at its highest level, just as it was at that time throughout Europe!

I could not give you a clear explanation of the causes of these events, but I can tell you what happens when the media says, "Attack on democracy!"

<u>The question we should all ask ourselves is this:</u>

Is there really democracy in countries that consider themselves democratic? <u>That automatically means</u> that if a politician were wrong and if his mistakes had harmful consequences for the nation and the citizens, he could also be tried just as any citizen is judged. I have not yet seen any politician from countries that consider themselves democratic. At the International Criminal Court in The Hague, they only judge African politicians or other politicians from Eastern European countries, but I have not seen any European politicians sitting on the dock. Only maybe in the Scandinavian countries! If there are doubts about the consequence or results of his bad policy, is usually allowed to him to defend himself, he will tell the nation a couple of arguments as if they were anecdotes to laugh at everyone and wash their hands and it is over... Then, history to oblivion and no more talk about it!

If there really was democracy, politicians should be justiciable, just as any citizen is, but unfortunately they are not! In France, they rarely judge politicians, but they end up making them pay a small fine of money and nothing else!

In the democracy of Athens, Socrates had to die for his philosophical ideas that clashed with the interests of the political class. There, true democracy was born in Athens, but it also had its faults...

Socrates was a philosopher; he did not want to be a politician!

It would be good for us to learn again from the philosophy and spirit of the true democracy of Athens, from Antiquity, and to seek where the failure lies in our democracies.

It is also necessary to consider whether the decision to exit the United Kingdom from the European Community is well or badly thought out. I am sure that this terrorist attack will leave many people pensive! They will ask the next question to themselves and say, "Now what is going to happen?!" Or the question will simply be asked: "And now, what?!"

I ask myself, and ask myself the same question: **"And now, what?"**

My answer is that we have to ask ourselves and, above all, the politicians themselves:

Why are these things happening?

Where is the ruling in the democratic system?

Where have we been wrong?

In order to answer all these questions, one should not only search in the archives for three months or three years or thirty years, but also have to look carefully at the errors in the history of each nation, the errors and the injustices committed for more than three hundred years. Then the teams of researchers will surely find many answers that will teach us that we have been wrong and have been unfair in all those situations and in all those historical moments where we have erred in the principles and foundations of human rights.

How could these serious problems of social injustice be solved?

It would try to start again the rebuilding of the political and social system, but with fewer errors and more moral and social justice. For this, our thoughts of peace, philosophy of good and social justice would be used!

This complex work is undoubtedly a work of research by wise people, historians and philosophers. It is not a politicians job; politicians should be inspired by such studies and should try to apply its spirit to reform and correct the failures of the democratic system.

On the other hand, there are open wars in the Middle East and in several countries of the world they call them "wars against terrorism". In Europe, east of Ukraine, there is also open war!

Since 1948, since the beginning of the Israeli-Palestinian conflict and for almost seventy years, there have been many wars in the world. There were millions of dead, of innocent civilians, children, women; old men and adult men; and continue to die daily...

The Arab-Israeli conflict has no end; it seems that there will never be peace in Jerusalem! Why? Because Jerusalem is three times holy: for Israeli Jews, for Christians and for Arabs (both Muslim and Christian).

There, in the place where the Lord Jesus Christ, the Messiah, was crucified and died on the cross and where the veil of the temple was torn in two, I do not think there will be peace any day!

"And when Jesus had cried out again in a loud voice, he gave up his spirit. At that moment the curtain of the temple was torn in two from top to bottom."(Matthew 27: 50-51).

It is a very difficult thing that could happen!

Where will there be peace?

<u>The Gospel of Christ gives us the answer:</u> There will be peace in the heavenly Jerusalem.

We can read carefully this wonderful biblical passage that describes it:

Revelation 21: 9-10. "*One of the seven angels who had the seven bowls full of the seven last plagues came and said to me, "Come, I will show you the bride, the wife of the Lamb." And he carried me away in the Spirit to a mountain great and high, and showed me the Holy City, Jerusalem, coming down out of heaven from God.*"

<u>We must also see the positive part of our world</u>:

In the last decades, there was really a lot of modernization, a lot of construction, a lot of positive and useful inventions. Medicine has made great strides thanks to science and the large and valuable work of researchers.

Life is more and more pleasant for those who can feel and live the wonders of this world. We can also enjoy many things, such as driving beautiful cars and traveling in state-of-the-art perfected aircraft. The world is very rich in everything, there are wonderful places where we can travel on vacation and enjoy nature and its landscapes. We can live unique and unforgettable moments...

Women are becoming more beautiful and more elegant, and men are also better, they all dress better and have a better appearance that pleases the eye. Many men today wear beards because wearing a beard is fashionable. I'm sure that in a couple of years the fashion will change, many of them will shave their beards again and perhaps will be more attractive, especially for women, they will know what is best!

On the other hand, there are many people in the world who suffer hunger, poverty and injustice. There is much more emigration and massive immigration of people of all ages and in many parts of the world. These are mainly young people, children and women who are fleeing from wars and areas of conflict; they flee from misery and persecution for ethnic and religious reasons. This produces an immense crisis and a great human tragedy that degenerate into major world conflicts.

Nowadays, it is necessary to be a professional or, rather, an expert. We must know how to walk the world with great care and we must earn enough money to face all kinds of expenses that may arise...

If you do not have enough money, you will not be able to travel; you will have to stay at home, face the daily expenses and resign yourself to what you have!

Besides all that, we need angelic protection. Without the blessing of God and without the angels of God, the human being will be lost because he is very vulnerable by nature! That is why prayer is necessary before leaving home, before eating and before bedtime.

There are people who do not want to recognize God, because they think that they themselves are capable of solving everything with their own means. That is possible as long as they can but someday they will encounter problems that they cannot solve! There are tragedies in every family, as I said many times with my dear English friends Lin and Steve: "*In every family there is a tragedy*"...

For example, a relative or a known person commits suicide! Then one asks the question of "and why did he commit suicide?" They look for an insufficient reason and illogical, they say that it was depressive.

Where does the depression come from? It comes from lack of faith in oneself and in God, from the lack of love for oneself, God and one's neighbour, lack of experience of faith, lack of emotional balance.

A few months ago, I heard my sister Ketty speak of a neighbour from Beirut, where I used to live before and whom I knew as a child. He was a little younger than me and his name was Joseph. Joseph had committed suicide. He was single, lived with his mother and his sister in his apartment, in a building opposite ours, in the neighbourhood of Achrafieh, where he had been raised, I also grew up there! But I left when I was very young and he stayed! He threw himself from the balcony, from the sixth floor. Why did Joseph commit suicide? Because he had lost hope in life, and in everything. How can you live in a country at war for more than forty years in a row?! Although the war was over many years ago, the traces continue and have not been erased. Problems have accumulated in the daily lives of citizens. There are infrastructural problems that have not been solved due to lack of resources and corruption. The problems have become increasingly heavy, and have become unbearable! These consequences intoxicate the daily life of the Lebanese people. Thus social and vital problems have accumulated, day after day and year after year, without anyone being able to solve them. It was not possible to solve the first, nor the second, nor the last. I think it is necessary to be able to overcome the problems of daily life, it is necessary to realize oneself; to be free and to find oneself, to start if possible a family, to find God and to find true love.

People also commit suicide in rich countries where there is peace, because of boredom and because individuals lose the desire to live and keep fighting for survival, and above all because of a lack of faith and hope in God.

Our vision of the world, as the Germans say, "Vision für die Welt", must always be positive and optimistic whatever happens.

We have to take things with joy and trust in God knowing that He would never leave us, here on earth and in eternity. We must pray to God, thank Him and always recognize God before others, since God is not a taboo!

In God there is the truth and the reason for our existence!

In political messages, they all read atheistic messages! They speak only of the nation, of democracy, of human rights and of the constitution. Talking about all this does not satisfy the soul or fill the spirit because it is full of lies, mistakes and hypocrisy.

<u>Finally, I had great joy:</u> I read in the news that the new President of Brazil, Michel Temer, who is the son of Lebanese emigrants who left Lebanon in Brazil in 1920, said the first speech with an unexpectedly spiritual formula: "*Thank you, good luck and may God bless us on our way.*" God had appeared in many official speeches for the last thirteen years, but this Wednesday was the first time that a president entrusted Him with the future of the country.

I do not know this politician personally or read much about him, so I cannot give opinions. Lately many critics have been reading in the news that go against him, there were great popular demonstrations in *São Paulo* and other cities of Brazil against his social policy!

I honestly do not know what to say: What really happens? I am so far from Brazil! However, I like it, it gives me great joy and satisfaction to know that there is a president of a country, a nation as big as Brazil, which recognizes God in his speech to the nation and in front of all citizens.

In Europe and Western countries, presidents almost never speak of God in their speeches to the nation; it is as if God did not exist. It is apparently taboo to speak of God, it is frowned upon!

It would be very good if the presidents of the countries and the rectors of the universities recognized God in their speeches and asked for help and protection. Because the man alone is not capable of solving big or small problems, nor wars, nor conflicts, nor economic or social problems.

As long as we live, all human beings will need God until after death and eternal life. We will also need God and His mercy.

This is my vision of the world. "Meine Vision für die Welt."

Final chapter: This book has been a dialogue about the truth

It is important and necessary to talk about the truths and the deep things of our life. However, that could lead in many occasions to collide with others, with those who disagree with our way of thinking and seeing things. In general, they refuse to argue; they consider the subjects as taboos, because they are not yet prepared or sufficiently experienced and mature in their knowledge or did not have enough time to meditate on them. They have not yet reached the philosophical age in order to understand and digest our ideas. That is why they simply refuse to dialogue.

That is why it is necessary to dialogue to arouse interest. Hence it comes the Socratic philosophical dialogue that breaks the ice of discretion and removes the fear of speaking about truths.

Socrates was an autodidact. He spoke in the Agora of Athens, that is, in the market, where every day people of all colours, all ages, trends, cultural levels and social classes passed.

I am an autodidact and each one of us, the readers who read the words and reflections of the different chapters of this great little book and feel identified with their thoughts and conclusions, we are also autodidacts!

We all are autodidacts, who believe that the truths of the things of life are simple and their secrets are easy to discover. As my father said, God save his soul: "The secrets are hidden in some corner of your house. Maybe in the kitchen behind a dry leaf of onion. Simply lift this onion leaf to reveal the truth, which we have been looking for a long time. What was once secret is now a discovery, an invention, a truth!"

The truth is in God, who, with his power, created this world so great and wonderful. The truth is also in each one of us!

Jesus Christ said: "I am the Alpha and the Omega, the first and the last, the beginning and the end."

Jesus Christ also said: "I am the way, the truth and the life; No one comes to the Father except through me."

This is the divine truth and doctrine in which we have been educated all who believe in Jesus Christ, because we simply believe in Him. He is the Saviour;

He is unique, eternal and undisputed. He is above all things earthly, heavenly, divine and eternal.

We must look at ourselves, to the truth of each one, the truth of our life on earth, which is the daily struggle to survive and keep ourselves worthy before God. This dignity we try to keep firm, every day and every moment, through our love and our trust in God and through our love for others.

Thus, we try to keep and improve our human qualities. To do this, we daily struggle against many contradictions and difficulties that come from our weaknesses. They also come from the intervention of the evil spirits, who want, at all costs, intoxicating and spoiling our spiritual relationship with our God, the Father and the merciful.

I hope you have enjoyed reading the book and that you have been able to learn something new from my reflections and my fantasies, since they are based on my thoughts and the experiences that I have lived through the different schools that I had to go through, through my long journeys and stays in several countries of this small great world. In them, I have been able to observe and analyze the different situations that interested me, those that attracted me and, in which I have been able to distill the ideas, make my synthesis and collect and store their valuable essences.

I have tried, in these thirty-three chapters, to explain to you some of the ideas and conclusions of my analysis, of the topics that I consider to be the most important of our existence and our life on earth. I tried to explain them clearly, the one I had at my disposal, using my simple and direct language. I hope that it has really served to enrich you in your knowledge. I hope that you have been able to take advantage of my lived experiences in the different schools that I had to go through and the wisdom of this wonderful world that I have been able to know and live. I hope above all that you have enjoyed reading and that you have felt joy and satisfaction when reading it.

I hope that you, the readers of my book, in reading some chapters, my arguments have seemed to you my somewhat satiric, perhaps very critical, even rare and funny. I hope you have felt the desire to laugh! That is good!

It was what he indirectly wanted to get: to make you laugh occasionally! Because many situations in our world, in which we live, are illogical and absurd, we often want to cry. This comes from our inability to solve, with our mind and imagination, the everyday problems of the equation of our life. But then, once we have discovered and understood their deep truths, we want to deeply laugh, and this time with great joy and great relief, because we have already been able to decipher their secrets and understand their meaning!

I hope with all my heart that reading this book has served you well and that it has really been constructive. I hope that, after a certain time, some of you, the readers, those who really feel passionate about the deep things of our life, those that you know perhaps more than I, you can develop some deep aspects of these ideas. They are the basic, modern, and contemporary philosophical ideas that I have tried to analyze, to debate, and from which I have tried to draw my own conclusions, which come from sensibility, observation, spirituality and human experience.

I am sure that each one of you will develop the ideas in your own way, using your own language, according to your own criteria and experience and according to your own way of thinking and seeing things.

I am sure that I was wrong in some analyzes of the topics that I have developed in this book, where I tried to talk about the most immediate, about the first thing that came to my mind, what I had been worrying for a long time, what I have gone analyzing and discovering throughout my life. In the philosophical themes developed, I have tried to explain you with words, in the best possible way, so that you could see and feel what I saw and felt, and that you could follow closely the story of my personal life through my stays and travel. For this, I chose the most outstanding moments, so that they could serve as an example and testimony in your life, in your travels and personal experiences.

This book can be obviously criticized, because I am a human being like all of you, the readers. I am not perfect nor do I pretend to be and criticism is always good and constructive.

This work will continue if God wants and depending on His help. This book is the first of a trilogy. As soon as I publish this first book, I will begin to work little by little in the second book of the trilogy, which will follow the same path. I will continue to talk about my trips and my outstanding stays, my thoughts, my reflections and meditations since 1990 and as far as I can. I hope to publish it within a year.

For this dream to be possible, I will put it every day in prayer, so that the beloved merciful God hears my prayers, inspires me enough and helps me to realize it. I hope also to count on your support, that of the readers of this first book. Without your moral support, I don't think I'll get to do it!

I hope this work, this trilogy that I am preparing with this first book, may someday become a complete and beautiful work that many readers in the world may like. Perhaps, it comes to be described as precious or even come to be considered as a masterpiece! Who knows! That will depend on the judgment of each one of you, the readers of my books, but it can never become a perfect work!

The perfect work is the Gospel of Jesus Christ. We are all imperfect and we are wrong a few or many times. I consider myself the first to be mistaken one and more times, which is normal for a human being!

Therefore, it is good that we often look at ourselves in the analytical mirror to realize our own mistakes and try to correct them every day as much as possible. It is also good that we try to do our own self-criticism and learn to accept the criticism of others.

That is what I did in writing, meditating, reading and reviewing many times my book "Diary of an autodidact" since its introduction, its 33 chapters and finally this last final chapter.

I especially thank my dear friend Germán Ubillos, the great writer, novelist, playwright and essayist from Madrid. He has supported me and helped me for months to carry out this book, my first written book, for which I am very grateful and consider myself a very lucky man.

I hope that all this work and the content of this book, of analysis and developments, which have been made with sincerity, love, passion, imagination and spirit, help us all, both readers and the same author, to serve us in improving our interior every day a little more, and thus we can get to improve our human quality.

Best regards to all and thank you with all my heart for reading my book, *Diary of an autodidact.*

The author,

Wangeli Chaaraoui

.

INDEX